D1233675

BLACK
CAPITALISM

E185.8
C9

THEODORE L. CROSS

BLACK CAPITALISM

*Strategy for Business in
the Ghetto*

New York

ATHENEUM

1969

OCT 27 1969

144852

COPYRIGHT © 1969 BY THEODORE L. CROSS
ALL RIGHTS RESERVED
LIBRARY OF CONGRESS CATALOG CARD NUMBER 72–80268
PUBLISHED SIMULTANEOUSLY IN CANADA BY MC CLELLAND and STEWaRT LTD.
PUBLISHED SIMULTaNEOUSLY IN CaNaDA BY MC CLELLAND AND STEWART LTD.
MANUFACTURED IN THE UNITED STATES OF AMERICA BY H. WOLFF, NEW YORK
DESIGNED BY KATHLEEN CAREY
FIRST PRINTING MAY 1969
SECOND PRINTING AUGUST 1969

FOR

Sheilah, Amanda, Lisa

and M.A.

Introduction

THIS BOOK does not offer a specific blueprint or timetable. Although, at some point, most of the enriching programs industry has so far devised for the relief of the poor will be mentioned, this is not a handbook for businessmen who wish to become involved in the problems of the ghetto. Rather, my effort has been to develop certain guidelines and examples which seem to make sense and seem to have worked. Also, I suggest principles which I think are fairly universal—or should be.

This is a book about poverty, but not in the sense of what specifically can be done about the thirty millions of our citizens who live in family units whose annual income is less than $3,300 a year. I know little about this subject, and would not care to suggest solutions to the incredibly complex problem of how to get money into the hands of the poor.

The dangers to America are too great to permit 163 ghettos to continue to build with impoverished blacks at the rate of five hundred thousand people a year. The preamble to the Economic Opportunity Act of 1964 declares that it is "the policy of the United States to eliminate poverty." Men of great intellectual capacity, economic power, and innovative talents such as Joseph C. Wilson of Xerox, Joseph L. Block of Inland Steel, and David Rockefeller of the Chase Manhattan Bank, together with fifty or more of the nation's leading economists—conservative as well as liberal—affirm the need for a national system of personal income guarantees and supplements. Solid opinion is behind the view that our rich nation will not ruin itself by taking care of its poor. Now it is likely that Congress will take major steps toward abolishing ghetto poverty in the not too distant future.

This book is concerned with a different face of poverty—not the view that proclaims that almost everyone in the ghetto is poor

—but rather the reverse face of poverty that states that almost nobody in the ghettos of America is rich, or even affluent.

The leader of the National Urban League, Whitney Young, Jr., states that he marvels at the creativity in the white economy, however distorted, which has consistently and effectively excluded blacks from participating in executive and blue-collar jobs. The focus of my thinking is on the extraordinary qualities of the ghetto economy which allow it to banish all the ingredients of wealth— the ghetto's stubborn economic conservatism, its miserable patterns of credit, its ability to crush incentives and the development of risk capital—and the failure of its residents to marshal talent for production, marketing, and the ownership of capital.

One million blacks live in the New York City ghettos of South Bronx, Harlem, and Bedford-Stuyvesant, yet those slums are presently operating only twelve registered Negro-owned businesses hiring ten or more people. The most deprived and undeveloped economies of Latin America have greater elements of entrepreneurial affluence.

Even as the nation succeeds through some system of guaranteed income maintenance in abolishing poverty in its conventional form, many of the same patterns of economic conservatism, credit illiteracy, and undeveloped entrepreneurial talent will remain. This is inevitable since the generous act of sharing our wealth with the poor does not add to their wealth. Lifting income to a legally predetermined level does not make the beneficiary productive; it does nothing to improve his entrepreneurial skills or to build his capital. Corporate or public charity through the creation or donation of more jobs for blacks does not expand the meager capabilities of the black slum to use labor for productive goals. Even if backed by a federal mandate that family income shall not fall below $3,300 a year, there is no assurance that the head of the family will be wanted, or needed, as a producer in our economy, any more than he is now. Although it is clear that the nation must first provide a program of legislation to lift family incomes of almost thirty million of its citizens above the level of poverty—thereby crushing poverty in the conventional sense— it must also remove the unique ability of American ghettos which prohibits the development of wealth by successive generations of American blacks.

The British economist Barbara Ward promises, "We will abolish poverty if the rich are willing to become even richer—but at a slower rate between the months of Christmas and Easter." But just as important as sharing our wealth, we must share the secret of how we become wealthy. We must identify those qualities of the ghetto which prevent affluence from entering that society. We must banish the extra costs of doing business—those crippling tariffs which preclude normal patterns of commerce in the slum. National goals should provide every able worker with a job, and make certain that the income of every household of four is brought above the poverty level. Yet, clearly an equally compelling goal of the United States must be a true economic emancipation of impoverished blacks—achievable only as they acquire the ownership of capital and the mastery of credit—the essential tools in the affluent man's kit of magic.

Many people, both within and outside the ghetto economy, will question this book's basic premise—that the skills and benefits of entreprencurship must be transferred to the residents of the black slums. This view attacks the roots of enterprise capitalism. Others will concede my objective of "normalizing" the ghetto economy; and they will wisely contend that the ultimate economic emancipation of the blacks cannot be achieved if ghetto entrepreneurship is dependent on white "colonialism"—on white capital, credit, or managerial control. Yet, the archives of the Small Business Administration and the equal-opportunity loan programs of metropolitan banks are replete with examples of money pumped into ghetto businesses which failed to stick— money which, through the process of white foreclosure, found its way back into the "safe" economy downtown. The black community not only lacks adequate capital and credit to go it alone, but also the aspiring ghetto businessman—dependent and unskilled as a result of one hundred years of entrepreneurial segregation—cannot presently retain and thrive on capital or credit imported from Main Street. He cannot use the wealth-building techniques of leverage and financing unless his business is temporarily shielded by reliable markets for his production or services, and by managerial skills possessed exclusively and abundantly by the white economy. Therefore, I offer programs for whites to assist black entrepreneurs in production and marketing. Black capitalism grounded on credit and skills borrowed from the white economy is a temporary but necessary foundation for creating viable and enduring business in the black slums. Despite the outcry of militants in the ghetto, this seems to me the only sure and sensible route to pursue. What other way can infant black business get off the ground when faced by competition from the world's most successful vehicle for the production of wealth— the white economy of the United States?

If much of our society suffers from the disease of a dreary middle class concerned only with material values, the Negro does not. The residents of the ghetto may have abolished wealth, but no one there has taken a vow of poverty. Let us sponsor in the ghetto the "sickness of riches" that now exists in the mainstream economy. Then black Americans can elect for themselves whether they will move in the total market as producing employers and employees, sell in the whole economy as entrepreneurs, and enjoy the benefits of credit and a taste of wealth and affluence like the rest of us. The black American cannot be denied the option to reject these material values in favor of a new dream or a new opportunity; yet this option will be meaningful only in an economy which provides a chance at affluence as well as freedom from poverty.

THEODORE L. CROSS

New York City
February, 1969

Contents

Contents

VI: TWELVE MAGNETS OF PROFIT:
A PROGRAM FOR CATEGORICAL CORRECTIVE INCENTIVES

Injections of Leverage

Front-End Incentives

Imparting the Skills of the Entrepreneur

Conclusion   203

Appendices

Index   259

PART ONE

An Identity of Needs

Not by Philanthropy Alone

DURING THE WEEK OF July 23, 1967, soldiers watching for snipers in Detroit saw two figures on the top of the General Motors Building. They raced to the roof and found General Motors' two chief executives, Frederic Donner, Chairman, and James Roche, President, of the world's largest manufacturing company. These men had witnessed an event which, ten years ago, no businessman would have dreamed could have occurred —gunfire in the streets, snipers on rooftops, and a mushroom of smoke rising over Detroit's Twelfth Street ghetto.

Today, America watches in amazement as the world's most selective and efficient industrial economy pursues a nationwide program for recruiting, hiring, and training five hundred thousand hard-core unemployables. Since that hot summer of 1967, we have seen a national revolution in corporate employment procedures. Orders to the personnel department of one of the nation's most successful corporations now encourage or even require hiring trainees with police records "if the applicant shows little likelihood of repeating prior criminal or anti-social acts." For more serious offenders, employment interviewers at Xerox are instructed to "note whether the applicant spontaneously indicates

3

remorse because of the anti-social effects of his behavior." A Lockheed Aircraft Corporation subsidiary formed in the Watts section of Los Angeles uses a standard employment application, but the company "does not insist that they fill in the blanks." Sixty or more companies, including General Motors, have spurned Department of Labor training subsidies, budgeting instead hundreds of millions of private corporate funds to bring into our economic system people who were previously considered unemployable—totally devoid of productive value to the American economy. Dozens of major corporations are contemplating new plants in slum areas, facilities that will stand for many years as monuments of good corporate citizenship but not as centers of corporate profit and wealth.

Why should all this occur? Why should not business, exercising its traditional mobility, withdraw to the suburbs and seek insulation from core areas threatened by encroaching ghettos? How long will individual companies voluntarily tax themselves to support efforts for hiring hard-core unemployables, if competing companies drag their feet and save the costs, sharing nevertheless in the benefits of cooling riots in the ghettos? Why should mortgage lenders make new loans or extend old ones in the slums? Why should not fire-insurance companies continue to "redline" large areas and cancel policies in the ghettos? Why should a businessman act to rebuild the home of a Negro who burned out his last one? Why should businessmen adopt an attitude of high statesmanship and abandon the pursuit of the interests of their stockholders? Is the problem of the impoverished black any different from the problems of air pollution, the outflow of gold, increasing crime, the explosion of population, the threat of atomic war? Are not all of these public problems that should be solved by government action?

There are many practical reasons why businessmen commit stockholders' funds to hire hard-core unemployables. There are many convincing reasons why companies voluntarily "tax" their treasuries in electing to locate a new assembly plant in the Brooklyn Bedford-Stuyvesant ghetto rather than in suburban Westchester County. Yet, there are also many more powerful

4

forces which discourage, if not forbid, permanent and substantial commitments of private capital for the relief of poverty. The truth is that the economics of the ghetto prevent an industrialist, a stockbroker, or a banker from doing business or investing capital in the ghetto, or even hiring in the slum, on a basis that is equitable both to ghetto residents and to the owners of the business enterprise.

Despite all the exhortations at business symposiums, social and economic threats inherent in racial schism and violence in America have not yet reached the crisis proportions which would make business anti-poverty efforts a vital business need—essential to the continuance of corporate profits, the preservation of capital, or the survival of commerce. As long as this is the case, a major and sustained effort by private business to rehabilitate and normalize the ghetto economy, and bring the ghetto resident into the main economy, will fail since the effort does not fulfill essential corporate needs.

Since this is a vital point, let us consider a few examples of how it operates. The American construction industry has an urgent and continuing need for capital, credit, and building materials. The industry will do battle to protect its sources of supply for these items. But the industry does not need a new low-income housing project in the ghetto. Such projects are hopelessly involved with government red tape and almost always unprofitable.

On a broader scale, industry throughout the country needs trained labor, but it has no immediate economic need for the services of millions of hard-core unemployed. Downtown urban banks need corporate loans at the prime rate. Hundreds of bank officers travel the country begging for the privilege of lending money, but these banks have no need to build loan accounts in the ghettos. The great corporations have no compelling need to recruit and train Negro entrepreneurs. General Motors does not need a sub-assembly plant in any of America's 163 ghettos.

Since the Detroit and Newark riots in 1967, a closer identity has sprung up between the needs of the ghetto economy and the needs of the normal economy. The riots now reach beyond the

5

black or "gray" areas of the cities and threaten the entire American economy. Curfews and enforced closings of businesses undermine downtown real estate values. Riots now mean massive losses of profits, millions in forfeited wages, and canceled conventions for entire cities.

Our apparent inability to cope with violence at home has had a disastrous effect on America's prestige abroad. World-wide publicity of burning and looting in our cities has given a new political dimension to the crisis of America's impoverished minorities. These events have reshaped the needs of American business, whose future is inevitably tied to the political success of the United States. With each riot, communist propaganda exploits the evidence that in the world's great capitalistic society, Negroes and other minorities are victims of economic discrimination. America's political and commercial prestige is severely damaged—a poor advertisement for the emerging nations of Africa who are choosing between communism and the enterprise system.

Because of the rioting and violence, the need of the Negro for jobs and housing, his need to become an owner of capital and part of our economic system, have become more everyone's need than in the past. The ghetto's threat to all Americans has brought about a closer identity between the poor man's needs and the needs of the affluent.

But memories of riots fade. As the public sector moves to "cool the riots," business efforts in the ghetto begin to flag. Since the Detroit and Newark riots, and the riots after Martin Luther King's assassination in April, 1968, we experienced a summer of relative tranquility in the slums. The presidential election almost by-passed the problem of poverty. Yet the ghettos continue to fill at the rate of five hundred thousand impoverished people a year. In any case, it would be insane to rely on virtual insurrection in our cities as a catalyst to bring about necessary new business programs for training, hiring and—hopefully— enriching the nation's poor. Now, under conditions of ghetto rioting or tranquility, there is no impelling business need capable of producing sustained industry programs for the reconstruc-

6

tion of the slum. The ghetto economy is so hardened in its overkill of profit and incentive, so hopelessly lacking in the ability to attract credit, so charged with business and investment risk, that the only hope of correction or rehabilitation lies in framing national goals that create an identity between the ghetto's needs and the needs of the normal economy.

(1) There must come a time when the needs of the Negro for front-end money, risk capital, and credit coincide with an identical need on the part of people who possess risk capital and credit to dispense it to the Negro;

(2) Conditions must be created in which the needs of the Negro for jobs and entrepreneurial skills are matched by need on the part of businessmen to provide jobs and impart their production and marketing skills to the black poor;

(3) The needs of the Negro for new shopping centers and other ghetto-enriching facilities must become the needs of the nation's supermarket chains, hotels, and manufacturers.

Fifty years ago a German philosopher and sociologist, George Simmel, suggested why corporate charity, and now even our private business programs for relieving the plight of the poor, are failing. These programs almost always confuse the economic needs of the poor with the philanthropic aspirations of the rich: "When Jesus told the wealthy young man, 'Give your riches to the poor,' what apparently mattered to him were not the poor, but rather the soul of the wealthy man for whose salvation this sacrifice was merely a means or symbol. Later on, Christian alms retained the same character; they represent no more than a form of asceticism, of 'good works,' which improve the chances of salvation of the giver." [1]

At an American Management Association seminar in June, 1968, on the role of the businessman in urban problems, one speaker, a Negro, noted that he had attended dozens of similar symposiums and seminars. He stated his belief that white businessmen attended these meetings to hear black men "tell them

---

[1] George Simmel, *The Poor,* in Chaim I. Waxman (ed.), *Poverty: Power and Politics,* Claire Jacobson (trans.) (New York: Grosset and Dunlap, 1968), p. 7.

like it is" and "flail" the whites for discriminations of the past. He said the businessman, after this chastising, returns to business as usual. This commentary unfairly assesses the motives of thousands of businessmen who sincerely wish to learn how they can help. Yet, this Negro's comment focuses on a basic misdirection of the efforts of many industry leaders who are engaged in massive and costly programs to relieve the problems of the ghetto.

This essential principle of matching the affluent man's needs with the poor man's needs is difficult to implement. Indeed, it often is difficult to determine the real economic needs of the poor and separate them from the psychic non-economic needs of the affluent. Instead of helping the impoverished black, the businessman is often helping himself. Instead of identifying and concentrating on the specific needs of the ghetto economy, the white entrepreneur is concentrating on his own needs, and only tangentially implementing them to help the Negro.

Virtually every corporation of any stature has aggressively recruited and hired one or more black executives in recent years. Companies point to their Negro assistant vice president to convince the public of their liberal hiring practices. When Negro executives are acquired merely for prominent display on the bank loan officers' platform or in the executive suite, and are not employed to fulfill a productive position, whose needs are being advanced? If the black executive is merely a subject for public-relations releases, employed in a showcase job, are the entrepreneurial weaknesses of the ghetto being cured? For every Negro who is drawn into a managerial position on Wall Street, deduct from the ghetto a man who might develop an insurance agency, a new bank, or another wealth-producing business in Central Harlem or South Bronx. If the Negro grows in wealth and affluence downtown, an important step has been achieved in the economic integration of blacks and whites. But if the Negro becomes merely "window dressing," in a white-collar job, he is just a useless appendage of the underdeveloped ghetto community.

For decades, charitable foundations associated with great in-

dustrial corporations have given millions to the poor. These gifts
have achieved no record for helping the underskilled poor man to
acquire incentive, risk capital, credit, and wealth-making skills.
Every spring, hundreds of corporations in New York City con-
tribute services and money to the Mayor's Summer Task Force,
which will enrich the lives of Negro youths and keep them active
in projects off the streets. This has been a magnificent program
—one of the critical factors in "cooling" rioting in the world's
largest ghetto during the summers of 1967 and 1968. Hundreds
of thousands of young Negroes have benefited; yet fundamen-
tally whose needs were being served? Does this program cut
deeply into the roots of ghetto poverty, or is this an anti-riot
holding action? A major national corporation recently established a fund to train Negro policemen. Training minorities in
skills is probably the single most constructive effort any corporation can undertake. But in this case who benefits the most?
Spurred on by riots in thirty American cities, American industry,
through the National Alliance of Businessmen, is conducting a
vast community-chest program for Negro jobs. In the first six
months of the program, fifty thousand jobs were "pledged" at
a projected cost of hundreds of millions of dollars. These job
programs are valuable when they carry training and opportunity.
But in too many cases companies are simply donating jobs—like
contributions to the United Fund—to buy peace in the ghetto.
Jobs for hard-core unemployables are an improvement over
"care packages." But when they are handed out like welfare, or
as "reparations" for discrimination of the past, whose needs are
being satisfied—those of the businessman who likes to feel he is
"doing his part" or the needs of the impoverished, untrained
black? The "Jobs Now" program of the National Alliance of
Businessmen finally buries the black-nationalist argument of employer discrimination which has shut out the Negro from our
economy for a hundred years; yet who needs to bury this argument—we or they?

Corporations most active in operating federal Job Corps centers and in conducting programs for ghetto hiring are also high
on the list of the nation's largest defense contractors. These com-

panies accept responsibility for carrying out national needs to relieve poverty as a condition to enjoying the privilege of federal-contract benefits. But what happens to the needs of the slums if the nation should succeed in negotiating an important missile-reduction treaty with the Soviet Union?

Since the Negro unemployable is not needed by our economic system, the simple act of providing him with a job must remain a form of charity. Jobs keep the dropout off the streets. Free hot dogs, Cokes and country outings keep the teenagers from rioting and looting—a form of fire insurance. But whose needs do these programs basically satisfy, theirs or ours?

I do not deprecate job programs of ghetto hiring which involve agonizing efforts to train the unemployable and offer him new avenues for economic progress and enrichment. Yet I do suggest that business must change the direction of its effort. It must focus on the specific economic needs of the blacks. It must direct attention away from our needs—away from how we can benefit from helping the black man. It must identify and correct the precise weaknesses and needs of the black economy—the specific conditions which have permitted the ghetto system to abolish the creation of any vestige of wealth.

But if, for example, one of the vital missing ingredients is leverage provided by credit, how is a situation created in which the First National City Bank, a bank controlled by a group of extremely able and fair-minded citizens, actually needs, in an economic sense, a loan in Bedford-Stuyvesant. Under what conditions can it move urgently needed low-priced loans into the ghetto on a basis satisfactory both to bank examiners and to bank stockholders? How can we as a nation produce an identity of needs so that successful national franchise companies such as Holiday Inns, Kinney Shoes, or Midas Muffler will risk a valuable, nationally advertised brand name on an inexperienced Harlem businessman who needs the franchise? How is it possible to create the economic conditions which would cause General Motors to need a new assembly plant in Harlem as badly as it needs its new facility in suburban Tarrytown? How it is possible to develop conditions in which the Safeway Corporation not only needs a supermarket in the Hough ghetto of Cleveland, but also needs to sell minority common-stock shares in the store to the market's customers? How is it possible to create circumstances which foster a need on the part of securities underwriters in New York City to bring to the markets of State Street or Wall Street a new debenture issue to finance a cluster of service establishments in the Lawndale ghetto of Chicago? Is there a possibility of creating conditions in which treasurers of national corporations, controlling billions of dollars of demand and time deposits, could actually need to shift a hundred million dollars in deposits to sound interracial banks operating in ghetto communities?

Human nature being what it is, the affluent man does not easily forget his own needs. Yet, in recent years a new generation of corporate leaders has developed new flexibility and understanding of the problems of the ghetto. However, they face an impossible dilemma: at the moment the weaknesses, risks, and tariffs of the slum economy are such that there is no way that a concerned businessman, except as a token gesture, can commit his company to marketing, production, or hiring in the ghetto on a basis which is fair to the owners of the business and to his customers, whether they are inside or outside the ghetto.

A new supermarket branch in Watts must either establish low retail prices competitive with markets outside the ghetto and accept operating losses, or it must increase retail prices (or reduce quality) at its ghetto branch and report profits. The company must either "gouge" the black customer or cut back operating results. Since the dilemma is insoluble, the supermarket chain rejects both options and shuns all operations in the slums.

The system of categorical corrective incentives, which is discussed in Part Six of this book, builds on the emerging desires of American business to take action in the ghetto. The system focuses on the specific crippling weaknesses of the ghetto economy —its lack of credit, risk money, and business skills. Having identified these needs, a corrective money incentive is provided as a bridge to the main economy. This system of incentives therefore removes the businessman's dilemma. It creates new economic forces which help a business enterprise to develop projects and facilities for enriching the slum which operate fairly—both for slum customers and the business owners. This system of corrective incentives matches the needs of the affluent with the needs of the poor.

Sharing the Secret
of Wealth

In *Le Défi Américain,* a best-seller published in France in 1967
and recently brought out in the United States as *The American
Challenge,*[2] French journalist J.-J. Servan-Schreiber takes the
French to task for allowing American businessmen to outwit,
out-invent, and out-produce the industry on the Continent.
Servan-Schreiber scorns the Frenchmen who explain away American business success "because Americans are rich." This attitude,
he says, is French rationalization for their own failure. Americans
are successful, not because they are rich, but because they act
like capitalists. They act like entrepreneurs. "They borrow money
from us in France," Servan-Schreiber explains, "and then turn
around and buy up control of our industry."

A shrewd Frenchman's view of what his country can do about
a receding economy on the Continent takes us a long way toward
the correct approach to the economic problems of the slum. The
Frenchman may admire his factory more than its profits. His
failure to achieve material success, in the American sense, is his
election. He *chooses* not to behave like an entrepreneur. But in

[2] *The American Challenge,* J.-J. Servan-Schreiber (New York: Atheneum,
1968).

13

the American ghetto it has been impossible for the black American to behave like an entrepreneur regardless of his personal wishes.

Unless we are content with future generations of minorities in which nobody is poor but few are affluent, we must also build equities, foster the ownership of capital, and create wealth in the ghetto. We must finance and develop Negroes who know how to borrow money, use risk capital for business, marshal talent for production and marketing. We must seek out and develop Negroes who, in Servan-Schreiber's words, "behave like entrepreneurs." We must recruit and develop Puerto Rican Americans who can produce and market in the big leagues. If Americans are successful because they act like capitalists, then we must move heaven and earth to recruit, finance, and train Negro entrepreneurs. If wealth and success come from the agile use of credit and leverage, we must find nimble minority borrowers and lend them money.

The affluent man in the normal economy is one who knows how to invent or accomplish, or one who knows how to organize a job and get it done; perhaps he has special skills in taking "businessman's risks," in making an informed decision and then seizing economic power. Conditions must be created in the ghetto to attract and build these entrepreneurial opportunities and talents.

How have poor white men in America become rich? How have they accumulated capital? How have they learned to "act like entrepreneurs"?

As I have observed men grow rich, I have noted three ever-present ingredients:

(1) The essential secret of borrowing and using other people's money to multiply the value of an initial stake.

(2) Risk capital, "front-end" money, or margin money—the initial stake itself. This is discretionary funds or savings (money not needed to pay for rent or groceries) which can be committed to an opportunity to own equities or capital.

(3) The skill and ability (often exercised by men of only modest intelligence) to mobilize risk capital and leverage and

combine it with a talent for production or marketing of a product idea.

Almost every issue of the *Wall Street Journal* reports examples of how the ownership of capital of great value is created practically overnight by the use of leverage combined with a minor stake of risk money. New security issues capitalizing earnings, or even losses, by the process of multiplication build new and fantastic value from the operation of a rather pedestrian business enterprise. Applying financial magic unknown to the slum economy, the market "decides" that a company's annual earnings of fifty thousand dollars are worth one million dollars. This is the essential "secret" of finance or leverage. Scores of business franchise systems, based on such unglamorous restaurant businesses as Dunkin' Donuts and Kentucky Fried Chicken, have "gone public" in recent years. Their entrepreneurial sponsors have built great personal fortunes erected entirely on a modest risk stake plus a sophisticated use of leverage. This leverage is the labor leverage—the work and effort of other people operating hundreds of franchised restaurants and paying privilege fees to an entrepreneurial profit center. This leverage is then boosted by the financial leverage supplied by a predictable market in the white economy for new stock issues that build wealth by capitalizing earnings at thirty-to-forty-times annual income.

Even the remarkable capital stock values of innovative corporations such as Polaroid and Xerox rest not only on entrepreneurial skill combined with a revolutionary product, but on leverage—the injection, under the system of corporate equities, of other people's money. If Edwin Land's net worth approximates half a billion dollars, the dominant element of his wealth is that the public market has set a value on Polaroid's public shares of sixty times annual earnings. Without the equity leverage of public ownership, the capitalization of Mr. Land's share would be priced at a much more modest figure.

Outside the world of entrepreneurial finance, billions of dollars of wealth for staff executives has been created through executive stock options—the most sophisticated instrument our economy has developed for using leverage to build wealth. Few

15

Americans who at some time have owned a home (20 per cent equity and 80 per cent mortgage) have not experienced a 100 per cent growth in their equity through only 20 per cent increase in the value of the property.

If (1) leverage, (2) risk capital, and (3) entrepreneurial skills for production and marketing can combine to create such vast wealth in the normal Main Street economy of America, surely the same techniques can be adapted to build equities and wealth in the urban ghetto.

In the past, we have made only passing efforts to build wealth and equities in the ghettos of America. At no time have we used the proper techniques to do the job. Influenced by reformers such as Jacob Riis, we have taken profits out of the slum when the real objective should have been to build profits into it. We have insisted that Federal Housing Administration projects for low-income housing be owned by non-profit churches or charitable corporations. Real estate entrepreneurs, with the agility to make low-cost housing actually work, have been charged by Congress with unconscionable profits. Speculation, the essential lubricant for production of wealth in the normal economy, has been banished by law from federally subsidized real estate projects in the slums. To keep the "quick buck" speculators out of low-income housing, we have adopted strict and impractical safeguards against corruption, which assure us that the legitimate wealth-makers will not participate.

Since we have failed to liberalize usury laws, we have excluded responsible small-loan companies and even banks from lending in the slums—to the lasting pleasure of the ghetto loan shark and credit merchant. Motivated by social justice, we have abolished or curbed the "holder in due course" rule on ghetto installment paper. By restricting its liquidity and negotiability, we have also discouraged legitimate credit from entering the ghetto and enhanced the monopoly of the hip-pocket lender. The highest court in New York State recently handed down a landmark decision absolving a Negro from time payments on furniture bought under an unconscionable merchant credit plan. The decision is correct and just; but the court order does not assure fair credit for the residents of the ghetto.

In response to pleas to build capital and equity ownership in the slums, the government creates another federal agency, forgetting that complicated enabling laws and regulations of the Small Business Administration and the Federal Housing Administration freeze out the wealth-makers in our economy, and thus guarantee that the ghetto will remain credit poor.

We have clung to a traditional and destructive system of welfare under which life-preserving but incentive-killing payments have been poured into the ghetto while leveraged equities and "front money" have been neglected. We have hung on too long to the federal investment-guarantee programs for the ghetto of the Small Business Administration, which have failed because the process of creating wealth has been entrusted to the public sector of our society—all sincere and able people, but possessing the least possible skill in generating the ownership of capital.

Anyone with even the most rudimentary knowledge of ghetto economics knows that no Puerto Rican American who wants to go into business could improve his lot or the value of his capital with the aid of the Small Business Administrations, whose regulations forbid start-up loans for "small grocery, beauty parlors, or carry-out food shops." Moreover, no one in the normal economy has ever started down the road to affluence through a short-term residential lease in an FHA project. Programs for urban renewal or public housing do not produce Negro ownership of a real estate equity any more than Supreme Court decisions which have opened public schools to blacks teach them how to marshal capital, production, and marketing to produce wealth. We have confused the talent of our government that can produce social innovation and just conditions of equal economic opportunity with the talent for building private capital and affluence.

Congress can appropriate, subsidize, and make laws against discrimination in marketing and employment, but Congress cannot create capital or wealth. The government, by legislation, can ultimately achieve a system of equal business opportunity in which the Negro will be encouraged to save, and perhaps multiply his capital by investing it—but the government cannot, by

17

legislation, force or create this kind of capital or savings.

Confronted with the black community's emerging power to destroy commerce and property values in non-ghetto areas, the white businessman will move heaven and earth to eliminate the will or need to riot. But if we are to cut deeply into the roots of ghetto poverty, we must build productivity in the slum. To combat the ghetto's determination to banish affluence, we must see to it that motivation, capital, and wealth become a part of ghetto economy. Before proceeding with specific proposals for a business strategy to correct the economic problems of our ghettos, it is essential to understand the conditions that prevent the slum economy from functioning in a normal way. Part Two explains why black slum economies have not been able to build credit and leverage into their systems and why they have been incapable of generating wealth and the ownership of capital.

PART TWO

The Ghetto:
An Economy That
Abolished Wealth

A Mindless Marketplace
of Anarchy

THERE IS A PARABLE, well known in the Middle East: One day in Iraq a field caught fire. All the animals and insects began to dash for the river. Just as a camel was about to slip into the stream and swim to safety, he was accosted by a scorpion. "Please," pleaded the scorpion, "I can't swim. If I stay here in the field, I will die in the fire. But you can swim. Won't you please ferry me to safety on your back?" "Oh, no," snorted the camel, "you will surely sting me, and I will die." "Why should I do a stupid thing like that?" countered the scorpion. "If I sting you and you die, I'll drown. That doesn't make sense." So the camel, a logical beast, gave in. The scorpion clambered aboard, and the camel, bearing his lethal burden, began to swim across the river. Midway across, the scorpion stung the camel. As the camel sank, he groaned, "Why, Why?" The scorpion, giving a final shrug before he too went below the surface, answered: "This is the Middle East."

High-minded business leaders who offer new jobs or propose new plants in the ghetto, only to be greeted by threats or even guns, should remember the parable of the camel and the scorpion. The ghetto, like the Middle East, is a crazy complex of anomalies

21

and paradoxes. Its economy borders on anarchy that defies all orderly rules of supply and demand. Gunnar Myrdal spoke of this in *An American Dilemma:* "The economic situation of Negroes in America is pathological." This inherent sickness of unpredictability in the black economy is illustrated in all aspects of its feeble commerce.

Economic anarchy is most visible in the important matter of jobs and employment. Basic to the high rate of ghetto unemployment is a paradoxical and equally high rate of unfilled job opportunities. The ghetto poor do not respond to the simple opportunity of a job. Ford and Chrysler have virtually dragged young dropouts off the streets of Detroit's Twelfth Street ghetto into company employment offices. The militant and status-conscious young man in East Harlem calls his neighbor an "Uncle Tom" if he takes a job—especially a menial one. He doesn't line up at the employment gate, because he believes it is a waste of time and he won't be hired. He is certain that, for blacks, all jobs are dead-end jobs; he would prefer to live as a hustler. The cry of youth in the ghetto is "I can't take this black face off, just like I can't tear up my prison record. . . . No one wants a nigger in his factory."

Like the poor whites of Appalachia or northern California, Negroes established in the ghetto are unwilling to move from abject poverty to a job a few miles away. For generations, there has been a migration of black people to northern cities from rural areas in the South. First they wanted higher wages, and now they migrate for more liberal welfare benefits available in Chicago, New York, and Philadelphia. Yet once a southern Negro gets off the train at Chicago's Central Station and takes the five-dollar cab ride to Lawndale (his first encounter with the special tariffs of ghetto economics) his mobility and motivation end. The ghetto becomes his home and he won't leave, regardless of how squalid conditions may be. The original motivation and drive which persuaded him to leave the South is gone. He soon joins the ranks of welfare and the hard-core unemployed. In 1967, Chicago enjoyed the tightest labor market in the country, with only 2.4 per cent of its total work force unemployed.

22

Yet Illinois Bell Telephone studies estimate that there were some blocks in Chicago slums where unemployment ran as high as 48 per cent. In May, 1968, *The New York Times* reported 20,000 or more unfilled low-skill positions available in New York City, despite 135,000 unemployed. These contradictions of jobs going begging while job-seekers are idle highlight the insensitivity of the ghetto labor market. Even creating more jobs outside the ghetto does not absorb the unemployed inside.

In the normal economy, there is a logical and predictable correlation between education and later success in life. This rule does not hold in the slums. The *Kerner Commission* reports that the Negro high-school dropout between the ages of sixteen and twenty-one has an unemployment rate of 20 per cent. The Negro high-school graduate has an even higher unemployment rate. Whitney Young of the National Urban League concludes, "It is almost dangerous for a Negro to get a high-school education. His chances of being unemployed are greater than if he dropped out of school."

In the slum economy, many commonplace events interfere with a man's ability to get or hold a job. Ghetto residents are constantly fighting off finance companies and arguing with car dealers who have cheated them. Their cars break down and are towed off the street. These conditions not only interfere with an employee's on-the-job reliability, but they also build more theft, crime, inability to meet rent payments, evictions, and bad credit—the very obstacles that prevent people from getting and holding jobs. Plainly, the system of anarchy is self-perpetuating.

This anarchy of the ghetto economy is reflected in the breakdown of its communications. In the normal economy, traditional rules of supply and demand operate efficiently because the existence of a demand is effectively communicated to the sources of labor, goods, and capital—and these supplies make their presence felt on the market. The ghetto economy is in chaos because many slum residents, including the hard-core unemployed, are barely literate. A job offer, a lower rate of interest on an installment contract, or an offer of better quality or less expensive merchandise is rarely heard; it certainly isn't read.

23

Even when established in jobs, the ghetto poor often do not respond to the usual wage and economic incentives. Watts Manufacturing Company, the tent-fabricating factory established in the Los Angeles curfew area after the riots of 1965, planned to offer stock ownership to its employees. The workers ignored or rejected the stock program because they did not understand or attach personal benefits to the process by which equities compound in value at a greater rate than piecework bonuses deposited in a savings bank. The plan was abandoned in favor of production incentives and cash payments. Still, even cash payments as a reward for effective work will not always lure or hold a man who has a habit of going on the dole.[1]

Some years ago, Reynolds Metals Company built three hundred moderate-priced cooperative housing units in an all-Negro slum in Cincinnati. Down payments were nominal and monthly maintenance came to eighty or ninety dollars. But it was almost impossible to sell the units because of the basic slum stigma. The Negro who could afford a down payment wanted something with greater prestige.

Government hearings on "truth-in-lending" legislation recount endless examples of irrational purchasing habits in the slums. Even where there is a convenient supermarket, a resident of the ghetto will frequently trade with the high-priced credit merchant one block nearer home. In 1965, a neighborhood grocery-

[1] Louis O. Kelso, the brilliant analyst and sponsor of plans to develop "universal capitalism," cites an example of how to stimulate an appetite for equities under almost impossible conditions: "A *New York Times* correspondent from Khartoum recently described how one of the Sudan's leading businessmen overcame the negative economic effect of 'the extended family of cousins, aunts, uncles, parents and children [that] may saddle a successful person with a whole retinue of relatives or retainers.' Conceding that 'the traditional system of having the more fortunate members of the family support their poorer relatives often discourages the ambitious and encourages the idle,' Sir Abbas met the challenge 'creatively.' 'In 1964, he set up the Anzara General Trading Company, Ltd., with his own capital, and gave shares in the company to selected members of his family and a few long-time employees, a new twist for all but a few Sudanese families. His idea was to put his relatives to work as part-owners of a family-dominated business rather than simply let them come to him for handouts. Today, this company engaged in imports and commission work, directly benefits about 70 persons. Mr. Abbas believes his scheme is proving itself not only by encouraging initiative and industry, but also by developing a sense of responsibility among otherwise dependent relatives. . . .'" *The New York Times,* July 24, 1966.

purchasing cooperative was organized in San Francisco by residents of one of the city's poverty areas. The cooperative was owned by 2,700 shareholders, most of them Negroes. The project was a total failure because, as the president of the cooperative stated, "We cannot get our members to shop in the store. The prices are competitive with other supermarkets, but we have not been able to pull people in. The members do not seem to understand that when they shop in the store they can help make a profit and will share in the profit."

Another aspect of the anarchy of the slum economy is its hardened ability to ignore interest rates. In the normal economy, a one-half-percentage-point interest-rate premium on thrift accounts in Las Vegas banks moves millions of dollars of capital across a continent in accordance with the rules of Adam Smith. Unfortunately, there are no such rules in the economy in the urban slum. In the black ghetto, interest rates of at least 100 per cent per annum are commonly built into the retail price of ghetto appliances and furniture. Former Under Secretary of Commerce Howard J. Samuels reports that in Harlem a retailer pays $109 wholesale for a portable television set and sells it on time payments for $255 in the slums. Downtown stores sell the same set for $159 in cash. Premium prices do not discourage purchases in the ghetto, nor do they persuade the ghetto resident to shop at discount houses in other areas. The five-block strip from 116th Street to 125th Street on Third Avenue in East Harlem supports 67 furniture and appliance stores run by credit merchants; yet low-priced discount stores are only a fifteen-minutes subway ride away in mid-Manhattan.[2]

The normal laws of supply and demand probably never applied to ghetto real estate. In the Brownsville area of Brooklyn,

---

[2] For cash items such as food, ghetto residents are increasingly turning to supermarkets in white neighborhoods. A Wharton School study found that 90 per cent of 520 residents of a predominantly Negro area did most of their shopping for food in supermarkets in adjacent fringes of white neighborhoods. Since ghetto neighborhoods have been a dumping ground for inferior products, the Negro shopper increasingly relies on brand products available in white markets as an assurance of quality (*Business Week,* May 18, 1968, p. 94).

For high-priced items requiring financing, the unavailability of credit at downtown department and discount stores protects the business of ghetto appliance dealers, who build credit charges into the price.

25

row after row of modern brick-and-masonry buildings have been completely deserted.[3] Since the stable Jewish middle-class families moved out after World War II, these properties, although perfectly sound, have no present economic use or value; yet dilapidated warehouse space a few miles away outside the ghetto commands annual rentals of several dollars a square foot. In a typical ghetto such as Brownsville, property owners pay only enough taxes to avoid foreclosure; there are no equities, no values[4]—just a vague hope that someday the city may condemn the properties for urban renewal.

In the normal economy, real estate tax assessments usually bear some reasonable relation to real estate values. But in the anarchy of the ghetto economy, studies show that real estate taxes are higher in relation to fair market value than in downtown areas. Typically, ghetto properties have decayed and diminished in value over the years, but taxes have not been readjusted. A study at Harvard [5] concluded that homes in the Roxbury ghetto of Boston are assessed at about 75 per cent of market value, whereas houses in affluent West Roxbury and Hyde Park are assessed at about 33 per cent of market value. In downtown Boston, commercial and office buildings are assessed at about 66 per cent of market value. As a result, the slum dweller, directly or indirectly, bears the largest share of the city's property tax.

The economic anarchy of the ghetto is matched by the mindlessness of its riots. The academician in the normal economy is quick to assume that riots occur in cities or areas where the greatest deprivation, racism, and police brutality exist. He mistakenly applies logic to a basically anarchical condition. Dr. John P. Spiegel, director of Brandeis University Lemberg Center

[3] *The New York Times* reported on March 7, 1968, that five hundred sound buildings have been completely deserted in Brownsville.

[4] On July 28, 1968, the New York City Real Estate Department took possession of 152 Harlem tenements under a New York Supreme Court seizure order. The properties were taken after the owners failed to pay real estate taxes for more than four successive years. The city announced that it had the unhappy distinction of being the largest slumlord in New York, operating about eight hundred tenements (*The New York Times,* July 29, 1968).

[5] By Oliver Oldman, Professor of Law, and Henry Aaron, a former Harvard economist.

for the Study of Violence, told the American Psychiatric Association in 1968: "The chances for riots are least likely in cities in which there is 'sincere recognition' of ferment, more likely where there is 'insincere recognition' and most likely where there is 'massive denial' [that a serious racial problem exists]." But there is no evidence that the ghetto behaves in such a logical fashion. On the contrary, the riots are rarely planned, occur at unpredictable times and places, and are frequently triggered by a seemingly insignificant event. In the summer of 1967, the arrest of a man for speeding in Newark and a routine raid on an after-hours bar in Detroit set off two of the most destructive riots in American history.

In Detroit the mayor and the police authorities have been considered the most progressive in the nation. Detroit's automotive industry supports the highest Negro wage rate of any city in the country. Detroit's United Auto Workers in considered the most enlightened large union, with aggressive programs for building membership among minorities. Yet so far Detroit has sustained greater violence and destruction than any other city in which rioting has occurred. The *Kerner Commission*'s report informs us that rats cause riots, but before the 1967 riots Detroit had implemented an advanced two-million-dollar rat-control program heralded as a model for the nation. The disorders after Martin Luther King's assassination in 1968 showed a similar senseless pattern. Looters, presumably out to destroy merchant credit records, spared those doing substantial credit business; burning occurred in guarded stores while unguarded stores were passed by.

The only predictable rule in the anarchy of the slum rebellion is that 90 per cent of riot damage occurs *inside the ghetto*.

Businessmen framing programs for new industry in ghetto areas are frequently bewildered by another unpredictable aspect of the slum economy—the implacable and illogical Negro opposition to programs for enrichment of the slums. One influential group in the Watts ghetto used every effort to discredit and insult the constructive programs of a former head of the Los Angeles Chamber of Commerce, H. D. McClellan, who arranged for twelve thousand or more jobs for residents of the Los Angeles curfew area after the 1965 riots.

Shearson Hammill & Co., Inc., announced in July, 1968, that it had signed a ten-year, five-hundred-thousand-dollar lease for space in a Harlem furniture store to operate a branch brokerage office. The Wall Street brokerage firm also committed 7.5 per cent of the slum branch's gross commissions to a foundation organized to provide capital for ghetto businesses and new job opportunities. This is the first effort made by a major stock-exchange house to enter the ghetto market in a generation. However, an official of the Congress of Racial Equality charged that the Shearson plan was a "conspiracy by state, municipal, and Wall Street interests to take over Harlem. White power sees Harlem as the potentially most valuable piece of real estate in New York City. . . . Harlem is too valuable to remain in black hands." The determination of black militants to remain credit poor is so great that insurance companies such as Equitable and Prudential, with a commitment of hundreds of millions of company funds for investment in ghetto areas, have been obliged to conceal the source of these funds by channeling them through Negro mortgage correspondents in slum areas.

The automobile industry has been at the forefront of industry programs for hiring the hard-core unemployables. It is estimated that the labor forces at Ford and Chrysler are better than 20 per cent black. But in 1968, five hundred Negro workers, charging that racism was prevalent throughout the automotive industry, led a wildcat strike which stopped production at the huge Chrysler assembly line at Hamtrack, Michigan.

One of the elements of the success of the American entrepreneur has been his ability to plan and predict his costs of supplies, labor, and production. This is assured by the relatively stable and reliable economy in which he functions. So long as it is possible to predict costs, American industry overseas has produced successfully in the most hostile environments of Africa and Asia. In the slum economy, however, labor is totally unpredictable and unreliable. Credit and capital costs for ghetto projects are not simply excessive, they are completely uncertain and widely variable. Fire and vandalism insurance may not cost more in the ghetto economy; it simply is not available—unless the "rioting profile" of a particular city is satisfactory.

The merchant, banker, or contractor in Chicago can assess his operating or construction costs in a politically unstable city in Latin America. An oil producer in Dallas can calculate within 2 per cent error limits the cost of assembling a drilling rig in the Sahara Desert or five hundred miles from the Arctic Circle. But it is impossible to set up a reasonably accurate *pro forma* projection of the capital costs or operating expenses of an assembly plant in the slums of our cities.

The ghetto economy spurns new plants or job facilities; it cherishes and protects the high-cost credit merchant and hippocket lender; it rejects the low-cost grocery cooperative in favor of the high-cost "bodega" or carryout food shops; its residents contest programs for private local ownership of the plants where they work or the apartments where they live.

Therefore, those who work toward rehabilitating the black economy must understand that the ghetto market is not just a poor economy with economic drives that are the same as, but weaker than, those of the main economy. Businessmen should not be surprised when sincere programs for Negro hiring do not attract job applicants and when new supermarkets not only are not patronized but are burned. Traditional money incentives and stimuli are ignored in the slums; creative programs for economic enrichment are met with either total inertia or implacable opposition.

The Negro economy is not simply underdeveloped, it is determinedly so and hostile to efforts to change it. The anarchy of uncertain expenses means that American business cannot undertake a commercial project in the ghetto economy without establishing contingent cost items and reserves which are either too large (and consequently unfair to the ghetto consumer) or too small (and so unfair to the entrepreneur or his stockholders). Thus, neatly packaged and finely tuned incentives or adjustments to the ghetto economy will not operate to make it normal or attractive to outside capital.[6] A 1 per cent interest-rate subsidy

___

[6] In August, 1965, Congress reduced the interest rate for certain low-income FHA housing projects from 4⅛ per cent to a flat 3 per cent. The rate change

payment to ghetto residents will not generate savings accumulations in its interracial banks; a minor income tax credit will not persuade a home owner in Watts to improve his house. In view of the hazards and uncertainties involved, a 10 per cent federal subsidy for hiring hard-core unemployables will not reduce slum unemployment.

Only massive incentives or benefits will be sufficient to convince the white businessman that the needs of the ghetto economy are indeed his needs. Only when the reward is manifestly large enough to cover all the risks and uncertainties involved can the merchant, banker, or businessman move capital, credit, and business expertise into the economy of the slum.

---

had no appreciable effect in stimulating interest in the FHA ghetto housing program. Yet, as we have seen, in the normal economy, hundreds of millions of dollars will move across a continent chasing a .05 percentage-point interest-rate differential.

The Separate Subsidiary
of the United States

THE PAINFULLY APPARENT FEATURES of the ghetto economy are its economic weaknesses, a low level of productivity, and the poverty level of its consumers. Not so obvious is the economic isolation of the ghetto—its complete separation from the normal American mainstream economy—of which it is a sick, dependent, and almost wholly owned subsidiary. Within the United States there is a separate nation of the poor, containing twice as many people as the population of Canada. Among these poor are four million Negro families, of which almost exactly one half have incomes under $3,000. Most of them live in the country's 163 urban ghettos.[7]

The pattern of developing economic isolation is illustrated by the growth of Boston's Roxbury slum. Twenty years ago, white middle-class residents moved out as the Negroes moved in. Local ownership became absentee ownership; business properties

[7] This is routine poverty. For a look at hard-core poverty, consider the profile of the average young adult Job Corps enrollee: Reading and math achievement of fourth-grade level. Eighty per cent have not seen a doctor or dentist in ten years. Almost always these factors are present: (1) broken home, (2) head of household unemployed, (3) family on relief, (4) sub-standard housing, (5) asked to leave school, (6) both parents with less than eighth-grade education (Clark Senate Subcommittee Examination of the War on Poverty, 1967).

31

were "milked"—cash siphoned off and invested more profitably elsewhere. Local real estate fell into decay as the black population steadily increased. In June, 1967, Roxbury residents rioted and burned their community. After this, nearly all business was suspended. The remaining stores became vacant and the vestiges of white capital withdrew entirely. The same pattern of decay has been repeated in the ghettos of Bedford-Stuyvesant, Hough, and Cincinnati's Avondale. In 1967, a Los Angeles realtor testified before a Senate Committee: "Watts has no economy." In almost all respects, the slum marketplace has become a foreign market—entirely distinct, deprived, dependent, and undeveloped.

Nowhere is the isolated character of the ghetto more evident than in the tariffs it imposes on life's necessities. Free markets in real estate rentals do not cross the barrier of the slum. Whitney Young reports that most of Chicago's one million Negroes (living in its two major ghettos) pay about thirty dollars a month more for housing than do whites who reside only a few blocks away. Statistics are unnecessary to prove the consummate skill of slumlords in "blockbusting" white neighborhoods and extracting greater rental profits from the suddenly isolated Negro or Puerto Rican poor.

Since the income profile of the Negro family does not generally meet the standards of lending institutions, the Negro home buyer, too, has been practically shut off from low-cost FHA mortgage loans. The National Urban League estimates that 30 per cent of Negro homes are puchased through loan speculators whose interest rates start at 10 per cent.

The sharpest differences in America's two economies are reflected in real estate values. In 1968, a report to the Society of Real Estate Appraisers stated that commercial property in the central business district of Watts was selling at an average of $4.75 a square foot. At the same time, bids for prime commercial sites in Manhattan ranged upward from $500 a square foot. In the normal economy, tax assessments are regularly increased to reflect the spiraling real estate values; but assessments are rarely reduced as property values sink in the ghetto. The higher real estate tax per dollar of actual fair market value is one of the punishing qualities of the isolated ghetto.

Closely tied to real estate taxes are expenditures for public education. The large disparity in expenditures for education is the most divisive aspect of the separate economies. Most cities base their educational expenditures per pupil on the assessed property values of the school district. For example, in the Robbins ghetto of Chicago, which is 99.1 per cent Negro, the assessed property value per child is $7,300. The tax rate is $2.02 per hundred dollars of valuation, and the annual expenditure per pupil is $300. In the city's affluent Kenilworth section, the assessed property value is $55,000 per child, the tax is less than $2 per hundred dollars of valuation, and the annual school expenditure is $800 per pupil.

Putting aside issues such as enforced integration of public schools and bussing of students from one district to another, very powerful economic forces are built into the fiscal systems of our cities, which resolutely maintain a kind of apartheid in education and job-training opportunity. Under these systems for allocating city real estate tax money for education according to the resources of the neighborhood, the weak and valueless ghetto economy cannot generate sufficient internal wealth to permit it to train and educate its children to read, tell time, or even make change well enough to permit them to enter the normal economy. As a result, the ghetto economy becomes even more isolated and deprived.

The isolation of the ghetto economy shows clearly in the tariffs it imposes on consumer goods. The price of oranges in East Harlem may be 15 per cent higher than in Manhattan markets catering to the Upper East Side carriage trade, fifteen blocks south. Studies by the Federal Trade Commission show that prices are substantially higher in the Bedford-Stuyvesant section of Brooklyn than they are in nearby Flatbush, a middle-class area. In St. Louis, a Catholic church in a Negro area has been bussing residents to an open-air market four miles away where they can save 10 to 15 per cent on vegetables.

Price differentials persist for many reasons. The ghetto mer-

33

chant is burdened by higher costs resulting from pilferage, curfews, and threat of riot damage.[8] His credit and collection costs are spectacularly high. The Federal Trade Commission reports that in depressed areas there is one garnishment suit for every $2,600 of consumer sales. This compares with one suit for every $232,000 in the national economy. The ghetto merchant is able to crank these extra costs into his retail prices, since he frequently enjoys a trading-area monopoly, with no competition from supermarkets or chain stores. The normal retail distribution system shuns the ghetto for more productive and safer markets downtown.

National brand products are frequently unavailable in slum areas. Presumably, the ghetto merchant will not handle these products unless he is permitted to inflate the retail prices, reflecting his higher costs and risks of remaining in business. National manufacturers, in turn, will not tolerate any form of price discrimination of their branded products. Also, the well-known appliance manufacturers are reluctant to permit their products to be sold in areas where deceptive sales practices are common. Since the ghettos have often been dumping grounds for spoiled or inferior products, the Negro cannot rely on brand names as assurance of quality unless he shops "outside." The result is a further division in our national economy: the ghetto merchant stocks off-brand items, and the Negro consumer pays the jacked-up prices.

Rioting has further reinforced the separation of the two consumer economies. Because of the threat of looting, ghetto stores operate with short inventory. The ghetto merchant has ceased to purchase in volume. Savings to the consumer through quantity discounts are therefore lost. Since the Newark riots, merchandise is delivered on a limited consignment basis to appliance and furniture stores on Springfield Avenue, the main shopping street in the Negro Central Ward.

---

[8] *Business Week* reports that in the Spring of 1968, the average store in Newark's Central Ward area had five employees instead of the three normally needed to service customers. This was so, even though the shops in the Central Ward were no longer open at night, formerly the period of greatest volume. The extra staff was needed for protection.

34

Division between the two economies is sharply reflected in labor markets. During the post-World War II period, when the national economy expanded quickly, there was a tendency to absorb and blend more Negroes into the employment mix, because industry was actively bidding for labor. This trend toward integrating the two economies has stopped. Increasing automation primarily affects unskilled blacks, whose jobs now can be performed by machines. In many instances, Negro unemployment increases when meager job skills are not equal in value to the existing minimum wage.

The ghetto economy is so isolated and so unresponsive that a massive increase in national spending barely dents slum levels of unemployment.[9] Former Secretary of Labor Willard Wirtz stated in a report to President Johnson on slum employment that "No conceivable increase in gross national product would stir these backwaters." Federal government statistics show that average individual income in New York's central Harlem actually dropped from $3,997 in 1960 to $3,907 in 1966. This occurred during a period when national income rose at a remarkable rate. The National Urban League notes that during 1960–65, when nationwide unemployment dropped 20 per cent, unemployment in Watts dropped 1 per cent.

Thirty five years ago the unemployment rate of Negroes and whites was about the same. Today the Negro rate is twice as high. In 1948, the 8 per cent unemployment rate for Negro teenage boys was actually less than that of whites. By 1964, the Negro unemployment had grown to 23 per cent, compared to 13 per cent for whites. In January, 1967, when the unemployment rate in the country was 3.7 per cent, the rate in Hough was 15.6 per cent; 13 per cent in Bayside, Oakland; 12.9 per

[9] It is conceivable that if the government abandoned 4 per cent unemployment as an acceptable norm and injected enough money into the economy to reduce unemployment to 3 per cent, a massive reduction in the current 33 per cent unemployment among ghetto teenagers might take place. At the moment, the risk of inflation and gold drain is so great that the government is moving toward higher taxes and, on other fronts, is pursuing a deflationary policy. The program of saving the dollar necessarily has the collateral effect of increasing unemployment. Some of the more militant blacks say that the government's desire to prevent inflation and to curb the gold drain is "crucifying our ghetto teenagers on a cross of gold."

35

cent on the north side of St. Louis; and 12 per cent in South Los Angeles.

Although the economic isolation of the ghetto is often a reflection of sharply lower job skills and frustrated opportunities, many cases exist in which the barriers are more tangible. The Watts curfew area in Los Angeles is physically isolated from the central city. Here major physical barriers block acquiring jobs, pursuing normal consumer purchasing, and recreation. A Watts resident who does not own a car must take three buses to get to a moving-picture theater in central Los Angeles, or four buses to get to his job in an aircraft plant in Burbank.

A resident of the Philadelphia ghetto—"the Jungle"—commuting to a suburban job in nearby Montgomery County changes buses three times each way and pays $6.60 a week for commutation. This weekly tariff is about 10 per cent of median ghetto family income after taxes. To go from San Francisco's Hunter's Point ghetto to new equal-employment-opportunity jobs in Contra Costa County requires four transfers, fifteen dollars a week carfare and five hours a day travel time. Chicago industry has virtually abandoned the city's central core, and residents in the city's two ghettos have no public transportation to Cook County's five new industrial areas.

Inadequate transportation may reinforce the economic isolation of the ghetto, but convenient transportation does not necessarily help. New York City's Bedford-Stuyvesant and East Harlem, two of the nation's most pernicious ghettos, are within fifteen minutes of midtown Manhattan by subway. Venice, California, a small but ever-persistent poverty area, enjoys a magnificent physical location directly west of central Los Angeles, on the Pacific Ocean. It adjoins prosperous Santa Monica on the north and Playa Del Rey on the south. But, ironically, nature's beauty doesn't bring "bread."

The economic isolation of the ghetto is also reflected in the absence of normal flows of capital and credit. The black slums are starved for these essential ingredients of a healthy economy. This condition is worsened because the ghetto credit system is almost wholly controlled by underworld lenders. The extra credit risks of the core areas require a drastically higher interest charge to cover bad-debt losses. Downtown banks refuse to lend at these higher interest rates. Therefore, conventional outside capital does not flow into the slums in response to a normal investment opportunity. If money does enter, it must leap over the "tariff" barriers impelled by an uneconomic allocation of government resources, or by a willful, benevolent and uneconomic infusion of private capital or of job-creation opportunities.

The pervasive split between the ghetto economy and the normal economy is reinforced by divisive influences within the groups themselves. After the 1967 riots, the New Detroit Committee of Businessmen negotiated with a militant Negro group to create a program for technical assistance to strengthen the black community, particularly in housing, education, and community services. Many white businessmen in Detroit accused the Committee of rewarding riots and blackmail, of selling out to black separatists. Although Negro moderates agreed that the New Detroit Committee was trying to buy off the black militants, they were willing to accept ghetto-rehabilitation programs that provided administrative controls by the Committee. The black militants, on the other hand, refused to accept the program since these "strings" violated the principles of Negro "self-determination." The Negro militant-moderate split was matched by an equally sharp division of opinion among white businessmen.

An identical pattern of divisive attitudes developed in 1967 over a proposed thirty-five-acre industrial park for the burned-out area of Watts. The whites pointed to the benefits of increased real estate values and new jobs in an area where real estate was dilapidated and 12 per cent of adults were unemployed. The blacks charged fraud, a land grab by the Southern Pacific Company, and job discrimination in existing plants in Watts. They threatened to bring out their guns if the industrial park materialized. A vice president of the Fund for the Republic assessed the situation: "Benevolent whites were startled when the residents of Watts said that they wanted no part of an industrial park in their city. To the benevolent white an industrial park looked like a humming job market. To residents of Watts it looked like

37

another generation of dirty, low-paying, and uncertain jobs. The ownership of the factories would be light-miles away and likely to close up shop for bad reasons and good. Watts had experienced this before, had called it exploitation, and decided it wanted no more of it." [10] The proposed industrial park was postponed. Such Negro-White dialogues about what is best for the ghetto produce a complete breakdown in programs and further reinforcement of the two separate economies.

The separate nature of the black economy takes on special significance in relation to ghetto rioting. Consider the important difference between such rioting and even the most violent labor dispute. A labor strike has a direct and fundamental effect on the national or a regional economy. The use of the strike weapon in Pittsburgh or Schenectady usually evokes a strong management response. But the labor strike always occurs within the legitimate framework of the normal economy; it is one part of the collective-bargaining technique our economy permits and our laws protect. In 1967, Milwaukee Negro boycotts of white businesses occurred within the fabric of the white economy. A direct economic pressure was brought to bear on the businessmen of the community to achieve the political goal of integrated housing. Even slave revolts in the South before the outbreak of the Civil War occurred within the economy, because the slaves were an integral ingredient of the southern agrarian system.

However, the Negro ghetto riots of past decades have had a limited impact. The black slums were so physically and economically insulated that the white economy was never seriously affected by violence in the ghetto. Business in Los Angeles proper was barely interrupted when Watts rioted for a week in 1965. Riots in Harlem have rarely had a direct effect on commerce downtown. But for the first time, in the summer of 1967, the rioting in Detroit and Newark infected the greater urban economies. Hotel and department-store business dried up during the 1967 burning in Detroit. In the spring of 1968, following the assassination of Martin Luther King, Jr., retail stores in the best

[10] W. H. Ferry, "The Case for a New Federalism," *Saturday Review*, June 15, 1968, p. 15.

38

locations lost their earlier insulation from damage. In Washington, looters swept down F Street, only a few blocks from the White House. Riots are no longer confined to the ghetto, where 90 per cent of the damage is to Negro property, and have therefore acquired a new immediacy.

Ironically, burning and looting in the cities may lead to a first step in an eventual merger of the two economies. Riots and the threat of future city-wide violence have provided an urgent need for business to make plant investments and provide jobs in the ghetto. These measures are becoming a matter of economic necessity and business self-preservation. Proposals for the allocation of business capital and credit can no longer be dismissed as an "uneconomic allocation of resources to the wasteland." Businessmen, being practical men, see a sounder business basis for taking corrective action to break the isolation of the ghetto— action which formerly might have been considered only in the public interest.

Resolute Safeguards Against Profits

COMMENTATORS IN EUROPE, and even our critics behind the Iron Curtain, have extolled the extraordinary quality of our American economy and the almost universal opportunity it offers its people to profit and grow rich. But next to the economic mainstream of America is the unprofitable economy of the ghetto. Not everyone agrees, of course, that the ghetto is an economic wasteland. Black nationalism teaches that the Negroes of America are a kind of subjugated colony, potentially rich but undeveloped. Militant blacks charge that the whites in America maintain the black ghetto's "economic dependency" because it is contrary to white economic interests to train and finance the blacks so that they may share the white man's secret of wealth. They argue that if the Negro is educated or trained ("liberated" is the word black nationalists use) a large reservoir of cheap industrial, domestic, and service labor would be lost to the white American industrialist or housewife.

These specious but appealing arguments are fortified with statistics about the vast buying power of the Negro economy. The ghetto economy, so the argument runs, is being exploited and bled from the outside. The unfortunate fact is that the ghetto economy, with undeniable assistance from white racism, has now banished all profit opportunities or investment attractions. There are, indeed, very powerful conditions and safeguards which guarantee to keep the ghetto poor, but these conditions only partially support the black nationalist creed.

Certainly, the contemporary American ghetto has a superficial resemblance to the subjugated colonies of Africa and Asia in the nineteenth century. Like a territorial colony, the ghetto is isolated and dependent on the "master economy." Both are economically undeveloped. But here the analogy ends. The African colonies were developed and maintained for their vast natural resources and cheap labor. The American ghetto offers neither. Its commercial real estate is virtually worthless. Money invested in new ghetto construction or in rehabilitation does not yield the capital-gains profit readily available elsewhere, since the value of property in the slum is most likely determined by the condition of surrounding buildings rather than by its own condition.

The slum's residents are rejected as potential employees by a free-market economic system whose extraordinary productivity requires both education and skill. Increasing automation and higher-minimum-wage laws have further reduced the ghetto resident to an unwanted and unprofitable labor commodity. A hundred years ago, European nations developed colonies to provide new markets for manufactured goods. There are no such markets in Lawndale, Avondale, or Hough.

Years ago, the nation's financial institutions withdrew from the profitless Negro districts. The darkest ghettos of America, such as Watts and Bedford-Stuyvesant, have no important branches of downtown banks. The basic leverage opportunity— to use credit or other people's money to build affluence or acquire the ownership of capital—is therefore missing. Life-insurance companies have long ago recognized the lower life expectancy of Negroes and have not sought out life-insurance contracts in the ghetto.[11] Some of America's fire and casualty

11 Blacks have a saying: "My mother used to tell me, 'If you live to be twenty-one, you know the Lord's been good to you.' " The White House stated

41

companies have sustained massive underwriting losses as a result of fires and rioting in urban areas. Basic disaster protection, an essential background against which all normal business activity operates, is thus missing from the ghetto. Even before the riots and profit-killing curfews, the incidence of fire and inventory theft was much greater in slum communities such as Brownsville than across the East River in Manhattan.

The giant American retail and supermarket chains are either not present or, at best, not profiting in any important way in slum areas. A Safeway store was burned out in Watts in 1965 and hasn't yet returned. A&P, which has substantial and commendable operations in East Harlem, has been called on the Congressional carpet with allegations of overcharging and selling spoiled meat and vegetables. It is doubtful that top management of either Safeway or A&P could find profit nourishment in pursuing policies of price or quality discrimination in the ghetto. Even a 15 per cent retail price differential would not compensate national merchants for the additional costs of doing business in Negro core areas. The national supermarket chains, which remain in the ghettos stay there either through inertia, a sense of civic responsibility, or fear of a bad press if they withdraw.

General Motors and RCA profit handsomely on the sale of new cars or television sets in what militant Negroes call the "master economy." But how much does it matter to these companies' profit-and-loss statements that the impoverished Negro community provides a tenuous and unreliable "after market" for second-hand automobiles and appliances?

Unquestionably, isolated pockets of profit exist in the ghetto. But crucial to any corrective program is for blacks and whites to recognize that these profit centers belong only to the marginally legal or underworld business operators. There are profits in the illegal sale of narcotics, in slumlording, and in real estate

in 1967 that the estimated life span is 71 years for whites, 64 years for non-whites. The death rate is 40 deaths per thousand non-white children, 21 deaths per thousand white children. There are 90 maternal deaths per 100,000 deliveries for poor Negro mothers, 22 maternal deaths per 100,000 for white mothers. The infant mortality rate is so high in the American ghetto that it has increased the national average (24.7 per thousand in 1965) to a point where it is twice the rate of Sweden.

42

"blockbusting." The loan sharks and the white numbers racketeers who come daily to the ghetto to settle accounts are making a profit.[12] But since the rioting, even the slumlord and the gouging furniture credit merchant have a difficult time finding buyers for their businesses. The capital of the predatory businessmen is now locked into the ghetto as securely as are their victims.

In the ghetto the low levels of individual income and skills (twice the normal labor turnover rate), the unsettling effect of riots, higher real estate taxes, yards of red tape on FHA or SBA loan applications, canceled fire policies, sick real estate and absence of reasonably priced credit have all provided guarantees and safeguards against legitimate business profits. These ghetto "safeguards" make it nearly impossible for an aspiring Negro merchant or business entrepreneur to find start-up loans. The ambitious Negro with talent has very little idea of how to construct the cash-flow or net-worth statement required by the bank examiner. Patterns of discrimination, particularly in the labor unions, make it difficult for the Negro entrepreneur to locate his office or plant in the more desirable areas. Skilled white managerial personnel or salesmen will rarely work for a Negro. Other Negroes lack sales or management experience. It is almost impossible for a Negro to operate or market products in the normal white economy. The ambitious Negro businessman is therefore confined to the profitless market of the ghetto.[13]

The straightforward project of organizing a new business becomes an agonizing puzzle. Consider the history of a new cooperative supermarket launched at 147th Street and Seventh Avenue in Harlem during the spring of 1968. After working eleven years in the cooperative movement without seeing one cooperative market materialize in Harlem, Cora T. Walker recruited seventeen teenagers from the Federal Poverty Program and promised them a party if they could sell $10,000 worth of

[12] Leonard Hunter, the Negro deputy sheriff of Chicago's Cook County and a keen observer of ghetto economics, says, "Money comes into the ghetto at nine in the morning; and all of it leaves again by five at night."

[13] The most notable exception is H. G. Parks, Inc., of Baltimore. This Negro-owned firm markets about $7.5 million of sausages a year under the famous TV slogan "More Parks Sausages, Ma." Seventy-five per cent of the firm's retail consumers are white.

co-op shares at $5 each. They sold the shares, and she leased land at a cooperative housing site. Then she went to Litton Industries for a loan of $150,000. Litton supplied the credit in the form of refrigeration units. She arranged bank financing through New York City's Economic Development Council, and persuaded the Shop-Rite chain to serve as consultants. "It was so complicated," she explained, "that I never would have gone even part way if I hadn't been a lawyer." [14]

The formation of new businesses, a process which is achieved easily and rapidly outside the ghetto, barely operates in the slum society. This inability to sponsor and build new entrepreneurial profit centers—a vital method by which people become affluent in the normal economy—is an important force in keeping the ghetto poor.

[14] *The New York Times,* May 26, 1968, carried an extraordinary account of how nine Puerto Rican factory workers with $9,000 in front money struggled to become the owners of a steel fabricating plant in Brooklyn. The project was brought off through herculean efforts of the Economic Development Administration, the Small Business Administration, First National City Bank (two officers assigned to work up the SBA loan application), Gibraltar Factors (a commercial finance company), Consolidated Edison and Brooklyn Union Gas (waived utility deposits), management consultant Henry E. Allen (recruited by First National City Bank), a Brooklyn City Council leader, and at least three Brooklyn community anti-poverty agencies.

Frozen Arteries
of Credit

A HARLEM CIVIC LEADER used to say to his New York City radio audience: "I remember listening to a white bank president in Hartford who said in my presence that he had never known a Negro in whom he had confidence for more than a three-hundred-dollar loan." This statement cannot be dismissed as simply the bigotry of a white banker. Today, three hundred dollars has much less value than when the statement was made, but the Negro credit profile has not changed.[15] A bank's routine credit check on a ghetto borrower finds nothing—not bad credit, but simply no credit. Of the more than twenty-three million Negroes and Puerto Ricans in the United States today, only a minuscule percentage can execute an unsecured note for three hundred dollars which is bankable at even an interracial lending institution. Moreover, when measured by credit risks in the safe economy downtown, there is virtually no interest rate high enough to compensate a lender for the average unsecured or commercial

15 Perhaps it has been modified. Most installment credit officers used to consider only the income of the head of the household, ignoring the income of working spouses. This rule excluded hundreds of thousands of Negro families from credit, since two working parents is more common in the ghetto economy. Some banks are now revising their lending manuals.

45

credit risk in the ghetto. The Negro businessman is not credit-worthy because of the inherent weakness of his business and his marketing skills. At the same time, he is unable to establish a strong business tradition because of his inability to attract credit. Thus, he becomes involved in a cycle of total entrepreneurial failure.

Months before the bankruptcy of his company, William Zeck-endorf, one of the most sophisticated and nimble borrowers of our time, was taking down millions of dollars in loans at interest rates of 20 per cent and higher in order to pay other pressing creditors. He was fond of saying to his detractors, "Better alive at twenty per cent than dead at the prime rate." When the final crunch came, Zeckendorf had seven mortgages on his estate in Greenwich, with interest rates moving downward from 49.29 per cent.[16] Zeckendorf's credit plight might seem to be similar to the Negro borrower in the ghetto who desperately pays his tribute of "vigorish" every Friday to his favorite loan shark. The situation could not be more different. Zeckendorf operated in the sophisticated money markets of America, where credit is almost always available at a predictable rate—the interest rate always depending on the repayment terms and on the credit risk.

The Negro business borrower operates in a credit-isolated economy where loans are always expensive. Just as important, funds are frozen and unresponsive to credit risk. The single great pathology of an urban ghetto economy is its weak and miserable patterns of credit.

Moneylenders report that when they repossess a property in the ghetto, an important cause of the credit failure is that the owner has burdened the parcels with two, three, or more home-

16 *The Wall Street Journal*'s account (May 10, 1965) of the Webb & Knapp bankruptcy is a tribute to the unique ability of the mainstream economy to extend credit suitable for almost any risk: "Marine Midland's petition declared Webb & Knapp 'is insolvent and unable to pay its debts as they mature.' As of March 15, the petition said, these debts—excluding conventional first mortgages and the debentures—totaled $31.8 million, carried interest rates as high as 49.29% and were owed to about 75 big and small creditors, ranging from major banks, leading industrial companies and prominent financiers to accountants, architects and landscape gardeners. It added that these creditors held an assorted variety of collateral ranging from most of Webb & Knapp's securities in its affiliated companies to personal guarantees by Mr. Zeckendorf and—in one case —a seventh mortgage of his Greenwich, Conn., weekend estate."

46

improvement loans. The ghetto economy lives on short-term, high-interest-rate second and third mortgages. In the normal economy, secondary liens are rarely used except by the sophisticated borrower seeking maximum leverage and advantage for his capital. In the ghetto economy these mortgages are the indicia of credit desperation rather than planned leverage.

In the normal free-market credit economy, every credit risk commands a compensating interest. The normal credit market is so fluid and precise that the appropriate rate can be found in a banker's manual. For example, automobile-purchase loans command a pegged rate of 6 per cent in advance (about 12 per cent per annum). This rate is generous enough to allow banks a profit—with good and bad credit risks averaging out. Banks, like insurance companies, have long ago learned: "You take 'em or you turn 'em down." There are no first-, second-, or third-class private citizen borrowers or insured persons. But the ghetto borrower or insurance applicant is excluded from the actuaries' calculations.

White businessmen, on the other hand, are more sophisticated and accept credit ratings. There are hundreds of layers of varying credit risks, all commanding a fairly precise and predictable interest rate that measures the risk in a free-credit market—6 per cent for collateral loans secured by federal government securities, 7 per cent for prime business borrowers, 7½ per cent for commercial borrowers who are "less than prime," and 12 per cent for "non-bankable" fledgling business borrowers at regulated and responsible commercial finance companies. This is the magnificent liquidity of normal credit markets which supply a basic element of our national affluence.

In the normal economy, commercial paper (a short-term promise by a large corporation) is saleable on the telephone in denominations of millions of dollars, at a price or rate that may fluctuate only a fraction of a point from one day to the next. A bank that is overloaned can readily "warehouse" or sell its mortgages and commercial loans without great sacrifice. This liquidity exists because money is almost always available at a rate, and moves freely through hundreds of arteries chasing a

47

higher interest rate, a shorter repayment term, or a lower credit risk.

A leading New York City bank recently offered its customers "A Red Rose Loan." Along with the proceeds of the loan the borrower received a red rose as a memento of the bank's generosity. Another bank fatuously offers "A Fairy Godmother Loan," and another, "An Aladdin's Lamp Loan." Banks can't feed out credit fast enough in the normal economy; yet there are no "Red Rose Loans" in Bedford-Stuyvesant—for housewives or businessmen. In every area of ghetto borrowing, credit costs more or is completely unavailable. This is what Negroes call the "tax on being colored." The interest charge is 20 per cent a month for business people and typically "six for five" [17] for hotel maids.

However unjust, the "color tax" is only a symptom of a fundamental problem that goes beyond discrimination in white lending institutions. Ghetto credit is isolated, it is frozen, it does not flow, it does not respond in rate to individual differences of credit risk. In the ghetto economy, there are no free-credit markets. In the banker's lexicon, all loans and credits are "soft." There is no free-market bargaining for a loan. The banker "grants" a loan to a Negro businessman. The bank or insurance company "pledges" loans for slum housing. Because a loan to a Negro is "soft" and does not originate from an arm's-length bargaining credit transaction, a credit to a Hough businessman (without a Small Business Administration guarantee of repayment) or a conventional home mortgage in Bedford-Stuyvesant is basically unsaleable by the lender except at a sacrifice. The institution lending in the ghetto is "locked in" to its loans, even if the borrower is sound and real estate collateral is good.

Credit is not exported to the ghetto because the ghetto borrower is risky, unpredictable, and unreliable. The downtown banker's aversion to getting stuck with a soft loan is reinforced as soon as the aspiring Negro businessman enters a branch to apply for a business loan—itself an unlikely act of bravery. Many of

---

[17] The borrower takes down five dollars on Monday and repays six dollars five days later on payday. The effective annual interest rate is 1000 per cent!

48

the most able and intelligent young men in the ghetto economy dress in the African style and have a "cool" manner of speech —an approach hardly likely to inspire the confidence of the lending officer. Moreover, no downtown banker wants to hold the note of a Negro businessman, because he doesn't want the bad publicity that may ensue if he has to "pull the string" on a minority borrower. A responsible banker today would no more close up on a struggling Negro entrepreneur than he would foreclose on the homestead of an impoverished widow or on a church. National sympathy for the Negro's plight and strong national commitments to equal rights and opportunities have therefore further restricted the flow of credit to the ghetto. Political and social equality has actually aggravated the Negro's credit plight.

The weakness of credit in the ghetto is paralleled by heroic but almost hopeless efforts to establish indigenous, locally owned banks in black slums. In the later part of the nineteenth century, a vigorous Negro banking movement existed in this country. Following the Civil War, the black-owned-and-controlled Freedmen's Bank was established to encourage thrift among newly emancipated slaves. At one time the Freedmen's Bank had thirty or more branches, with offices in Washington, Philadelphia, and New York, servicing only Negro depositors and businessmen. Negro banks were particularly strong in the South, where economic segregation gave them an umbrella of protection from the competition of white-owned banks. But in the North, the Negro was always permitted to trade at white banks. Ironically, this competitive sharing of the Negro customer's deposit, loan, and thrift business weakened Negro banks in northern cities.

Most black banks failed along with thousands of the nation's banks in the panics and the depressions of the past seventy-five years. A contributing factor to this failure was that the ghetto banks were not sustained by low-cost commercial-loan portfolios, which are the profit backbone of American banking. The Negro economy of small shops, service establishments, and funeral parlors did not require commercial credit. When the commercial banks moved into the field of retail and personal credit in the 1930's, they naturally avoided high-risk ghetto areas.

49

In the past there have been occasional experiments with so-called "interracial" banks. In 1928, John D. Rockefeller opened the interracial Dunbar National Bank at West 150th Street and Eighth Avenue in Harlem. While Rockefeller retained ownership, his objective was the operation of a bank that employed Negroes and accepted their deposits. The bank was liquidated in 1938. Today the sources of Negro-operated-and-controlled bank credit are severely restricted. There are twenty Negro-owned-and-operated banks in the country. Their total assets are $162 million, compared with $334 billion for all banks in the nation.

The strongest and most aggressive black credit institution operating in the American ghetto today, an outstanding monument to black credit power, is Harlem's Freedom National Bank, with a branch in Brooklyn's Bedford-Stuyvesant which represents 20 per cent of the bank's total business. Freedom National claims to have made more Small Business Administration-insured loans to Negro businesses than any other bank in the country. A television program, broadcast after the assassination of Martin Luther King, reported dozens of commercial loans made by Freedom National Bank to Negro hardware stores, druggists, and restaurants. All of these loans had previously been declined by the large metropolitan banks of New York City.[18]

The American Bankers Association can take little comfort in the bold efforts of Freedom National Bank to move commercial business credit into the slum. Three hundred banks in the United States have deposits exceeding $160 million each. Freedom National, the largest Negro-owned bank in the country, has deposits of only $30 million; it currently ranks 1,733 among the 14,000 commercial banks in the country. As F. Scott Fitzgerald once said, "Large banks are very different from small banks . . . they have more money"; the money in the large banks is barely

[18] Kenwoods Furniture Store, 125th Street, Harlem; four Negro partners doing business as Embassy Pharmacy (customers were "slow pay" and receivables were not "bankable"); Strachan's Hardware Store, Eighth Avenue, Harlem (lost business to competing white establishments because inventory was inadequate; loan for expansion of inventory declined); Oliver Clark, Bedford-Stuyvesant, for home improvement ("The banks said they would see; they never saw"); Richard Rujo, Myrtle Avenue, Bedford-Stuyvesant (declined loan for Chicken Delight franchise—his gross volume now exceeds $100,000 per year).

trickling into the slum economy.

The credit plight of the ghetto is aggravated by the bad press downtown banks command in the slum areas. Negroes are distrustful and suspicious of the money society. During 1967 hearings, a Senate Committee disclosed that only about 10 per cent of Puerto Rican-American businesses (usually food retail outlets—"bodegas") have bank accounts; only 5 per cent use any type of bank credit. A large number of them initially started in business with the financial help of loan sharks.

David Rockefeller, President of the Chase Manhattan Bank, tells of the experience of one of his credit men who visited three hundred retail establishments in Harlem to find out what additional business services the bank could supply to ghetto businesses: "Almost everywhere he went, he was viewed with suspicion and felt hard pressed to find ways of countering it. He took to keeping the flaps of his coat open to indicate that he was not carrying a gun. Frequently, he had to begin his visit by explaining that he was not a policeman, a tax collector, a social worker, or a holdup man."

Black nationalists teach that the large metropolitan banks are financing the slumlords, the gouging credit merchants, the loan sharks. The banks have not successfully refuted these charges. Hostility of many Negroes to the banking community is illustrated by the organized efforts now being carried out to encourage mass voluntary bankruptcies as a means of punishing local merchants, banks, and finance companies. Meetings of black militants teach the advantages and techniques of bankruptcy. Even though the Chemical Bank New York Trust Company in New York City has been financing open housing for ten years, few people have heard of this splendid program.

The dearth of ghetto bank credit does not mean that Wall Street and other metropolitan banks do not have branches in slum areas, although they are few. In Manhattan, the ratio of commercial banks is about one for every 5,000 residents of the city. In Harlem, the commercial center of the Negro economy, the ratio is one commercial bank for every 30,000 residents. In Los Angeles, in the fall of 1967, I could identify no commercial bank among the boarded-up shop-fronts of Watts. The Brooklyn Bedford-Stuyvesant ghetto, a major city in itself, of 400,000 inhabitants, has one commercial bank.

The ghettos of America are underbanked partly because of discrimination on the loan platform; but the dominant cause is the massive credit tariffs built into the slum economy. The high costs or tariffs of ghetto banking are built on the principle that these banks must service a large number of customers who have small and active savings accounts. These banks invariably have a low ratio of low-cost demand deposits or checking accounts to high-cost time deposits or savings accounts. At three New York City ghetto branches of Puerto Rico's Banco de Ponce, passbook savings deposits account for 87 per cent of total deposits. At the hard-core Brownsville branch, the ratio is 98 per cent.

In the normal economy, bankers accept and absorb the cost of heavy activity on special checking accounts because (1) the bank charges for each check drawn on the account, and (2) the banks have successfully guarded their legal privilege not to pay interest on checking accounts. But in the ghetto economy, even the small businessman maintains a savings account instead of a special checking account. The ghetto bank must therefore absorb, without a compensating fee, all the extra-activity costs of withdrawals and deposits in savings accounts.[19]

An example of the punishing extra costs of banking in the ghetto is Harlem's Freedom National Bank. The bank's thirty million dollars in deposits requires 85 employees. A typical bank of this size operating in the normal economy would have half that number on its payroll.

In the normal economy, a commercial loan to a small businessman may be simply an unsecured note or a note secured by a pledge of securities, inventory, or accounts receivable. A million-dollar commercial loan made to a prime borrower is committed

---

[19] Ghetto banks are even denied the larger and more profitable deposits of the more affluent members of the black economy. Robert L. Davis, executive vice president of Houston's black-controlled Riverside National Bank, suggests that Negro professional men feel that some sort of stigma is attached to dealing with a bank operated by members of their own race (*Barron's*, January 13, 1969).

on the telephone without the cost of any credit check. In the ghetto economy, making each commercial loan is a struggle. Collateralization of the loan is usually a mixed bag of basically unmarketable and unbankable items: a second mortgage on the borrower's home and car; a wage assignment from his wife, if she works; a pledge of accounts receivable owed by customers who are inherently slow to pay. If the ghetto loan is to be guaranteed by the Small Business Administration, the delays in multiple credit checks and approvals are intolerable. A ghetto businessman told the Kerner Commission: "By the time the loan comes through, the borrower is dead or it doesn't matter any more."

The cost burden of banking in the ghetto is further increased because the commercial borrower has no financial experience or training. The President of Freedom National Bank states that a major problem of his loan officers is to determine exactly how much the borrower needs to borrow in order to save his business.[20] The ghetto bank is ineffective unless it can render or call in management consulting services not usually required in the normal economy.

The same extra cost patterns exist for consumer loans in the ghetto. In Harlem, the average installment loan is very small; the collateral is second-hand and unmarketable. The borrower's credit profile is held unbankable by downtown standards. The ghetto borrower's bad-debt loss is very high. According to a 1968 report by Federal Reserve Governor Andrew Brimmer, 10 per cent of the outstanding paper held by black banks is, on average, past due.

In our urban economy the downtown branches skim off the cream of the desirable consumer loans. One mortgage banker states the matter frankly: "We are cream lenders, not creed lenders, and it has been damn difficult to switch to doing creed

[20] At an American Management Association Seminar in New York City in June, 1968, William Hudgins, President of Freedom National, described the negotiation of a typical commercial-loan application in the ghetto: "We talked to him and saw that he needed not $10,000 but $25,000 to get off the treadmill. We told him we would give him the loan provided he would: (1) use a certified public accountant, (2) cut his own salary, (3) set up a tax account, (4) keep a minimum inventory of $12,000, (5) see his bills were paid by the 10th of every month, (6) take a second mortgage on his home."

business." The marginal and submarginal loans are left for the financial institutions of the ghetto.

Nick Ortiz, Manager of the Banco Popular de Puerto Rico branch in New York City, cites the basic problems and costs in lending in the ghetto: (1) High promotional costs (75 per cent of their customers have never had any banking experience—a checking or savings account, or even a loan). (2) About 50 per cent of their personal loans (largest income-producing areas to these banks) are for $600 or less; a bank loses money on any loan for less than $300. (3) Income from commercial loans is very limited. (4) A lot of their energy is channeled into social activities, civic and general guidance, as part of their effort to uplift the community. (5) Highly competitive salaries[21] must be paid to maintain a civic-oriented, business-minded bilingual staff. (6) By servicing small businessmen and marginal clients in ghetto areas they face the consequence of greater credit risks.

Banks do not publish their profits or losses in slum-area branches. In 1968, a Federal Reserve study, conducted under the supervision of Andrew Brimmer, evaluated the nation's banks according to capital adequacy, asset quality, and management performance. Sixty per cent of white banks were given Class I ratings. Only 20 per cent of the Negro-owned banks achieved that status. The average white-owned bank returns a profit of 9.6 per cent on invested capital. Taken together, the Negro banks show a loss steadily increasing since 1964.

Thus, most ghetto branches of downtown banks are sustained as "demonstration projects." Their existence reflects bank management policy of never terminating a branch operation except under the most trying conditions. Burdened with the punishing extra costs of extending credit in the ghetto economy, the downtown banker faces the same dilemma as the department-store chain or the manufacturer seeking to sell or manufacture in the slum economy. To carry on business at even a break-even basis would require a massive compensating retail or wholesale markup. A national corporation will avoid all business activities

[21] The *Brimmer Report* states that the average employee salary in black banks was $4,290 in 1968, compared with $3,796 for all federally insured banks.

54

in the black poverty areas rather than impose such an extra tax on the black purchaser. The downtown banker also backs away from assessing the extra interest cost on a ghetto borrower.

Indeed, ghetto interracial banks charge a higher interest rate on ghetto consumer loans than prevails in the normal economy. For example, the effective interest rate on consumer loans at the New York ghetto branches of Banco de Ponce is about 1.5 per cent higher than the prevailing rate downtown. Banks controlled by a minority group are not vulnerable to charges of gouging or racial discrimination. Therefore, they may compensate themselves in part for the higher costs of extending credit in the ghetto economy. However, there is no possible way that the Chase Manhattan Bank can establish at its ghetto branches a higher rate on consumer loans than it charges at downtown branches in the normal economy, or an extra penalty charge for unusual activity in deposit accounts. This is the essential dilemma of the metropolitan bank, and the most fundamental reason that bank credit is not moving into the black slums. Until the differences in cost are adjusted or compensated in a manner which is just and ethically acceptable to the nation, the ghetto economy will continue to be ruled by the high-interest-rate credit merchants who prevent the formation of normal patterns of credit.

Federal and state laws in the United States now prohibit the refusal to deny credit on account of race or color. But these laws cannot legislate credit into the ghetto; they cannot restore credit to an economy whose tariffs of risk and unprofitability have resolutely banished all forms of reasonably priced credit. Fourteen thousand commercial banks have no functional need to extend credit in the slums. Under present conditions there is absolutely no basis on which loans can be exported to black areas on a basis fair to the lender and to his ghetto borrower.

The Failure of Savings and Front-End Money

A THIRTEEN-YEAR-OLD Negro boy in Detroit recently told a reporter: "There's nothing the matter with niggers that money can't solve." This statement contains a world of wisdom about ghetto economics. The slum economy works resolutely against the development of savings and the ownership of risk capital—the essential spark which white businessmen use to grow affluent in the outside economy. Never has any society, including the Soviet Union, broken the chains of poverty or underdevelopment without the aid of voluntary or involuntary internal savings.

At the downtown Dollar Bank for Savings, with branches all over New York City, the average savings account is $2,000 to $3,000. At the Negro-owned Freedom National Bank in the commercial center of Harlem, the average individual savings account is a few hundred dollars (including the accounts of hundreds of ghetto businessmen who use savings accounts as a substitute for business checking accounts).

On Main Street, the middle-class American saves in order to live better tomorrow. Capital means power and leads to social and economic progress. In the normal economy, adequate interest rates attract savings. The taxing economics of urban slums discourage and forbid the natural accumulation of savings and capital. Therefore the total failure to build savings and convert it into risk capital is surely one of the outstanding defects of the ghetto economy.

In the ghetto the usual generation of capital funds in the form of personal savings does not occur, since the slum dweller lives on an economic ragged edge where all money is spent to satisfy basic needs of human survival. Even when discretionary funds can be squeezed out, the Negro, Puerto Rican, or Mexican-American is not convinced that if he saves today he can earn or spend more tomorrow. The payment of interest as the conventional incentive to attract savings does not work. For a man who is borrowing from the credit merchants at a rate of 20 per cent or more, an interest rate on savings accounts of double the normal 5.5 per cent does not divert money from the numbers operator or make the difference between saving and spending.

Deferred gratification is one of the essential luxuries of the normal economy. The white man has confidence in a stable society; he is confident of his ability to hold a job; he takes risks with a part of his capital because he knows his family is secure; he has an opportunity to invest and progress. The resident of the ghetto may know that in America personal progress in business has frequently been the easiest route to social progress. Yet even if he puts money aside for savings, there remain those crushing patterns of unequal business opportunity that stand in the way of his translating this capital into new business ventures, ownership of real estate equities, or other profit possibilities.

Individual aspirations exist, of course, but the opportunities are not visible—they do not act as a catalyst to personal savings. A television set that goes into a pawnshop at the time of financial crisis and is reclaimed when the welfare check arrives indicates only a weak and primitive instinct to put money aside for a rainy day. Instead of saving for new furniture, the slum dweller buys shoddy, second-hand tables or chairs. Instead of saving to buy anything, he borrows at usurious interest rates.

In the undeveloped countries of Latin America and Africa, the major "disincentives" to personal savings are weak banks and national inflations that frequently wipe out 20 per cent of personal capital in a few days. In this country, bank deposits are insured by government agencies in the ghetto as well as in the white economy. The risk of inflation does not discriminate against ghetto thrift accounts. Yet excess business funds generated in the ghettos are promptly withdrawn and redeposited or invested in the more hospitable and stable economy outside the slum.

This failure of individuals, businesses, or other ghetto-bound institutions to create an adequate pool of credit or capital in the urban slum is not compensated by capital exports from the outside. Only "hit and run" capital moves in and out of the slum every day to settle up the accounts of the loan sharks and the numbers operators. No profit opportunities exist to overcome the chaotic economic disincentives which act as a barrier to moving established and permanent outside capital into the slum. In recent years the threat of riots and curfews has caused a fresh and massive outflow of money from Watts, Hough, and the Central Ward of Newark.

In the mainstream economy, a man with business talent or a product idea who is shy of necessary front-end risk money with which to launch it turns to a number of sources of capital. The "seed money" may come from an affluent relative, a group of friends on the lookout for capital gains, a banker who is willing to "stretch a point," and (most importantly) that great American reservoir of risk capital—the markets for new security issues. In the ghetto economy, affluent friends or relatives are rare; discretionary investment funds are meager; the capital-gains opportunity holds little allure. There are no security markets either in the ghetto or downtown for new issues to finance the start-up costs of black business enterprises. Branch offices of stock-exchange houses were unknown in the ghetto until Shearson Hammill and Co., Inc. announced its plan to open a brokerage office in Harlem. Yet even this most farsighted and commendable ghetto demonstration project was founded on good will, not on good economics. Since stock-exchange commissions do not take into account the taxing extra costs of small transactions or the extra credit risks at a ghetto brokerage branch, there is no basis, at the

58

present time, on which a stock-exchange house can operate in the slum economy which is fair both to its partners and to its stockholders.

Therefore, all normal markets for front-end risk capital are excluded by the tariffs of risk and unprofitability. A witness testifying before the Clark Senate Subcommittee stated that a large percentage of new businesses established by Puerto Rican Americans in New York City were initially financed with funds borrowed from loan sharks. In the hard-core areas, an almost total lack of risk capital—the most vital ingredient for the development of business equities—is replaced by the staggering credit costs imposed by hip-pocket lenders whose astronomical interest rates and insistence on a short-term maturity prevent the potential ghetto entrepreneur from developing and sustaining a viable commercial enterprise.

Ghetto Entrepreneur:
A Missing Person

BEFORE THE CIVIL WAR, the American Negro was property, a legal chattel. Since he lacked legal power to enter a binding agreement, he was almost completely excluded from the commercial and business world. Now, more than a century later, the Negro has legal privileges and can become involved in commercial enterprises, yet he has totally failed to develop and sharpen entrepreneurial skills.

The statistic that only a dozen Negro businesses in Manhattan employ ten or more people is matched by the unfortunate fact that only an infinitesimal percentage of the national black community has developed the ability to organize capital and credit, and use them with marketing and production talent in such a way that wealth is achieved. The city of Newark, New Jersey, has approximately 400,000 people, of whom more than half are black. Of the 12,172 licensed businesses in the city, a little more than 10 per cent are Negro-owned. In Los Angeles there are 600,000 Negroes. Of its 121,039 licensed business establishments, an almost invisible fraction is owned by the most visible minority, and these are located principally in ghetto areas. Of the 800,000 residents of Washington, D.C., Negroes are a majority of 63 per cent. Yet, out of 11,755 businesses in our nation's capital, Negroes own only 1,500—less than 13 per cent.[22] Of the 17,500 authorized automobile dealers in the country, seven are black. Out of more than 6,000 radio stations, 108 direct their programs to black listeners, but only eight are owned by Negroes.[23]

Some blacks have made successful businesses. John H. Johnson is head of a publishing empire owning *Ebony, Jet,* and *Tan,* board chairman of Supreme Life Insurance, and owner of a cosmetics firm. Henry G. Parks, of Baltimore, sells $7.5 million worth of sausages a year to whites and blacks. His company recently pioneered in the Wall Street securities market, with a public offering of its stock through the prestigious firm of Allen & Company. Reverend Leon Sullivan of Philadelphia is building shopping centers and an aerospace company on a base of black self-help training centers.

For the most part, however, black businessmen have never succeeded in competing in the rugged markets of a white-dominated economy. Black businesses have been traditionally segregated, producing goods and services blacks can get nowhere else. There is a preponderance of restaurants, barber shops, hotels, funeral parlors, and other service enterprises; most of the few black manufacturers are cosmetic firms which sell in the black market.

The failure of Negro entrepreneurs is a recent failure, intimately connected with ghetto isolation and white attitudes which excluded blacks from entering or marketing in the main economy. When the blacks were emancipated, they had no property or schooling and were totally unprepared to earn a living, let alone build wealth. However, just after the Civil War, the Negro elite established a number of business enterprises. As a people no one could say that Negroes have lacked an entrepreneurial tradition. Many of the freed slaves became substantial owners of property in Philadelphia; Rochester, New York; Cincinnati, and many of

---

[22] 1968 Annual Report of the *Interracial Council for Business Opportunity.* These statistics have been confirmed by the *Clark Senate Subcommittee Hearings on the Examination of the War on Poverty* (1967).

[23] *Business and Society,* Vol. I, No. 13, December 17, 1968.

the cities of the South. The heart of the black insurance industry was Durham, North Carolina. Here were located the North Carolina Mutual Life Insurance Company, the Mechanics and Farmers Bank, the Bankers Fire Insurance Company, and the National Negro Finance Corporation—all founded by pioneering Negro entrepreneurs.

Unfortunately, few of the black banks started during that period have survived. A serious loss to the black economy, with effects that still mar the development of Negro business skills, was the failure of the Freedmen's Bank in the latter part of the nineteenth century. During its few short years, the bank suffered from mismanagement and manipulation of funds. Moreover, it was only after irreparable damage had been done that Negroes were brought into the control and management of the Freedmen's Bank. In June 1874, three months following the election as president of Frederick Douglass, the leading Negro of that time, the bank closed its doors.

A number of Negro-owned insurance companies have managed to continue from Civil War times.[24] But the success of the Negro in this industry is a result of discriminatory attitudes which guaranteed freedom from white competition. The low life expectancy of Negroes dissuaded the major companies from seeking life contracts in the ghettos. Progress of the insurance industry, never a growth industry for blacks, has now become even more difficult. As the Negro middle class expands, the Negro market has become increasingly attractive to the large national insurers. Many are now hiring black salesmen and agents to help them enter the black market. If this trend continues, black insurance companies, which have traditionally operated on a segregated basis, will have to compete in the larger market or face extinction.

In the past, black insurers were hamstrung in their operations because so much of their business was in industrial life insurance. Contrasted with straight life insurance, industrial insurance is usu-

---

[24] Combined assets of the country's 50-odd Negro life-insurance companies are 0.2 per cent of the industry's total. The largest, North Carolina Mutual Life, has assets of approximately $96 million.

ally sold in small amounts and requires frequent premium collection by door-to-door salesmen. As a result, black companies never accumulated the large reserves of other insurers. Andrew Brimmer of the Federal Reserve System has pointed out that black insurance companies play only a minor role in financing long-term capital development in the ghetto. Negro-controlled companies deal less in mortgages, and more in government bonds. Of the more than fifty black insurers, only two—Supreme Life and North Carolina Mutual—function nationally.

Today, it is estimated that only 100,000 or so Negroes in the country operate their own businesses or hold positions on the management level. The number of self-employed Negroes is decreasing. Government statistics show that in 1950 there were about 42,500 self-employed black businessmen in the United States; in 1960, only about 32,500. It is possible that this decrease (approximately 24 per cent) was due primarily to the elimination of small, weak establishments. Indeed, all small businessmen in America have suffered in recent years.

Personal-service businesses in the ghetto did not attract entrepreneurs or capital from the mainstream white community. In an isolated credit economy, where loans and risk capital were hard to find, the development of large capital-consuming manufacturing operations was impossible. An artificial umbrella of monopoly protected the Negro service businesses against white competitors. Instead of seeking out competition in the white economy, which promised at least a theoretical opportunity to achieve greater traffic and volume, Negroes have clung to business service activities in ghetto areas, which offer isolation from competitors. Now, as the barriers of race are hurdled, the protective monopoly of the ghetto is vanishing. The Negro entrepreneur is being buffeted by pressures from black militants and the growing affluence of his once-captive customers. The mortician, the beautician, the barber is finding much of his clientele deserting him for stronger and "more prestigious" white competitors.

The fate of the Hotel Theresa, at 125th Street and Seventh Avenue in West Harlem, illustrates how the gradual breakdown in racial discrimination actually undermines indigenous Negro business. For a number of generations this hotel was the center for Negro weddings, banquets, and business functions, as well as a residence for prosperous Negro visitors. Several years ago, when New York state law opened up all Manhattan hotels to Negro patronage, the Hotel Theresa's patrons moved to more desirable midtown hotels. As a result, the Theresa went into receivership.

Following the same pattern, good restaurants in Harlem lost their Negro clientele to the greater good and goal of integration. According to U.S. government statistics, the number of Negro-owned restaurants throughout the country declined by one-third between 1950 and 1960. While partially a reflection of an overall national trend to the highly capitalized corporate form of organization, much of the decline of the small businesses owned by Negroes has been caused by increased social and economic integration.

The Dilemma of
Black Nationalism

THE STORY GOES that when the miracles of American ingenuity finally succeeded in bringing a dead man back to life, his friends pressed him to say what God really looked like. "She's black," was the answer. The black nationalists do not insist on the double surprise. Adam Smith was not female, but surely he was black. And, they say, if black men are not entrepreneurs today, it is quite simply due to the economic colonialism of the whites.

This conviction on the part of black leaders that the National Alliance of Businessmen and other fair-minded white men are engaged in a fantastic conspiracy to take over the Negro economy is one of the great barriers to the reconstruction of the slums. Not only has the slum economy abolished all forms of credit, risk funds, and profit—thus becoming organically incapable of generating the ownership of capital—but it militantly resists white efforts to reintroduce into the ghetto any of the necessary ingredients for building wealth. This punitive quality of the ghetto economy is primarily reflected in the attitudes of black nationalists who assign ulterior motives to the most straightforward and sincere efforts of the white business community.

65

It is a baffling and complex problem for an outsider to understand and deal with the ghetto economy as he objectively views it. Once the reasons why the slum economy does not function have been identified, rational and carefully devised programs ought to work. Yet often they do not, and the usual reason is that outsiders with programs to invest, build, or hire in the ghetto do not have a clear view of the ghetto marketplace as the Negro believes it to be.

Many myths and distortions have evolved, but they are all rationalizations of the Negro's failure to achieve any degree of economic power or self-sufficiency. Black nationalists believe that the black ghetto is identical to a subjugated African colony deliberately exploited and maintained for the benefit of the white community. The endlessly repeated theme of Rev. Albert Cleage of Detroit's Central United Church of Christ is: "We are the biggest, richest colony the white man ever had, other than South Africa with the diamonds." If the white man does come into the ghetto to offer service, skills, and training, he is "fronting" for the colonial takeover. He is to be treated like a spurious white missionary.

Black militants say that the inferiority and dependency of the ghetto are necessary for the effective functioning of white business and banking. They believe the white society is so dependent on the services of blacks for menial positions that there is no motive to train or integrate them into the main economy—or to correct the economic malignancies in the slums. The Negro extremists preach that the greatest offenders are the institutions of capital and credit—the fourteen thousand American commercial banks. Many influential blacks believe that banking interests are engaged in a giant credit conspiracy with the gouging credit merchants, loan sharks, and ghetto slumlords. In 1963, the Negro author James Baldwin screamed to a group of Harlem rent strikers: "It's hard to find the landlord. It's hard to know where the enemy is. I know where he is. He's in the bank. He's in the bank!" Ivanhoe Donaldson, a powerful militant from Detroit, told a black-power panel in New York: "There's a Chase Manhattan Bank at a Hundred Twenty-fifth Street in this town. We're trying to get jobs in a bank we ought to destroy."

The black power structure teaches that, rather than seek the unsavory business of making loans directly in Harlem, the Wall Street bankers would prefer to avoid the opprobrium of ghetto loans and siphon off profits from Harlem by lending "wholesale" to factors, credit merchants, and small-loan companies who, in turn, "retail" or "bootleg" credit to the Negro at usurious rates. Banks are accused of providing plentiful credit for financing blockbusting acquisition of tenements by white speculators, but, they insist, money is not being made available to the Negro who wants to rehabilitate a deteriorating brownstone.

We are told that brokerage firms who are working to introduce the ownership of equities into Harlem are doing so only to bleed the ghetto of its meager supply of capital. New "demonstration" plants which outside firms establish in slum areas are suspect. Programs of the Urban Coalition for hiring Negro unemployables are cited as further evidence of exploitation.

The businessman or banker who would involve his firm in a project to enrich the ghetto is faced with an impossible dilemma. The risks of establishing a commercial facility in the slum are so grave that stockholders or bank examiners cannot ignore the inevitable erosion of capital. But if the banker or merchant sets a price on his production or capital which is high enough to cover the extra risks inherent in doing business, the consumer can justifiably complain of white discrimination. This reconfirms the allegation that the white man is exploiting the black poor for profit—a new obstacle to effective action to improve conditions in the ghetto.

The only potential resource of the ghetto is its manpower, but this manpower is currently unproductive and almost useless to the outside economy. A massive effort of refining, retraining, and reshaping is necessary to remove the "colonial" status of ghetto labor. But efforts by companies such as Ford in Detroit to send mobile personnel units into the Twelfth Street ghetto, with costly programs for "hiring now and training later," are looked on as confirmation of the white man's program for bleeding the ghetto of its talent. Industry programs which hire Negroes in middle-management executive positions are also the butt of this criticism. Hopes of re-establishing a viable Negro banking and insurance industry are smashed when black insurance agents are employed by white insurance companies. The white middle class, apparently, would prefer to safeguard the purchasing power of its life insurance and pension rights rather than to risk inflation by expanding opportunities for Negro jobs by running the economy at a higher level of employment.

New programs for breaking this destructive cycle of poverty by removing the cultural and educational causes which keep it alive are dismissed as a white man's excuse for not giving the Negro money. Efforts to show the value of personal savings as a route to capital formation are said to be another ruse for imposing on the Negro the decadent, middle-class ethics of savings and frugality. "Give us the money," they say, "and we will build a great Negro economy."

The most perplexing dilemma faced by the businessman who would build business and job opportunities in the ghetto is Negro distrust of any motive that is profit-oriented. Yet to justify a management decision to establish a new subcontracting plant in a ghetto of Brooklyn, Xerox is obliged to spin dreams of building markets for its products in the national Negro community. Avco must cite theoretical potential labor shortages as a "business justification" for undertaking a voluntary job-corps training program in Boston's Roxbury ghetto. A business must act for profit, and this presents a stumbling block to the white businessman who wants to become involved; he can do a job or spend money in the ghetto only when a profit opportunity is offered—when, with some plausibility, he can tell stockholders that there is a profit potential, regardless of how remote. Yet when a corporation publicly assigns a profit motive to what is really an act of good corporate citizenship, the Negro points to the profit motive as confirmation of the white man's program for economic exploitation. And so the profit myth that businessmen must fabricate to justify an anti-poverty commitment ironically confirms the Negro cry of colonialism.

The private business sector is damned if it moves into pro-

68

grams for enrichment of the ghetto; and it is equally condemned if it stands pat and pursues business as usual. The solution lies in ignoring the propaganda of black militants and in doggedly pursuing the route of clear logic and justice: the *forced* injection of credit, risk capital, and entrepreneurial skills into the ghetto economy. Every effort that the white businessman takes in the Negro community must, in fact, be done at the expense of *reinforcing* the irrational, but abiding, conviction that "he is being taken." Yet, if wealth and affluence—with its emancipating effect of creating new options, leisure, and mobility—can be nurtured in the ghetto, there will be an end to the colonialism which the black so correctly abhors.

PART THREE

Why the
Wealth-Makers Duck

The Businessman's Ethic and
His Prerogatives

FEW BUSINESSMEN do not profess a desire to become involved in the problems of blighted areas. Important industry leaders sign endless statements supporting programs for the rehabilitation of the ghetto. They declare their good intentions publicly, adopt policies of unrestricted employment, and support programs that reach out into the ghetto for hard-core unemployables. Business executives attend countless high-level conferences, committee meetings, and dialogues on urban problems.[1] Basically, however, the American businessman has a deep-seated reluctance to become truly involved. If the economic power of our private financial institutions and the technological, production, and marketing skills of American business hold the key to the regeneration of the slum economy, then it is important to know the background of the businessman's inertia.

In June, 1968, *The Wall Street Journal* commented that U.S. business is being dragged kicking and screaming "into the struggle to help improve the Negro's lot." Mayor Theodore McKeldin

[1] In June, 1968, over 600 businessmen each paid $150 tuition to attend a three-day conference in New York City on mobilization of business for the solution of urban problems, sponsored by the American Management Association.

of Baltimore stated: "When businessmen are asked to take action on these problems they will hide behind all sorts of smoke screens." He notes this typical reaction: "We are sympathetic. We want to do something, but we don't want to overpromise on something we cannot deliver."

A leading minority-group employment consultant stated that "job hunters who accept equal employment opportunity statements at face value receive one or another of the same old brush off. They find everyone is for motherhood until the time comes to meet responsibilities." [2] A Harvard Business School professor wrote: "Business's active involvement in these activities [anti-poverty efforts] is, as a proportion of the business population, so microscopic as to be almost invisible. Headlines have whipped a thimbleful of soap into a hogshead of lather." [3]

After the riots during the summer of 1967, the White House wrote to 500 major companies asking business support for ghetto hiring. Only 160 businesses indicated that they would do something about creating jobs in the slums. The government claimed credit for only 600 new jobs attributable to that effort.[4] A feature story on the Restoration Corporation, sponsored by Senator Robert F. Kennedy to build new business and real estate in Brooklyn's Bedford-Stuyvesant ghetto, reported one businessman's reaction to the Senator's prodding: "Senator, the afternoon I walk into my Board of Directors and tell them Bobby Kennedy was here today and thinks we should put a plant in Bedford-Stuyvesant is the afternoon they will have me committed." [5]

Businessmen of the old school are convinced that if a healthy man is out of work, it is because he is lazy. The notion of involuntary cycles of poverty from which even the most intelligent cannot escape is considered a theory of soft and unreliable "bleeding hearts." With compelling logic businessmen argue that if you guarantee the poor man a job or a living—a minimum in-

[2] Ulric Haynes, Jr., *Harvard Business Review,* May-June, 1968, p. 116.
[3] Theodore Levitt, Why Business Always Loses," *Harvard Business Review,* March-April, 1968, p. 83.
[4] *The Wall Street Journal,* December 15, 1967.
[5] In May, 1968, Thomas Watson, Jr., announced a new I.B.M. computer cable sub-assembly plant in Bedford-Stuyvesant. So far there are no reports that Mr. Watson has been committed.

come—you will reduce his motivation and increase his laziness. Some businessmen believe that poverty is inevitable and that the threat of poverty provides every man with a needed and desirable incentive for job achievement.

These business attitudes have shaped anti-poverty efforts, and the American businessman has been faithful to his ethic. For example, no urban program in America has received more enthusiastic support from business than Mayor John Lindsay's Summer Program for New York ghetto youths. The businessman recognizes that the slum child shares no moral responsibility for the poverty of his parents. In the same manner, business has always given strong support to anti-poverty programs for the handicapped, the aged, and the blind.

Even as personnel officers now reach out into the ghetto for unemployables, overlook prison records, excuse unreliable work, and forgive repeated tardiness, the businessman regards his effort as a kind of community-chest program—of "doing his part" in a "safe" public-service activity far removed from controversy.

However, the ghetto does not greatly need the anti-poverty efforts which the businessman's ethic encourages his company to pursue. The economic malignancies of the slum benefit little from either the businessman's charity or his debt of reparations for past exclusions of black executives. The businessman's sense of charity and his desire to make amends produces showcase Negro vice presidents, token loans to ghetto entrepreneurs, ghetto clean-up programs, and anti-riot holding actions. Instead, the ghetto economy calls on the businessman for massive infusions of credit, commitments of risk capital, and training in the entrepreneurial skills of harnessing production and marketing. These ghetto needs require the businessman to invest his money and skills not in the blind poor, the young poor, or the aged poor, but in the entire ghetto economy of poverty.

A traditional prerogative of the American businessman has been his right to buy labor, materials, and capital as economically as possible. This privilege of improving profits through efficiency and control of costs has been jealously guarded. Historically, business has always opposed minimum-wage laws, protective labor legislation, and other government restraints on the right to buy labor cheaply. This privilege of achieving maximum efficiency is basic to the current drive to automate American industry. The clear objective is to reduce labor costs, produce more efficiently, and either raise profit margins or maintain them in the face of increases in labor costs.

Businessmen are now exploring new areas where automation can achieve added efficiency; at the same time, companies are urged to hire the inefficient and hard-core unemployed. The business community invests hundreds of millions of dollars a year in labor-saving hardware to optimize labor efficiency; at the same time, it is asked to spend an equal amount on a civic effort on slum employment, the immediate effect of which is to diminish efficiency in the form of underproduction and absenteeism. It is estimated that about 1.5 million American jobs a year are abolished by automation; yet the nation's automobile companies alone are budgeting annually $3,000 to $5,000 per employee to train 20,000 to 30,000 of Detroit's chronically unemployed.

Hubert Humphrey, during his term as Vice President, frequently stated that the urban crisis can be immeasurably relieved by a massive "uneconomic allocation" of business resources to the ghetto. Whether a worthwhile enrichment of the ghetto can occur if the export of capital and business effort to the ghetto economy is "arbitrary" and "uneconomic" is debatable. In any case, the American businessman does not take kindly to Mr. Humphrey's proposition. It attacks a basic premise of business and fundamental prerogatives cherished by those who manage the enterprise system. Most businessmen and stockholders are appalled at the suggestion that their companies should pursue a policy of "uneconomic allocation of business resources" for the improvement of conditions in the ghetto. Businessmen may be only faintly disturbed by uneconomic allocation policies carried out by the federal government, but the private business sector does not budge when it is asked to operate a business, or commit its capital in a manner which is contrary to principles of profit.

A typical reaction to the suggestion that businesses in America

76

commit their resources to the ghetto is contained in a letter written in the spring of 1958 to the editors of *Fortune* by a Washington, D.C., insurance man: "One of the basic premises of our free enterprise system is that a corporation's officers and directors are employees of the stockholders. That is as it should be since they are operating with the stockholders' money. They should be required to explain and justify every action that is going to involve expenditure of stockholders' money and not be free to indulge in their own ideas of social engineering."

The challenge to the businessman's right to invest prudently and to hire efficiently is further complicated by the government's lexicon of poverty. The White House argues for a renewed "war on poverty." Robert Kennedy urged that "we mount an attack on housing and jobs." These are disturbing words for the businessman, for whom wars or attacks are invariably damaging to commerce. These projects connote economic anarchy, the worst possible environment for business achievement, since they deprive the businessman of his ability to plan his costs and his markets. The "war on poverty" is appealing rhetoric, but the notion of a businessman's war on poverty is absurd. It challenges the stability of the business world in which capital is committed and profits are earned in a rational and predictable economy.

Resistance to opportunities to locate new business facilities in the slum occurs because these projects interfere with the prerogative of management to decide how corporate funds will be allocated. Indiscriminate hiring of unskilled unemployables is written off by many businessmen as imprudent or improper allocation of business resources—an unwise interference with a manager's right to achieve maximum labor efficiency. The executive of the casualty-insurance company, trained in reducing underwriting losses in an industry which has been unprofitable for the past decade, views the reopening of ghetto areas to fire and theft as a blatant interference with his privilege to select the safest risks. Pressure on banks and other institutions to make high-risk mortgage loans in the inner cities violates the so-called "prudent man" investment rule which has governed investment policies of fiduciaries for centuries. The mortgage loan officer does not docilely re-

77

spond to a command to make a "soft" loan in order to accomplish a broad social purpose. He is not easily converted from a philosophy of "cream" loans to "creed" loans.

Businessmen's attitude of rugged individualism has actually restrained business programs for enrichment of the ghetto. Although this attitude has been weakened in recent years, it has been followed by an equally disabling philosophy—that of "the organization man." The rough-and-tumble philosophy of the tough-minded entrepreneur—in the tradition of Horatio Alger and Henry Clews—has been reinforced by a system where most new corporate projects, ideas, or innovations either originate with, or are tested by, corporate committees or staff.

At the staff level, unorthodox thinking in business is often discouraged. The lawyers and public-relations people in the inevitable chain of company command, asked to recommend or review proposals for new plants in ghetto areas, usually see more problems than potential. Regardless of political viewpoint, the staff plays it safe. Personal advancement dictates that it would be dangerously liberal to advocate a company demonstration store-front training project in the local ghetto. Not all this concern is misplaced; if the company becomes involved in controversial activities, customers may be lost or promotions impeded.

The traditional hostility of business toward forces or ideas which contradict a fundamental urge to "play it safe" is reinforced by an entrenched system of internal profit measurement. A plant in troubled areas will inevitably have greater built-in costs in the form of real estate taxes, insurance, pilferage, labor turnover, and interest charges. Ordinarily, too, any urban plant will be less efficient than a factory located in a suburban area offering skilled labor. Evaluating managerial performance, comptrollers and internal profit analysts traditionally eliminate items of cost beyond management's control, such as real estate taxes, interest costs, and other fixed charges. They see these as unrelated to measuring the comparative success of plant managers. However, I know of no internal profit-measuring system that "breaks out" from the normal profit-and-loss statement the excess and uncontrollable costs of recruiting and training hard-core unemployables. Two identical plants, one managed in the old tradition of limiting new employees to high-school graduates without police records, and the other hiring high-school dropouts with criminal records, show income statements with the same caption entries—but completely different results below the line.

Business accountants have not developed a component in the equation to allow for adjustment of comparative operating costs of plants with progressive hiring practices. Accounting systems do not allocate the extra payroll and training costs incurred to the public-relations department or to the company's "central-office overhead" activities. In most cases, the costs of anti-poverty efforts are simply charged to the division plant manager. When hiring the hard-core unemployed, the plant manager has on his hands not only labor inefficiency but also social antagonism. On a more personal basis, he faces the prospect that a program for hiring unemployables will handicap division profits—the measure of his own promotability.

The cautious attitudes of the staff are reflected in the endless repetitive themes at business symposiums dealing with urban problems: "There should be no panic solutions" and "patience will be required." How often have businessmen heard the view expressed at a recent conference: "Above all, calmness and judgment must be maintained, or effort will be dissipated without meaningful result; patience will be exhausted; good will may falter; the problem will keep on growing."

Before meaningful business programs for enrichment of the slums can occur, the able watchdogs at the staff level must be convinced. Even the most daring and innovative chief executive will rarely override the unanimous disapproval of his staff. He recognizes that great innovative growth companies made the grade because competent staff people protected the leader from mistakes that could have meant business failure.

As David Rockefeller has stated, it must become fashionable to advocate company commitments of capital and effort in the slums. Top management must set a mandatory policy of concern and action, and must communicate this policy to the younger men. The junior executive must be convinced that top manage-

79

ment will not think he is "getting soft" if he suggests a business project in the ghetto. The executive must be convinced that progressive views will cause no conflict with his promotion opportunities; that, on the contrary, he will be rewarded for suggesting creative methods in which the company can participate in solving a national social crisis. Now, all the arguments against extending ghetto-area credits and investments are on the side of the staff. Riots, looting, canceled insurance, unreliable labor, production, and markets and, particularly, black hostility to any white-sponsored project are conditions which call for a staff veto of a proposal for a new assembly plant in a local ghetto. The attitude at the staff level, which often correctly and logically opposes ghetto projects as an unprofitable and unwise business decision, cannot always be removed simply by executive order from on top. Views toward the responsibility of business to society are changing, but only gradually. The programs urged later on in this book are designed to accommodate the prescription for the ghetto economy to existing business attitudes toward investing in the poor. In hiring, manufacturing, or offering credit or merchandise in the ghetto, the staff analyst correctly sees no solution but to charge more to compensate for the inherent risk involved —yet this he knows is impossible. A successful program for business action in the ghetto must be so shaped that it removes the investment-risk dilemma without obliging the corporate comptroller to alter his basically mathematical view of the feasibility of accomplishing the objective.

Business Investment
in the Poor:
A Self-Inflicted Tax

IN THE MID-FIFTIES, the Seagram Distillers Company erected a Park Avenue office building on two acres of Manhattan's most valuable land. The company rejected conventional office-building design which takes maximum advantage of valuable ground-floor retail space. Instead, a forty-two-story tower was set back on an open plaza dedicated to public needs for light, air, and recreation. The company's reward was a massive assessment by New York City of a land-tax value equal to the commercial value that would have been realized had the company chosen instead to rent the ground-floor area at the present going commercial rate of forty dollars a square foot.

Industry has learned its lesson. Despite the hue and cry of outraged critics, the Penn Central Company has announced plans to construct a concrete box 800 feet tall by 310 feet wide by 125 feet deep on the Grand Central Terminal landmark. The building takes the maximum legal advantage of four acres of air rights. It is no monument to corporate avarice that the railroad has refused to sacrifice this sixty-million-dollar land asset for the greater good of New York City's citizens. Designing the new building to achieve maximum productivity is a frank recognition that a pub-

licly owned corporation in business for profit cannot sacrifice
such an asset for the public good. Community Chest gifts, do-
nations for summer recreation in the ghetto, and recruiting of slum-
area unemployables are desirable and acceptable practices; but a
major dedication of profits or assets to public use is simply a self-
inflicted tax on company profits that no businessman will impose.[6]

The experiences of Seagram and Penn Central bear directly on
the dilemma of American businessmen as they seek new projects
for enriching the ghetto. IBM can and will sustain a far-sighted
demonstration sub-assembly plant in Bedford-Stuyvesant. However great the losses sustained, this project cannot impair the
company's per-share earnings by more than a few pennies a year.
Ford Motor Company finds good corporate purpose for embark-
ing on programs for hard-core employment in the ghettos of Detroit. The cost of these projects would sink a smaller company;
yet they are barely noticed by Wall Street statisticians—especially when Ford's two principal competitors are engaged in similar ghetto hiring programs.

However, the economic failures of America's slums are so
massive that industry, as a whole, has neither the capability nor
the will to impair its capital or earnings to the degree that is necessary to reverse the crushing forces of profitlessness and risk that
the separate slum economy has built and nourished over a period
of many years. The smaller innovative firms, whose talents are
vitally needed to build enterprise skills, rarely have financial
capacity for more than a token effort.

Yet, not unlike Seagram's effort to dedicate a large corporate
asset for a public benefit, scores of the nation's corporations have
embarked recently on programs involving the hiring of tens of
thousands of hard-core unemployables. Some of the business
press has scoffed at these projects as "private WPA's," "make-
work efforts," or "private welfare." Ghetto hiring efforts have
even been denounced as a ruinous form of featherbedding.

[6] The concept of the self-inflicted tax as the major impediment to slum
hiring projects was first developed by *Fortune* in a series of articles published
in 1968.

Since many companies have job-training, rehabilitation, and educational efforts that involve hiring unemployables, these criticisms are neither accurate nor fair. Still, companies electing costly programs that break up skilled job functions into a number of unskilled components—thus permitting untrained men to find a place in our economic system—are voluntarily taxing their profit-and-loss statements to achieve a national objective in which everyone has an equal concern. Jobs that are not needed are being created artificially under onerous and painful circumstances. High-school dropouts are educated and rehabilitated at a time when trained labor is available. Unemployment rates in recent years have been running at or below 4 per cent. Under these conditions, private job-creation programs may be an acceptable commitment of shareholder funds. However, if the national unemployment rate goes to higher levels, trained and experienced labor will be rejected in favor of maintaining job commitments to the unproductive and untrained. A rising rate of unemployment places unreasonable demands on the businessman's willingness to tax himself by hiring and maintaining jobs for the hard-core unemployed.

I suggest that these programs, however commendable, cannot be sustained by American business over an extended period of time. Without government-provided money incentives, these programs remain an uneconomic allocation of capital resources for a worthy objective which is inconsistent with the maximum efficiency of business. Expensive programs for creating jobs are an effort on the part of business to tax itself to accomplish an objective which is public in scope and which, except for the threat of rioting, is not directly connected with the immediate aspirations of stockholder capital.

In viewing voluntary business projects for alleviating ghetto poverty, it is important to identify where the final economic burden of any anti-poverty effort falls.

Under the public-welfare system, the basic cost of poverty relief presumably is spread equitably among all the people from public funds. But in practice, since one dollar earned from labor by the man on relief also reduces his welfare check by that amount, the final impact of the system is a 100 per cent tax on his earned income. For this reason, the welfare system does not create jobs, marketable skills, or motivation—nor does it relieve any of the causes of poverty.

Under a system in which the businessman, either through moral suasion, or a sense of social obligation, acts to alleviate poverty, the cost of a company anti-poverty effort falls on the businessman involved. If he owns the business, he is voluntarily taxing himself; if he directs a business owned by others, he is voluntarily taxing his own performance and the profits of his stockholders.

The cost of job-creation and training programs can, in some cases, be passed on to the final consumer. The utility customer or insurance-policy holder must, in time, pay higher rates or premiums reflecting the additional cost to the utility or insurance company of hiring inefficient and unneeded hard-core unemployables. Equitable Life Assurance Society's massive program for hiring and training ten thousand hard-core unemployed in New York City adds millions of dollars to the company payroll. These expenditures are no longer in the same cost category as corporate charity or Community Chest, which are easily absorbed by a large business. The extra costs are now so great that, in the long run, they must be passed on to the consumer in the form of higher insurance-premium rates. But cranking these costs into consumer rates is possible only if competing life-insurance companies adopt similar anti-poverty efforts. If other companies choose to remain inactive, or if competing insurance companies located in smaller communities that do not have serious problems of riots or of hard-core unemployment "sit on their hands," Equitable is at a severe competitive disadvantage. Market conditions will inevitably prevent the company from continuing its anti-poverty effort.

Market conditions do not always prevent a company from taxing itself unduly for the public good. High-profit patent-protected companies such as Xerox or Polaroid more easily support training programs. Voluntary job-creation programs exist more readily in Detroit, where an oligopoly of three major automobile companies, presumably free of anti-trust restriction, have agreed to conduct a joint program for hiring the inefficient unemployables. If the automobile companies undertake these costly antipoverty programs in concert, and successfully crank the extra costs into the retail price for automobiles, the ultimate cost of rehabilitating the Detroit ghetto is borne by one sector of the purchasing public—the automobile purchaser. But this is hardly an equitable or durable solution.

Recent government efforts to persuade business to hire from the ghetto show that the key to a successful program is the partial or complete absorption by the federal government of the company's extra costs in slum-area hiring and training. When the self-imposed tax is reduced, company efforts gain greater momentum. For example, on March 15, 1967, the Labor Department introduced a voluntary concentrated ghetto-employment program known as CEP. The results of this program were disappointing. According to the Secretary's report, jobs were provided for only 6,900 people. Reasons cited for the failure were that on-the-job training programs provided a federal subsidy for the employers' direct training costs, but provided no extra compensation to the employer for lower worker productivity and turnover. Obviously, greater incentives were needed. The core-area employment campaign of the National Alliance of Businessmen for the creation of 100,000 jobs during the period from December 15, 1967, to July 15, 1969, achieved greater success because it was stimulated not only by the strong leadership of Henry Ford II, but also by the promise of Department of Labor subsidy contracts of $3,500 per trainee to cover pre-job and on-the-job training.

America's brief experience with ghetto hiring programs, together with the application of a little guesswork and logic, suggests some conclusions. Voluntary (subsidy-free) action by the private business sector, which involves substantial expenditures of corporate funds for job creation, cannot be sustained on a lasting basis unless:

(a) all competing companies in the industry involved elect to burden themselves in an equal way;

(b) the sponsoring company enjoys a product monopoly, or a special patent position in which very high profit margins permit

85

large public-benefit expenditures;

(c) special industry conditions permit the cost of the business anti-poverty effort to be passed on to the consumer in the form of higher prices.

Even when all these conditions exist, individual industries, single corporations, or special classes of consumers are singled out for taxation (voluntary or involuntary) to accomplish a national goal. The tax is spread more equitably when federal incentives or subsidies are offered for ghetto hiring. When none of these conditions exist—that is to say, when profit margins are narrow, competition is severe, extra costs cannot be "cranked into" consumer prices, or equalizing federal benefits are not available—ghetto hiring programs are usually undertaken merely for "window dressing" or as "demonstration projects." However, the addition of equalizing federal benefits eliminates the self-imposed tax and draws all industry and talent into the anti-poverty effort on a fair basis.

During the riots in the spring of 1968, branches of retail chains such as Ripley, Lerner, Mays, and Woolworth were looted in Harlem. In Chicago, Howard Stores was also looted and a Robert Hall outlet was burned. In Washington, a branch of Lerner was completely destroyed. Only basic guarantees against loss or an irresistible opportunity for profit will draw these stores back into these ghetto areas.

The key to the institutional investors' attitudes toward proposed ghetto investments is suggested in the 1967 publicity releases issued by more than a hundred of the nation's insurance companies. At that time it was announced that the life-insurance companies would "divert" one billion dollars of investments from normal channels to the cost of upgrading ghetto real estate and hard-core urban slums. The key word is "diversion." Inherent in the announcement is the concept that, however commendable in social terms, costly anti-poverty efforts by the private business sector violate what businessmen consider to be classical economic principles which guide their business decisions—namely, the maximization of profits.

The commitment of the life-insurance companies to one billion

86

dollars of new slum investments in FHA mortgages was made at a time when the maximum legal yield on FHA mortgages was 6 per cent. How could the country expect these institutions to accumulate ghetto mortgages when prime triple-A mortgages were available to yield 7.5 per cent? As the moment, the going free-market interest rate on uninsured Bedford-Stuyvesant home mortgages (if you can get one) may be as high as 25 per cent per annum. Even if the banker or investor expresses his "ghetto risk aversion" by setting an interest rate that overcompensates for the hazards involved, this massive rate differential is a suggestion of the magnitude of the subsidy which may be necessary to persuade money to move into places which crush capital and profit.

Boycotts, Blackmail, and Blame

ONE POINT OF VIEW holds that American business should, or must, work to rebuild the slums because it was responsible for creating these conditions. James Reston wrote in *The New York Times:* "Big business has clearly made its contribution to the ugliness and slums of America's cities, but a new generation of corporate lenders is obviously trying to make amends."

This statement is neither an accurate assessment of responsibility for the slums nor a convincing argument for American businessmen to invest capital or effort in the ghetto. The genesis of slum economics is so incredibly complicated that no expert can assess original blame. If, as the Negro contends, the origin of the American ghetto is closely connected with practices of white discrimination, the businessman bears no greater responsibility than do other white citizens.

A generation or more ago the concentration of manufacturing activity in northern metropolitan centers attracted Negro labor migrating from rural areas. Now, many business firms are deserting the cities for the suburbs, and the blacks have been confronted with a critical problem of urban unemployment. Undoubtedly, a major contribution to the growth of the ghetto was a migration from the South of impoverished blacks chasing higher wages provided by northern industry.[7] But this reason hardly produces a condition of blame or guilt that will propel businessmen to do penance or make reparation in the form of framing necessary programs for the enrichment of slum areas.

Here is a more convincing case against business: To achieve greater efficiency through reduced labor costs, American industry is eliminating millions of jobs a year through new techniques of automation. Since the jobs eliminated are primarily mechanical or repetitive, they are usually held by the untrained worker. Consequently, the major unemployment impact of automation falls on inherently underskilled Negro labor. Business, therefore, should pay for these lost jobs through voluntary industry programs of job creation in black communities. In other words, the argument suggests that the very economies gained by automation should now be surrendered in order to re-create jobs which the computer eliminates. Even though this syllogism might look convincing, few businessmen will consider it a persuasive reason for funding a new ghetto plant or undertaking new-job programs in the slums. Ultimately, it serves little purpose to argue that private enterprise should have a vital interest in solving our urban problems because it bears a major responsibility for creating them.

Also grounded on a premise of the white man's blame has been the economic boycott used by Negroes to persuade business to adopt programs for ghetto enrichment or for new job opportunities. In 1967, civil rights groups in Milwaukee led by Father Groppi, a white Catholic priest, applied boycott pressure on the local business community to gain an open-housing law. A "Black Christmas" was announced. People supporting open housing were asked to forgo Christmas shopping until an anti-discrimination ordinance was passed. Nightclubs, small business, and hotels were badly hurt, conventions were canceled. Wisconsin now has an open-housing law, but so does the nation as a whole. Certainly, it is not clear whether Father Groppi's boycott was either

---

[7] In recent years, with national Negro unemployment running twice the rate of white, the southern Negroes are no longer seeking jobs, but rather higher welfare benefits available in northern cities.

appropriate or effective in Wisconsin.

Probably the most successful boycott in the history of civil rights was the Montgomery, Alabama, bus boycott of 1955–56. Yet, the success of a boycott in moving politicians and voters to political action in a matter of civil rights does not carry over to economic sanctions in which the businessman considers himself unfairly coerced. Moreover, the economic power of the Negro does not match his political power. Although blacks constitute one-tenth of our population, they make up a disproportionately smaller percentage of national buying power. For fifty years, in America, there has been a host of totally ineffective Negro boycott programs aimed at eliminating job discrimination: "Don't buy where you can't work." These economic sanctions have almost always failed, and the failure invariably stems from the Negro's lack of economic power.

Negro economic boycotts have often ignored the companies with hardened policies of discrimination in hiring. The boycott was considered most effective when directed at companies whose products were popular in the ghetto[8], or at companies with the most reasonable employment policies. The idea was to "knock off the soft companies" and hope that the others would fall in line. Often, therefore, the merchant or businessman felt he was innocent, and either stubbornly or conscientiously refused to respond to pressure he regarded as unfair.

The most effective device for "persuading" businessmen is the labor strike. Businessmen will move mountains to avoid or to settle a serious disturbance. The strike is regarded as a legitimate and acceptable form of exerting economic power, but the business community is not yet attuned—or constructively responsive —to a boycott demanding black jobs or economic power.

[8] Before his death, Dr. Martin Luther King's Southern Christian Leadership Conference planned a boycott against the Kellogg Company and National Dairy Products, whose sales of Kraft foods and Sealtest dairy items are important throughout the Negro ghettos. Southern Christian Leadership Conference actually concluded an agreement with Jewel Tea Company, which operates 250 grocery stores in the Chicago area. Jewel agreed to buy products from Negro-owned companies for sale throughout the chain. It agreed to hire a Negro contractor to build its next ghetto store. The agreement also called for the deposit of company funds in Negro banks, and for hiring fifty Negro store managers.

Sometimes the government, too, has adopted some of the coercive techniques of the economic boycott. There have been veiled threats of loss of government contracts, of mandatory allocations of private banking capital to ghetto loans, of rules assigning ghetto fire risks to insurers, of withdrawal of government deposit balances from "uncooperative" banks, and of compulsory programs for hiring unemployables. None of these announcements has cut much ice with the business sector.

An outside business sector now concentrating on equal-opportunity hiring programs to make up for exclusions of the past is frequently more concerned with whether a man's face is black than whether he is underskilled and chronically unemployed. Moreover, the forces of blame have not been sufficient to convince the ghetto-plant personnel manager of the greater wisdom of rejecting the skilled black applicant who asks for a job—favoring instead one whom the state unemployment office has certified as "hard-core." Indeed, the assertion of corporate blame—or the exclusive reliance on "a new generation of corporate leaders who will try to make amends"—will never provide the black with the tools he needs to become affluent.

Public Programs and Crushed Incentives

THE UNPREDICTABLE QUALITIES of the ghetto economy have created conditions of near economic anarchy which act as a massive "disincentive" against the import of outside capital investment and the internal accumulation of savings, as well as ensuring strangulation of profit opportunity. Important attitudes and conditions in the white economy operate as an additional disincentive or obstacle to satisfaction of the black economy's need for a chance at affluence. Programs and policies which federal and state governments have mounted to improve slum conditions have, in turn, created a structure of further disincentives and barriers to the progress of investment and business in the ghetto.

For many years, our national welfare system, reflected primarily in monetary aid to families with dependent children, has fed and housed millions of unfortunate people. Few will quarrel with the objectives and benefits of unemployment compensation and minimum-wage laws. Yet both liberals and conservatives concede that substitute earnings provided by the welfare system and unemployment-compensation benefits have often acted as major deterrents to the development of job and career ambitions of the

92

Negro poor. In too many cases it was more profitable to remain jobless and collect government-provided benefits than to work for the same payment.

At the same time, minimum-wage laws have set an artificially high level of wages which industry is required to pay for skilled labor. This screens out the unskilled Negro, who rarely enters the economic system. Although the welfare system and minimum-wage laws are humanitarian public programs whose original purpose was the relief of poverty, they have become major deterrents to the progress of Negro employment and careers.

For the fiscal year 1968, federal spending on programs for the poor was estimated by the Bureau of the Budget at $27.7 billion.

FEDERAL AID TO THE POOR

Major Programs	Spending Millions of dollars Fiscal 1968	Where the Money Goes
TRAINING AND EDUCATION		
Pre-college education [HEW]	$1,200	9.5 million students, 30% Negro
Head Start [OEO]	325	Pre-school help for 616,533 children
Job Corps [OEO]	285	Training, education for 98,000 school dropouts, 58% Negro
Neighborhood Youth Corps [OEO]	281	Jobs, training, education for 389,200 youths, 42% Negro
Manpower Development [Labor Dept.]	251	Classroom and job training for 179,-000, 48% and 32% Negro
College Work-Study Grants [HEW]	102	Subsidizes part-time work for 226,-300 needy students
Educational Opportunity Grants [HEW]	95	Grants to 170,412 poor college students
Concentrated Employment [Labor Dept., OEO]	55	Helps 94,000 hard-core unemployed, 85% Negro in 76 slums
Work Incentive & Training [HEW]	40	Trains or educates 32,000 welfare recipients for work
Upward Bound [OEO]	30	Pre-college help for 23,000
Vista [OEO]	30	Trains, pays 5,000 volunteers to work on 450 projects among poor
Migrants [OEO]	25	Education, housing, day care for 148,-500 seasonal workers
Follow Through [OEO]	15	Extra care in first school years

93

HEALTH

Health insurance for aged [HEW]	1,700	Medicare coverage for 6.3 million poor
Medical care [HEW]	1,400	Medicaid for 6.9 million welfare recipients and other poor
Vocational rehabilitation [HEW]	280	Diagnoses, treatment, services and facilities for 697,500 poor
Indian health [HEW]	99	Furnishes health care, education to 390,000 Indians, Eskimos
Child and infant health [HEW]	56	Furnishes care for 170,000 children, 75,000 mothers
Comprehensive Health Services [OEO]	33	Neighborhood centers help 223,000

HOUSING

Low-Rent Public Housing [HUD]	184	Helps finance 1.2 million poor people in 477,119 housing units
Neighborhood Facilities [HUD]	27	Grants to build or rehabilitate about 100 community centers
Rent Supplement [HUD]	4	Subsidizes 12,000 poor families or individuals in 3,350 units

CASH BENEFITS

Social Security [HEW]	7,900	Old-age and disability payments to an estimated 7.3 million poor
Public Assistance [HEW]	3,500	Grants to 8.2 million under state welfare programs

Sources: Bureau of the Budget and *Business Week.*

A large portion of these funds was employed in paying salaries of professional welfare workers whose job has been the administration of the system, including the prevention of welfare cheating. But the welfare worker has no skills for or concern with the fundamental problem of creating wealth, capital ownership, or savings in the ghetto.[9]

[9] A woman in Harlem describes how welfare workers preach "savings" but haven't the slightest idea how to go about building capital: "They keep on telling us, to take better care of our money, and to save it away and buy what is the best in the stores and do like they for dresses, and keep the children in school, and keep our husbands from leaving us. . . . Well, I'll tell you, they sure don't know what it's about . . . and let them start at zero the way we did and see how many big numbers they can become themselves. I mean, if you've got nothing when you are born, and you know you can't get a thing no matter how hard you try—well, then you dies with nothing. And no one can deny that arithmetic." Coles, "The Poor Don't Want to Be Middle Class," *The New York Times,* December 19, 1965.

Recent efforts to go beyond the income-substitute plans have developed a host of the new non-profit community action agencies which provide job training, recruiting, screening, and employment services for the poor. But these groups are beset with the same bureaucratic red tape and rivalries as the established anti-poverty agencies. The non-profit Inner City Business Improvement Forum formed in Detroit to build one billion dollars in black-owned business assets was virtually immobilized by a thirty-three-man board of directors composed of militants, moderates, educators, and clergymen—hardly a group versed in the problems of developing business and entrepreneurs in the black slums of Detroit. Throughout the country, agencies compete to get a program retained in their department rather than handled by another one. The issue is invariably one of position and power in the welfare administrative system rather than constructive aid for the poor.[10]

From its inception, the federal Model Cities program developed as a "poverty-preserving" political pork barrel. Of the fortunate 63 model cities which were chosen for federal funds, five were represented by members of the Appropriations Committee of the House of Representatives. One model city, Smithville, Tennessee, with a population of only 2,300, is the hometown of the Committee's chairman. Participation by the most skillful real estate entrepreneurs is discouraged as he finds that favored constituents of Congressmen are competing with him for a share of the profits.

The Atlanta Model Cities program illustrates how ghetto-enrichment programs undertaken by the public sector discourage business involvement. The Executive Director of the Atlanta's Model Cities program was Johnny C. Johnson, a Negro city planner. Calvin Craig, long-time Georgia Imperial Grand Dra-

[10] The New York State Department of Labor reports that in every large city there are between 15 and 30 separate competing public and private manpower agencies supported by public and anti-poverty funds. There are 91 such agencies in New York City alone. The personnel department of one large New York City retail store was visited by 70 different federally funded local job agencies. *Clark Senate Subcommittee Examination of the War on Poverty* (1967), p. 1814.

gon of the Ku Klux Klan, was elected Vice Chairman by citizens of his neighborhood. Federal HUD officials declared neutrality!

Many months after the enactment of enabling legislation, Model Cities' money was being spent in only a few cities—Boston; Cambridge, Maryland; and Detroit. In these three cities federal money was allocated to neighborhood groups for hiring planners and experts to make judgments on what was best for their community. Model Cities officials circulated hundreds of thousands of propaganda leaflets for the purpose of "stimulating citizen participation." In Detroit, the various poverty groups—blacks, whites, and Polish Americans—argued interminably about who would control the program and how the money would be spent. The Citizens Governing Board of Detroit was granted $32,000 to hire a planner to design improvements in the neighborhood ghettos. The unneeded planning bureaucracy is formidable and discouraging.

Universities have been enlisted to make studies of the ghettos and recommendations for remedial action. Columbia University, for example, is presently conducting a "manpower skills inventory" in Harlem. Studies are being made of the need for goods and services in Harlem, and how new businesses can be created to supply them. Any competent supermarket entrepreneur knows that East Harlem needs more supermarkets and that there are endless low-priced sites on which to place them. The ghetto's urgent need for new banks, automotive diagnostic and repair centers, theaters, wholesale supply centers, and a dozen or more specific types of franchised service business was cleary established a decade ago. Now we are past needing to preface our efforts with expensive and time-consuming studies of ghetto business needs. The pattern is the same in other cities—interminable dialogues, countless symposiums and committees, foundations, and "blueprints for the ghetto."

96

The Small Business
Administration:
The Reluctant Guarantor

IN OCTOBER 1966, Congress rescinded the business-development program of the president's Office of Economic Opportunity. This was an unfortunate decision. OEO had been the only federal agency in the history of the country to develop and experiment with innovative programs for developing equity ownership in poverty areas. Since 1966, responsibility for making loans to aspiring ghetto entrepreneurs has rested on the unwilling shoulders of the Small Business Administration. If Congress had checked the record (which would not have mattered, since Congress has always been bent on shifting the anti-poverty efforts of the OEO to other agencies), it would have found that the government had earlier reviewed, noted, and ignored the failure of the SBA to extend business credits to Negro businessmen. Over the ten and one-half years preceding the Congressional study, only seven Negro loans had been made through its Philadelphia office.

All agreed that the objective at the time was to take a little man with an idea, talent, or ambition and help him develop a small business. But, under the aegis of the SBA, the concept never got off the ground. In May, 1967, the Clark Senate Subcommittee Examination of the War on Poverty heard a parade of

97

witnesses who, almost without exception, cited the basic failures of the anti-poverty lending program of the Small Business Administration. The thrust of the Senate hearings was that the SBA was plagued with bureaucratic red tape and administrative delays, that it adopted unduly restrictive and conservative lending policies, and that it was basically reluctant to make loans to businessmen in poverty areas. The testimony was that SBA discouraged potential borrowers from applying for SBA guarantees. Banks and other potential lenders were reluctant to get involved with the red tape.

Under the so-called EOL program (the SBA Equal Opportunity Loan program for the establishment of new business for those with submarginal incomes) the total dollar volume of loans was $15.7 million for the fiscal year ended June 30, 1967. New York's Senator Jacob Javits commented during the hearings: "We all know this is a fly speck on the wall, considering what we are up against, especially in the effort to build effective leadership in the Negro and slum areas where the small businessman can be a very effective leader."

A former Director of New York City's office of SBA testified: "While I esteem the goal of the Small Business Administration, and respect its record of accomplishments on behalf of the already established small businessman, I must affirm that clearly the SBA's methods are not tuned to the needs of the ghetto. I say this as a former regional director of the SBA for New York. . . . It is simply not enough, gentlemen, to have government employees sit behind a desk and answer yes or no to a loan applicant. . . . Fewer than 1 per cent of the 215,000 businesses in New York City are controlled by Negroes and Puerto Ricans. Yet 28 per cent of the population belongs to minority groups. Obviously SBA's methods of aid are out of tune with daily realities of our minorities. We must devise more inventive and more forceful methods. . . . The SBA, with all the good will in the world, is hampered by its regulations and the frequent depletion of its funds for national disasters."

Another witness told the Senate Subcommittee: "Representatives of the Small Business Administration have admitted that their staff does not have the community outreach. . . . Bureaucratic idiosyncrasies restrain personnel from effectively implementing the program." A New York City bank manager testified: "Slowness in processing applications and red tape at the agency administering the funds [SBA] limited considerably the effectiveness of the program."

Senator Clark summed up the complaints: "We found in the course of our travels around the country . . . a strong feeling that the Small Business Administration was not playing the part in the poverty program which advocates of the poverty program had hoped. . . . The Small Business Administration has backed away from loans to the poor."

After the riots following the death of Martin Luther King, the Small Business Administration came under criticism from the District City Council of Washington: " 'Business as usual' in the bureaucratic procedures of such government agencies, we submit, must no longer be the order of the day, and red tape must be cut to a minimum, immediately if we are to rebuild our damaged areas quickly and responsibly."

Again, an agency of the federal government had demonstrated its innate, although unintended, power to preserve poverty rather than aid in building wealth in the ghetto.

The Small Business Administration has been handicapped by a self-defeating restriction: loans could be made only "when there was a reasonable assurance of repayment." If the SBA refuses a ghetto loan because the applicant cannot provide a reasonable assurance of repayment, the banks obviously have no need for SBA in the first place. The banks and the ghetto businessmen need the SBA loan guarantee because without it the loan is unbankable—indeed, there *is* no reasonable assurance of repayment.

On November 9, 1966, SBA issued a ruling to all area administrators: "While new businesses qualify [for loans to the disadvantaged business community] . . . we do not intend to provide start-up financing for a small grocery, beauty parlor, carry-out food shop, or other business of the type traditionally operated by members of disadvantaged groups unless there is a clear indi-

99

cation that such a business will fill an economic void in the community." Those who are only remotely familiar with the nature of the black economy know that this ruling effectively blocks the only opportunity many potential business owners in the ghetto have to establish themselves. The feeble and segregated personal-service establishment, sustained only by freedom from white competition, is often the only route open to the fledgling black businessman.

SBA regulations state that a loan is not ordinarily eligible for an SBA guarantee "if the purpose in applying for a loan is to effect a change in the ownership of the business." Absentee ownership and slumlord control of ghetto business[11] and real estate— one of the most insidious features of the slum economy—is therefore reinforced by SBA edict.

Other SBA rules show the dead hand of government lawyers, who in their determination to exclude "the bad guy" also keep the man they are trying to help from participating in the loan-guarantee program. For example, SBA instructions provide that a pledge or mortgage on inventory usually is not satisfactory collateral, "unless the inventories are stored in a bonded or otherwise acceptable warehouse." Any banker knows that this is an impractical way of collateralizing a working-capital or inventory loan for a grocery store, hardware store, or any other small business.

In addition to sorting out many onerous instructions and guidelines, the inexperienced SBA loan applicant must wade through instructions which were written for sophisticated borrowers in the normal economy: "prepare an estimate of how much you or others had to invest in the business . . . prepare a current financial statement, balance sheet . . . detail projection of earnings for the first year . . . list collateral to be offered for security of the loan and indicate your estimate of the present market of each item."

[11] It is estimated that in central Harlem at least 85 per cent of the 2,000 small businesses are owned by white merchants who live outside Harlem. The Negro's share of central Harlem's $50 million worth of business has not increased in thirty years. See "Putting the Poor Out of Business," Mark Levy, *The Nation,* June 12, 1967.

Admittedly, President Johnson's instruction to the economic loan development area of the SBA was to guarantee loans to minority entrepreneurs of uncertain credit standing. Only a government guarantee could make such soft loans bankable. But the SBA adopted the same credit standards as the banks; it required the borrower to have a credit "track record." By definition, if the borrower had a track record, the SBA loan guarantee would not be necessary. This ideological breakdown, combined with the fundamental error in delegating to bureaucracy rather than business the responsibility for recruiting potential Negro businessmen or borrowers, resulted in total failure of the program.

SBA's personnel have developed the usual dossier of reasons or excuses for the failure of the ghetto loan program. Congressional appropriations were said to be inadequate for maintaining an aggressive lending program. But in 1967, the head of SBA testified before a Senate hearing on poverty that the agency could not use additional funds. When the agency came under criticism for not making more loans to ghetto businesses in Detroit and Newark after their riots, the reasons cited were the inability to obtain fire insurance or the fact that businessmen did not want to go back into business once they were burned out. However, a few months after the Washington riots of 1968, many burned-out proprietors went back into business at the old stand.

In the final months of President Johnson's administration, former Under Secretary of Commerce Howard J. Samuels became SBA Administrator. During his brief period in office, Mr. Samuels liberalized SBA procedures, adopting a system of blanket loan approvals which significantly improved bank participation in the program. Throughout the banking community Mr. Samuels was commended for his innovative and constructive approach. However, the regional SBA administrators, whose appointments to office were more often a political reward rather than a reflection of business and financial talent, acted as a serious brake on efforts at reform. When Mr. Samuels left office at the end of 1968 the number of equal-opportunity loans approved by SBA had increased materially, but were still insignificant in volume or number.

101

The reason most frequently given by SBA for the failure of its slum business-loan program was that it was unable to recruit potential ghetto businessmen with sufficient business experience. The Negro's chronic entrepreneurial failure—the very risk which the SBA ghetto loan program was designed to blunt—was reinforced by the agency's insistence on judging the Negro's business experience by the same standards applied to the small businessman in the normal economy.

Like other agencies, the Small Business Administration has shown jealous opposition to constructive proposals for creating private organizations to make loans and guarantee credits in poverty areas where SBA has failed. Following the 1968 riots, the Washington District City Council proposed a new loan fund or pool of several million dollars to encourage new Negro business activity. SBA hostility to this proposal was predictable. Richard A. Salem, director of SBA's regional Washington office, said, "There is no panacea in such a fund. . . . In addition to funding, what is needed is a comprehensive management assistance program to enable individuals to operate their own programs."

Intelligently planned high-risk business credits are the foundation on which Negro entrepreneurship can build. But the Negro businessman is denied federally insured business credit because he lacks management skills and his business is not stable. However, his business is unstable, and in many cases he has failed to develop management expertise because he lacks access to credit and capital.

The Federal Housing Administration and the Under-Mortgaged Society

THE FEDERAL HOUSING ADMINISTRATION was born in 1934 during the nation's most critical money crisis, when people were forced to put up with swollen down payments, short-term mortgages, and high interest rates. The FHA moved quickly to guarantee housing credits, ease rates and repayment terms, and broaden home ownership in the United States. In its quarter-century of activity, the FHA has insured more than $112 billion in home mortgages. Under FHA programs, eight and one-half million people have become owners of home equities—often the first step toward accumulating personal capital.

Through most of its history, however, the FHA has been dedicated to building in suburban areas, virtually ignoring the inner city. Because of the high element of credit risk, the FHA has been reluctant to insure mortgages for low-income families. Its ghetto investment risk-aversion and its preference for stable neighborhoods date back to 1938. At that time, FHA advanced the use of racially restrictive covenants through "prohibition of the occupancy of properties except by race for which they are intended. . . . If a mixture of user groups is found to exist, it must be determined whether the mixture will render the neighborhood less desirable to present and prospective occupants." Until recently, the FHA actually refused to insure non-white mortgage applications in white neighborhoods. During a Congressional hearing in 1967, housing expert Charles Abrams stated that "it would be a market phenomenon" for a low-income Negro family to secure a conventional or FHA-insured mortgage. This background has caused many critics, such as Senator Edward Brooke of Massachusetts, to call for the use of other vehicles to aid the housing problems of the urban poor.

The important role of the Federal Housing Administration in the national program for developing home ownership among moderate- and lower-income families is shown by a recent study carried out by the Department of Labor.[12] This study reports that virtually all new homes erected by a building company and selling for less than $12,500 are insured by the FHA or the Veterans Administration. Yet, Senate committee hearings show that the per cent of existing one-family houses insured by FHA for families with an income of less than $4,000 has fallen from 42.8 per cent of the total in 1950 to 1.3 per cent in 1966. For new homes, the drop is even sharper: from 56 per cent in 1950 to 1 per cent in 1966. This drastic change cannot be attributed to inflation, since the proportion of families with an income of $4,000 fell from 63 per cent in 1950 to only 24 per cent in 1966. In 1966, families with incomes of $4,000 to $5,000 a year constituted less than 5 per cent of those with insured mortgages on existing homes.[13] Obviously, the sharply declining trend away from FHA insurance of low- and moderate-income residential equities would be even more severe if the non-white home owners were eliminated from those figures.

Recognizing the failure to develop new housing in the ghettos, Congress has enacted, in recent years, an array of new FHA schemes for new low-income housing—featured by the touted Section 221(d)(3) below-market-interest-rate program (BMIR).

[12] Newman, "The Low-Cost Housing Market," *Monthly Labor Review,* Vol. 89, p. 1362.
[13] *Hearings Before the Subcommittee on Housing and Urban Affairs of the Senate Committee on Banking and Currency,* 90th Cong., 1st Sess., pt. I, p. 530 (1967) (Testimony of AFL-CIO).

None of these recent programs has produced any significant volume of low-income housing either inside or outside the ghetto. Six years ago, when Congress was considering Section 221(d)(3), it was told that the proposed legislation would make it possible to build 60,000 apartment units a year. After the riots in 1967, Congress looked at the situation again, and found that a grand total of only 40,000 units had been completed under the *entire* program, in ghetto as well as in white areas. During the 1967 Senate Finance Committee hearings, HUD Secretary Robert Weaver testified that he did not know how many 221(d)(3) BMIR units had been constructed in ghetto areas; however, he noted that since the program began, an average of 500 family units a year had been constructed in Harlem.

The pattern of ghetto residential-loan failure at FHA follows closely the recent disappointments in the ghetto business programs of the Small Business Administration. In both agencies, insurance-approval procedures have been infected by such inordinate delays and red tape that, in many cases, the private lending institutions have refused to participate in the agency loan-guarantee programs. Experienced FHA lenders cite an unreasonable and impractical array of mandatory building specifications, lengthy appraisal procedures, unrealistic credit standards, and crippling delays which must be accepted by every FHA project sponsor.

The most serious criticism of FHA came during the 1967 Congressional hearings on a proposed National Home Ownership Foundation. A spokesman for the National Housing Conference testified that it takes an average of eighteen months to process 221(d)(3) applications. FHA requirements demanded for a major project of the HRH Construction Company in New York City caused a project-approval delay of three years. Meanwhile, increased building costs and carrying charges made the project no longer attractive to the sponsors.

Programs of Action-Housing, Inc., in Pittsburgh, illustrate the punishing effect of FHA regulation on important real estate efforts in the slums. This limited-profit corporation undertook rehabilitation of ten buildings in a Pittsburgh ghetto. Sponsored by

Westinghouse, National Gypsum, and Pittsburgh Plate Glass, the Action-Housing, Inc., project qualified for loans under FHA's 221 program providing for 90 per cent financing with 3 per cent interest, and principal repayable over forty years. After long delays, Action-Housing, Inc., offered to accept an additional 10 per cent risk on the 90 per cent FHA loan. In return, it was hoped that FHA would reconsider its cost restrictions, performance standards, and time-consuming inspections. In effect, the project sponsors sought to bargain their way free of FHA red tape by offering to impose on themselves an unwarranted portion of the loan risk. The *Harvard Law Review* reported that Action-Housing, Inc., found that delays in FHA processing almost defeated the entire Pittsburgh rehabilitation project.[14]

It would be too pat to lay the entire blame for ghetto housing failure at the door of the FHA. The bewildering complexity of the problem of slum real estate is only compounded by the confusion and delays of the government agencies. Consider a proposal to rehabilitate a famous eyesore in East Harlem. 311 East 100th Street in East Harlem has been labeled by the press, and featured on national television, as the most notorious tenement building in New York City. It has been visited and inspected by a parade of senators and mayors. Over the years, the building has had more than 150 owners. At present its ownership cannot even be established, since under the New York receivership law for abandoned slum properties, the city can correct violation, but cannot acquire title to the property. Frances Levenson, director of the demonstration rehabilitation programs in the Housing and Development Administration, points up other obstacles which must be overcome if the community is to rehabilitate No. 311. Even if the city acquired full ownership, elaborate administrative procedures would have to be pursued by the City Planning Commission and the Board of Estimate before the building could be condemned. After these approvals were obtained, there would remain the complicated problem of forming a community corporation under a new amendment to the Private Housing Finance Law of New

14 *Harvard Law Review,* Vol. 81, p. 1295.

York State. This corporation would then purchase the building from the city. Only then could the community corporation start down the long road of obtaining an FHA commitment under Section 221(d)(3).[15]

The FHA has been burdened, not only by these incredibly complex problems of building or rehabilitation of slum real estate, but also by the agency's special relationship and concern with the Congress. The FHA has been criticized by the more liberal Congressional committee heads for not moving forward aggressively with new programs for insuring high-risk ghetto loans. But at the same time, senators such as John Williams of Delaware have attacked FHA for taking undue ghetto credit risks, and allowing federal funds to be wasted in speculation windfalls for FHA project sponsors.

In recent Congressional hearings, Martin Frank, an FHA housing consultant, was alleged to have made a quarter of a million dollars in retainers, expenses, and fees for arranging non-profit housing projects. One journal stated that Mr. Frank was a genius in figuring out how to produce housing under a "virtually impossible program." [16] As a result of such "scandals," FHA programs designed to create new or rehabilitated slum-area housing are now "guaranteed corruption proof." FHA programs receiving the most favorable interest rates are those sponsored by unions, churches, and other non-profit organizations. The FHA rent-supplement program, instituted in 1965, provides direct government subsidization of individual family rent payments. This program was hailed as the solution to the low-income housing dilemma. But this program, too, is restricted by its demand of "limited-dividend," non-profit, and cooperative sponsors. These non-profit groups, of course, have neither the seed money nor the expertise to start a project. They lack experience in obtaining option and loan commitments, in engaging lawyers, architects, and builders. They simply do not have the entrepreneurial equipment

[15] The story of 311 East 100th Street is eloquently told by Woody Klein in "Why One of the Worst Slums in New York Hasn't Been Torn Down," *New York Magazine*, April 28, 1968.
[16] *Barron's*, December 18, 1967.

necessary to undertake and complete a complicated multiple-tenant slum housing project.

Even the most advanced proposals for tax incentives for investment in ghetto housing contain elaborate safeguards against windfall gains. Robert Kennedy's proposal—to by-pass FHA by offering project sponsors direct ghetto-housing tax credits—still would have required investors to hold property for certain minimum periods. Congress has considered that ironclad safeguards against speculation are a necessary feature of all FHA legislation designed to encourage construction or rehabilitation of ghetto housing.

The Housing Act of 1949 established official government policy of achieving as soon as possible "a decent home and suitable living environment for every American family." Yet, existing programs have built neither shelter nor the ownership of real estate equities in the ghetto. Dozens of new programs have now been advanced to deal with this complicated and confusing aspect of urban poverty. Although the state of slum housing is a dismal one, the housing failures of the past suggest certain principles which we must follow if we are to construct a comprehensive plan to break the grip of the ghetto economy.

First, we must abandon the system of "double approvals" which has produced such waste and delays in the loan-guarantee programs of FHA and SBA. Apparently FHA supports fifteen thousand employees and an annual administrative budget of $170 million. Much of this system is engaged in lengthy procedures of review and approval of loans which have already been approved and reviewed by experienced lending officers at private financial institutions.

If the system of federal loan guarantees is to be retained as a means of blunting the anarchy of the ghetto economy, and of providing income certainty to the private lender, then we must move toward a system of "self-executing" loan guarantees. Under such a system the lender is told that if he commits his capital to certain carefully defined programs for enrichment of the slums, the repayment of his loan or investment is assured. This direct procedure is necessary to avoid the protracted loan-approval delays which, at the moment, absolutely forbid the constructive participation of the private sector in federal programs for the enrichment of ghetto housing or entrepreneurship.

The procedure I suggest of self-executing loan guarantees is not without precedent at FHA. Under existing FHA procedures, thousands of banks and savings institutions regularly commit FHA repayment insurance to home-improvement loans without the necessity of securing advance approval. If ghetto loan programs are to move ahead vigorously, the government's right to police what it subsidizes must be exercised by federal-agency reviews through the vehicle of audits *after* the loan is committed. If the government's policing function is a prior condition to granting loan approval, the incentive is greatly diminished. The delay, waste, and disadvantage of continuous involvement with the bureaucracy requires a higher yield or incentive. More often the sponsor in the private sector who has the initiative, capital, and expertise to move ahead with a project simply throws up his hands and refuses to play the game.

High-risk ghetto programs of FHA have often failed because of the agency's dependence on Congressional approval and appropriations. Slum-area credits have been withheld by FHA because of its concern that a powerful faction in Congress would attack these projects as unbankable waste of federal funds. In other cases, with concern for the Congressional watchdogs who are alert to every windfall, FHA has adopted complicated rules for project appraisals and unreasonable building specifications. Project-loan approvals and construction procedures have become the despair of builders and bankers. Obviously, the credit and housing problems of the slums must be attacked through a new vehicle such as a federally chartered urban-development bank, or a new ghetto loan agency within the framework of HUD, or even through FHA itself. But the new organization must have the independence of the Federal Reserve Board. It must not be dependent on Congress for continuing appropriations or supervision.

Finally, an important secondary consequence of the failure of our national program to house the poor has been a total failure to develop any vestige of the ownership of equities in slum-area real estate. The wealth-building technique of leveraging little or no down payment with a big mortgage is not used in the ghetto. When the day comes to revalue real estate in Hough, Bedford-Stuyvesant, and Lawndale, we must make certain that the one million black residents of these communities are dwelling in a home (or condominium) owned in fee simple and leveraged with a 90 per cent mortgage. The ghetto blacks have no hope if government lawyers, the federal agencies, and the Congress cling to precedent which holds that the poor must occupy their homes under a short-term residential lease.

PART FOUR

Emerging Motives for
Business Action

Business, Riots, and the Encroaching Slums

IT ALL STARTED in Detroit with a routine police raid on a "blind pig," an illegal after-hours bar, at 9125 Twelfth Street in the early morning of July 23, 1967. When federal paratroopers left the city a week later, forty-three people were dead. A week of burning and looting, together with curfews—enforced closings of stores—cost the fantastic sum of two billion dollars in lost revenues, wages, and destruction of property. The president of an international hotel chain reported to stockholders that rioting during that same summer reduced chain-wide hotel occupancy to the point that an $800,000 increase in the hotel's profits gained at Expo '67 in Montreal was completely wiped out by rioting in American cities. Less than a year later, an estimated forty million dollars of tourist business was lost in Washington as rioting and concern over the Poor People's March persuaded tourists to shun the nation's capital. The *Wall Street Journal* reported that riots following the assassination of Martin Luther King in 1968 reduced American Motors' sales by thirty thousand cars during a ten-day period.

But the riots in Detroit had at least one positive effect. They demonstrated to the national business community that grievances in the ghetto were basically economic. Aside from the dubious and unproven theory that riots are the work of a minority of trained agitators, how else could one explain the fact that the nation's most destructive revolt had occurred in one of its most progressive cities? The riots in Detroit suddenly galvanized the great power of American business to deal with the problems of a massive city slum. The New Detroit Committee, composed primarily of business leaders of America's largest manufacturing corporations, immediately embarked on aggressive and creative programs to improve conditions in the city's ghetto. During the eight months ending November 30, 1968, General Motors recruited and hired 21,706 hard-core unemployed, at an average starting pay of $3.30 an hour. The General Motors total accounts for nearly one-fifth of the jobless hired under the national ghetto recruiting program of National Alliance of Businessmen.

The Newark riots spurred a commitment of Prudential Life Insurance Company to invest, in its home city of Newark and elsewhere, hundreds of millions of dollars of private capital for new construction and rehabilitation of ghetto housing and business. In 1965, the burning of Watts' "Charcoal Alley" led Aerojet General Corporation to establish in the curfew area a "high-risk" manufacturing facility in which only hard-core unemployable Negro and Mexican Americans are employed. It is no coincidence that Hotel Corporation of America announced at its May, 1968, stockholders' meeting that the company's Washington hotel operated at 15 per cent occupancy during Cherry Blossom Festival in 1968 (which coincided with the riots following the assassination of Martin Luther King), and that the hotel chain would soon construct a $4.5 million hotel in West Harlem.

Whether you choose to call it an industry response to blackmail, a high-minded business effort to correct justifiable grievances, or just good practical business judgment, the pattern is the same throughout the country. Rioting and burning have invariably been followed by industry commitments for new plants, training centers, and programs for job creation in ghetto areas.

Businessmen who would motivate their companies to take action in the ghetto, lawyers who would exhort their business clients to action, and government leaders who now recognize business as the most effective agent for proposing and implementing action in the slums must therefore study the particular threats and options of the businessmen they are seeking to motivate. A close look at the companies which have developed creative programs to improve the ghetto economy gives an insight into the kind of motivation that is necessary to produce a significant business effort in the slum. It is plain that the magnitude of any given business activity or response is directly related to the immediacy of the ghetto's threat to the particular business.

We start first with the businessman's response to a proximate and expanding ghetto that is not yet speaking through the technique of riot. Where a real estate or manufacturing corporation has a large investment in land or plant ownership adjacent to an encroaching slum, the immediate risk to stockholders is real. Civic obligations aside, the firm affected is perfectly willing to take appropriate financial measures to reverse the direction of an encroaching ghetto. This type of business response has been going on in many cities for many years. For a decade or more, Sears Roebuck in Chicago and Smith, Kline and French in Philadelphia, both with very large plant investments in the heart of ghetto areas, have been pursuing imaginative programs for improving economic and physical conditions in the areas where their plants are anchored.

The next group of firms that have shown a significant anti-poverty response includes companies whose plant investment or markets are essentially locked into the central core of the city, but not yet inside the ghetto. For the most part, these are the urban insurance companies and utilities.

Unlike the manufacturing firms which have moved out of Harlem, utilities in the cities cannot move their operations; they are totally committed to the urban core areas. Their property consists of immovable cables, telephones, and power plants. Their markets are almost wholly within the city; restrictive franchises and charters prevent diversification to escape the urban threat of an encroaching ghetto. The urban utilities must either make the best of conditions in the cities or work to improve the urban outlook.

Aside from the negative danger to markets and plants, other factors propel the anti-poverty efforts of the utilities. The companies operate under a price-protected umbrella provided by law. A specified return on invested capital is guaranteed. This means that telephone and power companies can engage in massive and expensive efforts of job creation for ghetto residents without a serious impact on profit-and-loss statements. The cost of anti-poverty efforts is simply cranked into the utility rate structure. Moreover, the utilities do not overlook the possibility that new jobs for ghetto residents will enhance over-all consumer income and open up new markets for selling utility services. The utilities stand to acquire additional revenues if the ghetto can achieve greater affluence.

However, the promise that programs for improvement of Negro job opportunities may expand utility sales in the ghetto, and the fact that the cost of hiring minority groups can be written off against the utility rate base, are secondary considerations. In most cases these opportunities merely provide a business rationale for anti-poverty efforts that are more directly connected with the immediate threat of the ghetto to vulnerable and immovable plants and markets. Undoubtedly the heads of our utilities are motivated by strong obligations of good corporate citizenship. Yet the immediate threat to business revenues has provided a major catalyst for the massive anti-poverty programs they have undertaken.

Consider a specific example. In recent years, the Bell Telephone System has become the most important training and educational organization in the world. The company has probably trained on a private basis more hard-core unemployables than has the Job Corps of OEO. The head of American Telephone and Telegraph Company stated in 1967 that Negro employment in the Bell System rose from 29,000 to 51,000 in three years, compared with a 13 per cent over-all increase in employment in the company. Based on Job Corps training-cost statistics, I estimate that the AT&T effort involved a possible training cost of up to $3,000 per employee, plus perhaps $3,000 per employee for additional payroll costs incurred during the period when the for-

116

mer high-school dropout was unproductive and made costly errors. Obviously the AT&T job program for black citizens is not ordinary corporate charity. Corporate efforts of this magnitude must find justification in an immediate threat to the company's plant investment and profits. The danger was articulated by Ben Gilmer, President of AT&T, in the report to stockholders in 1967: "The city is where the large central offices are located and where 80 per cent of your customers live. The big cities and metropolitan areas account for 70 per cent of total telephone plant investment located in the deteriorating central cities."

Nowhere is the risk to the business community, hounded by the encroaching and rioting ghetto, more imminent than it is for the great metropolitan banks and insurance companies. Virtually all of the physical assets of the First National City Bank are locked up in Manhattan in the form of a central office and branches. Under present law, the bank may not diversify geographically, to any important extent, through branches in suburban areas or in other states. The bank holds a kind of franchise in New York City and, unlike General Foods and IBM, it cannot pull up stakes and move to suburban Westchester if things get too hot in central Harlem. Ultimately, the repayability of the bank's vast portfolio of business loans is intimately linked to the future economic course of the great central cities of America.

Since the large banks are locked into the central city, they must become engaged in programs for improving the ghetto's economy. A pioneering Negro job-training program was initiated in the Watts curfew area by the Security First National Bank of Los Angeles, following the 1965 riots. Unusually aggressive bank-sponsored programs for infusing credit into slum areas have occurred in the expanding ghettos of Philadelphia and Savannah. Important business equal-opportunity loan programs have been launched by banks in dozens of other cities.

The life-insurance companies, too, are totally and uniquely involved with the crisis in the urban economy. The portfolios of the life-insurance companies are committed to billions of dollars in mortgages on core-area real estate. These mortgages run twenty years or more—into future periods when, according to computers at the Bureau of Census, dozens of the largest cities in America will be more than 50 per cent Negro. At present, there is no market big enough, at home or abroad, for the sale of mortgage investments in these vast amounts. If the income and value supporting these mortgages should decay, these investments could be next to worthless.

The fire and casualty companies have been even more directly affected by the burning of the ghettos. The insured loss in Detroit was prematurely and erroneously reported at $85 million. At first the insurance companies panicked when they estimated their losses in Los Angeles, Newark, and Detroit. Large sections of the ghettos were "red-penciled" by company actuaries and thereby rendered totally uninsurable. Cooler heads in the fire-insurance industry have now concluded that the inability to obtain insurance in the black slum simply compounds the hazards which the deteriorating inner city already presents to the investments held by insurance institutions. New investment programs in the ghetto, similar to those announced by the life-insurance industry—backed by an effort to obtain a government reinsurance program for riot risks—have now become the more practical and sensible reaction to the threat.

The response of the downtown department stores to rioting has been predictable. These merchants are uniquely vulnerable to looting and the expanding decay of real estate in the urban central core. Hudson's, Detroit's largest department store, has been a leader and innovator of business-backed anti-poverty programs. Aside from the hotels and small merchants, there is probably no single company in Detroit whose business was more seriously affected or threatened by the ghetto riots of July, 1967. The same pattern of action is repeated in other cities. Neiman-Marcus in Dallas was the first department store to announce that in selecting suppliers the store's purchasing department would consider potential suppliers' equal-opportunity hiring practices. A similar program was announced by F&R Lazarus Company in Cincinnati and Dayton Company in Minneapolis.

The motive most calculated to ensure that businessmen will work for the enrichment of the ghetto is the threat to their corporate plants and product markets. Logically enough, the intensity of the businessman's effort in the ghetto will be augmented when he is "cornered"—when he has no option other than a frontal attack on the economic and social cancers of the slums.

American business has frequently shown its greatest qualities of innovation and creativity when it is under a direct threat. This quality is sharply demonstrated by the technological and entrepreneurial achievements that followed Pearl Harbor and the launching of the Russian Sputnik in 1957. The urgent threat of rioting and burning ghettos of the late 1960's produced the magnificent "Jobs Now" program of the National Alliance of Businessmen. But, obviously, riots are an uncertain and unreliable social force for shaping constructive business programs for the enrichment of the slums. Although the riots may focus on the desperate economic needs of the black community, the anti-poverty response of the businessman must be guided by a force of greater reliability and logic. Corrective programs must be developed which not only identify the specific economic needs and defects in the black community, but also provide assurance that the businessman will satisfy just these needs and no others. In substitution for the threat of riots, new economic forces must be marshaled which will persuade the businessman to build programs that are both constructive and controlled; his efforts must cease to be a personal, often poorly planned, and ill-considered reaction to the anarchy of a burning ghetto.

Safeguarding Labor and
Executive Markets

FOR DECADES, business has been built on the premise that the public schools of America would continue to turn out the necessary qualified manpower to feed an adequate supply of high-school graduates for the labor needs of a growing industrial system. New capital markets and sources of materials were developed by industry as a matter of vital corporate need. But labor was always plentiful—trained at public expense. In recent years, however, the economy has been running at an unusually high tempo, with labor in short supply. For the first time, industry has been obliged to reach out for the untrained and formerly "unemployables." At the same time, labor shortages have been aggravated by the failure of the public school systems in many areas to provide proper training for its pupils. The problem is even more severe in our cities. The business community was shocked to learn in 1967 that a large percentage of high-school graduates in New York City show reading and arithmetic skills equal to fifth-graders in other communities.

The President of Chrysler Corporation recently described the miserable level of achievement of the hard-core unemployable American youth:

120

"These people can't read simple words such as 'in' and 'out' signs on a door.

"They have to be taught the letters that spell common colors so they can read the instruction card that tells them to put a blue or green steering wheel on a car as it comes down the assembly line." They must learn simple addition "so that they can count boxes of parts they take off a supplier's truck."

Some sign an "X" for their names, some fail to show up, and many come late.

"These people," he said, "were not only offered jobs, but the offers were made right on their own blocks or at the favorite corner for standing on, or in the church basement or the poolroom. So if they didn't show up, they didn't really want to work."

But checking showed that the answer "in many cases was childishly simple," he said. "If you can't read, how do you know what it says on the destination signs of the many buses that go by on a given busy street? And a grown man isn't going to get on— and be sent off—the wrong bus very many times before he stops getting on buses any more. So we showed those people, one by one, how to recognize the right bus to take, and in some cases how and when to transfer to another necessary route."

When Chrysler checked on why many were regularly late, he said, the company discovered that "only one in five owned an alarm clock. Why? Because they'd never had to be any particular place at any particular time before." [1]

In order to protect its labor market, American industry has now entered the business of basic education in an important way. Companies such as Corn Products Company are teaching basic reading, writing, and arithmetic to selected workers. American Telephone & Telegraph and General Electric have become two of the most important elementary educational organizations in the country. These educationally oriented corporate activities are not completely altruistic. They are simply a function of the most basic motivation of every business: to protect its supply of labor and its ability to stay in business.

Many years ago, the United Fruit Company is said to have

[1] *New York Times,* June 16, 1968.

121

initiated revolutions in Latin America to protect its sources of fruit supplies. With the same fierce determination to stay in business, companies continue to endure oppressive real estate taxes in the New England states in order to remain near valuable sources of highly skilled labor. Today, many companies mount important and expensive civic activities in the belief they will endear themselves to local citizens and produce the favorable image that is helpful for general recruiting of labor.

We must recognize, therefore, that recent business efforts to train the hard-core unemployed are due in large part to current labor shortages inherent in a high-speed economy which operates against a background of a basic training failure in our public schools.

Currently, therefore, business motivation to recruit and train personnel is strong; but the thread of motivation is tender and unreliable. At the moment, the federal government is moving toward higher income taxes and reduction of the supply of money —necessary steps to head off inflation and an unfavorable balance of international payments. This trend will inevitably have the effect of increasing unemployment—easing not only labor shortages but also the need of industry to train and employ the impoverished underskilled. Shortages of labor—one of the most important motivations for industry's training and education of disadvantaged people—may entirely disappear until the business cycle turns again.

Although not often articulated, another important motive for recent business anti-poverty programs has been the parallel need of American industry to protect its markets for young executive talent. The hostile attitudes toward business of some of our most able students is well known. "Business Is for the Birds" was the title of a *Wall Street Journal* feature story on the fact that many of our most competent young men are now turning to teaching, public service, government, or other non-business activities. The large Wall Street law firms specializing in corporate law must offer the young law graduate not only a salary of $15,000 a year but additional assurances that the firm is active and committed to programs of legal aid for the poor. Business has all but lost its post-World War II glamour appeal for the successful college graduate.

Many intelligent and dynamic young men turn away from business because they believe its values are incorrect. To the distress of executive recruiters, these youths often opt for the Peace Corps at a meager salary. A recent public-service advertisement for one of America's great corporations suggests that student leaders (with moderate haircuts and political views to match) believe businessmen are dull, money-grubbing, and self-centered. The monetary lures of pensions, high salaries, and stock options have lost much of their charm. Young men yearn to help solve the great issues of poverty and race relations. The founder of Dow Chemical Company recently expressed alarm that public identification of Dow with production of napalm was hurting the company's recruiting of executive talent. These attitudes are obviously relevant to business's programs for rehabilitating slum areas.

Leading business recruiters believe that unfriendly student attitudes toward business will change if business demonstrates greater interest in solving America's critical urban and racial problems. There is no question that the important contract recently signed by Litton Industries with the Greek government to develop new industry and find means of relieving poverty in a traditionally underdeveloped economy will attract to Litton in America many able young potential managers who might otherwise enrich the Peace Corps. College recruiting by IBM and Xerox has been aided by the strong public-service image of those companies.

To businessmen keenly aware of the vital conditions which permit their companies to prosper, the need for recruiting young executives has become one of the strongest arguments for a business commitment to solving the problems of the slums.

The Gentle Art of the
Federal Hotfoot

ONE OF THE MOST effective devices for moving businessmen toward greater participation in combating poverty has been the specter of possible federal intervention in business activities which were formerly reserved for the enterprise system. Congress and the White House know that the old bugaboo of "creeping socialism" still has force in corporate boardrooms.

In recent years, for example, the banking industry has developed programs for educational loans to needy students, unquestionably stimulated by the potential entry of the federal government into the field of direct educational loans. The suggestion that the federal government's Small Business Administration might make direct commercial loans to promising Negro entrepreneurs has stimulated business acceptance of a substitute program under which the banks do the lending to ghetto business ventures, but with repayment guaranteed by the Small Business Administration. The construction industry eschews low-income housing projects financed with loans guaranteed by the Federal Housing Administration, but these projects are far more acceptable to builders than is direct government entry into the field of residential construction in the form of odious public housing.

124

For most businessmen, a "voluntary" private program for training Negro unemployables, such as the kind being carried out on a massive scale by the National Alliance of Businessmen, is infinitely preferable to the Concentrated Employment Programs of the Department of Labor or the Office of Economic Opportunity's Job Corps program. While more than six hundred firms are participating in the National Alliance of Businessmen's voluntary JOBS program for training and hiring the hard-core unemployed, three hundred firms, including General Motors, have refused government subsidies of as much as $5,000 per man trained and given a job. Even in Job Corps centers, private enterprise has not surrendered its traditional and primary responsibility for training employees. The major Job Corps centers are operated under government contract by dozens of national corporations.

The businessman's fear of "creeping socialism" as a force to prod the private sector toward anti-poverty efforts becomes more vivid for those who are concerned about the increasing level of federal spending. Feeding the argument that "if we businessmen don't start new business ventures in the ghetto the government will" is the certainty that if the federal government does the job, costs will not only be greater but ultimately will be borne by the businessman in the form of either higher taxes or an eroding dollar.

The federal government has demonstrated that if approximately $6,000 is spent on training the hard-core teenage dropout, probably the trainee can join the employment market at a low entry level. But private industry believes it can do the same job on a reduced budget. The Security First National Bank in Los Angeles has opened a private skills training center in the Watts ghetto. In many cases the bank takes the untrainables who possess the deprived backgrounds of Job Corps inductees. The bank claims to be training profitably in Watts without the need for government subsidy.

The federal government can "blackmail" businessmen to move into anti-poverty projects by threatening them with new federal programs. In some cases, businessmen are not aware that they have been "had"; in others, they were eager to become involved in

125

ghetto problems but needed a push and an acceptable "business reason" to show directors and stockholders. Yet despite all the froth and publicity, these voluntary business programs barely touch the deprivation of American slums. If we are even to hold our own in the struggle to build new jobs, skills, and facilities in these decaying economies, the wealth-makers, the capital-builders—the sources of credit and leverage—must be provided with more compelling attractions and motives than a prod or a threat from the federal government.

Public Relations, Patriotism, and Prestige

IT IS TRADITIONAL in corporate boardrooms that civic and community projects find their business justification in building favorable images which are helpful in reducing company real estate taxes, staving off unfavorable town ordinances, and sustaining management through periods of long labor disturbances. The same public-relations benefits flow from corporate anti-poverty programs in the slums. Ling-Temco-Vought and Litton Industries, two of the most aggressive and successful companies in the country, do not have corporate institutional advertising programs; yet they support strong public-relations departments which make certain that Negro-hiring and other company programs in slum areas become well known to the public. Announcement of IBM's Bedford-Stuyvesant sub-assembly plant made the front page of *The New York Times,* whereas a much larger IBM plant in a suburban area would have been noted only in the business pages. Westinghouse staged a lavish press conference to announce its new ghetto project in Pittsburgh.

Before the riots of the late 1960's, Chase Manhattan Bank decided to open several bank branches in Harlem. Once put into effect, this decision was virtually irrevocable. It would be impossible for a large bank such as Chase Manhattan to abandon a branch in a ghetto area. There could be no explanation for a visible banking withdrawal from the underbanked slums that the public would accept. Indeed, the bank has indicated that its Harlem branches are profitable. Stockholders and bank examiners could accept nothing less. Yet, it is certain that these branches are much less profitable than alternative downtown branch locations which the bank could have chosen at the time.

It is unlikely that the bank chose to open branches in Harlem simply for the reason that its management is headed by a brilliant team of fair-minded citizens. For a large Metropolitan bank, ghetto branches perform an important corporate function. For one thing, Chase Manhattan does a large volume of business with Negro depositors and borrowers in many areas of New York City, including the more prosperous sections of Harlem, Brooklyn, and Manhattan. The bank regularly lends money to successful Negro businessmen of the city. Since the banking industry is highly regulated, the ability of Chase Manhattan to grow and expand in other areas of the city (and, it is to be hoped, even in suburban areas) is critically affected by the attitudes of the Negro community, which exercises considerable political influence in Albany and Washington. The ever-present threat of new federal or state laws which could compel a bank to devote a fixed percentage of its loans and investments to slum areas is blunted as the bank establishes voluntary programs for the credit enrichment of the New York ghettos. Establishing in Harlem a marginally profitable branch bank, or even a loss operation, is therefore justified by hard business considerations which are unrelated to the social and civic responsibilities of a great banking corporation.

The same considerations apply to the large life-insurance companies and public utilities. In formulating the nation's most dramatic and expensive program for training and hiring hard-core unemployables, the Bell Telephone System is certainly mindful that telephone rates are established in places that have a very keen interest in moving industry into greater involvement with the problems of the ghetto. Similar corporate considerations must have entered the deliberations of almost two hundred large state-

regulated life-insurance companies that announced in 1967 a billion-dollar program for new mortgages on slum real estate.

The argument that patriotic considerations alone justify a massive effort by American business to find solutions to the crisis in
our cities was stated by Hubert Humphrey at the meeting of Businessmen's Plans for Progress in May, 1967: "I know that everyone in this room is a member of the establishment, including me.
We have more to lose than anyone in this country if things go
sour. We have everything to lose and everything to save."

In theory, the critical damage to United States prestige abroad
caused by the violence at home should provide an important impetus for new business programs for regenerating the slums. But
the argument does not carry much impetus for starting new business programs in the ghetto. The reason appears to be that most
businessmen regard riots and poverty as a national problem.
Only a still small, but increasingly influential, group sees ghetto
unemployment as a by-product of industry—and therefore as a
direct responsibility and obligation of the enterprise system.
Businessmen argue that the cost of solutions should be borne by
government and not by private business alone. The responsibility
for framing and financing programs in the ghetto becomes all the
more "public" as the crisis of American poverty and racial schism
acquires international political significance.

I suggest that the appeal to the patriotism of American businessman will become effective only as he comes to realize that the
federal government is almost powerless to deal with the basic
economic problems of building wealth and entrepreneurship in
the slums.

More potent than an appeal to patriotism is one directed toward civic responsibility. Efforts to improve conditions in America are striking responsive chords among many business executives. What is now happening is repeating a historical pattern.
Twenty or thirty years ago, if a national corporation had made a
large contribution for constructing a cultural project such as Lin-
coln Center in New York City, the executive in charge would

have been accused of harboring a suspicious and unreliable senti-
ment for the arts. Today, these projects are almost never characterized as the act of a liberal businessman who cannot be trusted
by his customers and associates. Although the benefits of these
projects to society are great, the nexus or direct benefit to the
contributing business enterprise is small. But, nonetheless, it has
become popular for business to make such gifts and investments.
The fact that the business establishment makes these cultural investments is important because smaller business will follow and
make similar commitments.

David Rockefeller suggests that, just as a pattern of increasing
corporate interest in cultural projects has developed, so business
investment and involvement in urban problems will develop as it
becomes fashionable.

The Anti-Poverty Power Innovators

IT SHOULD COME as no surprise that the corporations which have mounted aggressive programs for ghetto hiring and enrichment are not those controlled by staff organizations and committees. The most creative urban projects have originated with organizations of the "free-form" entrepreneurial type, often dominated by an innovative businessman who is skilled in taking risks and in entering unpredictable market situations. These are the pace-setters, problem-solvers, and makers of public opinion. These men are the first to recognize discrimination or injustice and take bold corrective measures.

Of all the business conferences on poverty that I have attended, I have seen no group of businessmen so aroused and angry as those at the June, 1968, meeting of the American Management Association. Preston Lambert, the black owner of a Chicken Delight franchise in the Bedford-Stuyvesant section of Brooklyn, spoke harshly: "Six weeks ago I bought my second Chicken Delight franchise. I called up my broker and told him I wanted insurance on that store. He said what's the address? I said 855 DeKalb Avenue. Last Friday he called me and said, Lambert, I have all of your insurance except for fire. I said what are

131

you talking about? How can I run a business without fire insurance? . . . I've got to have fire insurance. Chicken Delight [franchise] costs $13,700, plus another $7,000 to decorate your store. Then you must start out with at least two cars. I said my business has around a $32,000 value. I've *got* to get insurance. My broker says, well, I'll try to get some, but the cost will be excessive. Well, I'm a little smart guy. I just can't lie down and take a thing too well. I asked the other business people on the block, who happen to be white. I'm looking for an insurance broker to cover my store, I told them. Can you help me? Oh yeah, use my broker, they said. Do you have all of the insurance you need, I asked. They said, oh yeah, I have everything—liability, fire, everything. So now here I am at 855 DeKalb since last Friday, and I have checked the stores on either side of me and around me, and they have fire insurance. I happen to be the only Negro in one of those stores, and I don't. That is downright discrimination any way you figure it out. I can't get insurance. Why? Only because the white people own all the insurance companies. And they won't give it to a Negro. You're preventing him from being in business. If I have a loss, can I sustain that? Do you want to do something? Then go back home and do something. And when a little black guy like me comes along, give him the same thing that you would give to a white guy if he can pay for it."

This kind of intolerable discrimination is quickly rooted out when it comes to the attention of the business pace-setters. They have no petty anxieties about "playing it safe." International Business Machines' innovative project for manufacturing computer cables in Brooklyn's Bedford-Stuyvesant will barely dent the massive army of unemployables in that fast-growing ghetto. But this example of IBM's Thomas Watson, Jr., will inevitably set the style for others.

Aerojet General's pioneering tent-and-container factory in Watts, ITT's commitment to the politically hazardous Job Corps center at Camp Kilmer, Control Data's program for a sub-assembly plant in the Negro north side of Minneapolis—all illustrate that the most dramatic business programs in the blighted areas come from the highly innovative and successful companies.

The forces of innovation are also effective at some of the old-line financial institutions. In the fall of 1967, it appeared almost impossible to persuade over a hundred life-insurance companies to agree on a common one-billion-dollar program for investment in slum mortgages; yet two dominant and determined industry leaders, Orville Beale of Prudential and Gilbert W. Fitzhugh of Metropolitan, took the bit in their teeth and unilaterally committed their companies to 40 per cent of the billion-dollar package. Their promise was quickly adopted by the rest of the life-insurance industry.[2]

To achieve a viable equal-opportunity hiring policy in a suburban town, one company called in local realtors and stated unequivocally that the company would go to court on behalf of any of its employees who encountered discrimination in seeking housing.[3] Since the company was the major employer in the community, it had sufficient power and determination to effect significant change.

There is a new breed of businessmen who see the risks in a growing class of poor who, through no fault of their own, are underskilled and undereducated. These business leaders are not burdened by all of the arguments against involvement which seem to impede many firms. Moreover, these leaders have the power, the desire, and the confidence to take action. Still, a large and powerful element of the business community continues to engage in endless dialogues about urban problems which offer as

---

[2] Some sectors of the insurance industry are not so eager. After the riots following the assassination of Martin Luther King in the spring of 1968, there was a massive exodus of business from the ghettos of Washington, Baltimore, Chicago, and Cincinnati. Most merchants who had been looted, vandalized, and burned out said they were leaving for good because they could no longer get insurance. The expected "staff" reaction came from the insurance industry's General Adjustment Bureau in Chicago: "The right kind of people are still able to get insurance." The Bureau, which represents 300 insurance firms, went on to say, "Those who haven't got it are uninsurable anyway for some reason." (See *Time*, April 19, 1968, page 76.) The real answer is that the riot in the spring of 1968 cost the industry $45 million, and in 1967 the burning of Detroit alone produced claims against the fire companies of $45 million. Without government reinsurance, "red-lining" the ghetto risk is simply a business and actuarial necessity.

[3] See "Equal Opportunity: The Creditibility Gap," Ulric Haynes, Jr., *Harvard Business Review*, May–June, 1968, p. 113.

solutions only "community chest" projects of Lilliputian proportions. Many educators, professional men, and other members of
the private sector have a strong desire to assist in the ghetto. But
their ineptness in building capital and their lack of business skills
is matched by their lack of economic power. Unfortunately, large
numbers of businessmen who do possess both the power and the
skills to build wealth and capital in the ghetto (and who have the
most to lose if they don't act) suffer from a basic reluctance and
uncertainty.

PART FIVE

Bridging the Tariffs of the Slum

"Exits from Poverty" or "Enrichment of the Slum": A Choice of Strategies

SHARP DIFFERENCES of opinion are held as to whether the prime objective of business anti-poverty efforts should be directed at building new facilities and businesses in the slums, thereby "enriching" the ghetto, or whether these efforts should immediately disperse the slum and integrate the Negro into the mainstream economy.

Programs for establishing new plants in the slums, new inner-core housing projects, ghetto store-front training centers, and new credit institutions are basically associated with the enrichment theory. This theory emphasizes that when business fails to move into an area and employment is not available, the most capable people will leave, since this is the only way of finding opportunities commensurate with their abilities. The departure of the more ambitious and able members of the ghetto further depresses its economic conditions.

On the other hand, programs for constructing plants outside but near the ghetto, and increased efforts to make jobs for Negroes in the suburbs and downtown, are aimed at providing new exits from ghetto poverty and at integrating the Negro into the normal economy. Businessmen who are for economic integration

137

of the Negro argue that any program which significantly improves life in the ghettos will, like welfare benefits, only draw more poor Negroes to the problem areas—and intensify the social problem. Therefore the enrichment plan should have as a companion, or substitute plan, an effort to disperse Negroes to other parts of the cities and to the suburbs.

The theory of immediate economic integration has much appeal. It focuses on the basic evil of economic apartheid represented by communities such as Hough, Harlem, and Watts. The approach derives sympathy from its close association with the unassailable policy of our government to integrate the American Negro socially through open housing and open schools.

Supporting the integration or dispersal approach, Thomas Paine, General Manager of General Electric's "Tempo" research organization in Santa Barbara, California, states that efforts to attract industry into the slums "is a movement to gild the ghetto." He believes in reasonable efforts to improve conditions in the ghetto, but emphasizes its fundamental economic obsolescence. He also believes it is impractical to bring a modern factory into a slum area and expect it to compete with a modern suburban factory. Paine proposes the alternative: to move ghetto residents "after we give them some training" to the suburban areas where there are clean houses near factories that offer job opportunities. He adds that "There may be people in the city who might not like to move—and I realize a lot of lily-white communities don't want them to—but I would like to give these people some real options. . . . Let's make exits bigger and the aisle wider. Harlem is just a plain horse-and-buggy place for a large number of sweatshop people who once worked in the downtown lofts. The things that made it are gone, but the structures are left."

The integration or dispersal theory finds some support from American business because it opposes black-power concepts; it focuses on developing total American economic power, rather than a kind of economic federalism which tolerates and even encourages the development of Negro or other minority economic-power centers in the United States.

I believe that the basic emphasis of our business effort must be directed, in the first instance, at programs which enrich the ghetto economy. This view recognizes that the ghetto economy is separate and that it encompasses millions of acres of urban real estate which simply cannot be abandoned. The enrichment theory brings jobs, capital, credit, and new entrepreneurial skills to the black slums. It corrects and builds upon what we now have— however undeveloped it may be.

By no means does this theory seek to perpetuate racial segregation. But it does recognize inexorable patterns of discrimination and geographical segregation which are reinforced by Negro poverty. The enrichment choice states that disadvantaged Negroes cannot achieve economic opportunity or power through an immediate migration into the white economy.

Consider three essential weaknesses in the Negro economy: (1) obsolete and unjust methods of retail distribution; (2) inadequate sources of credit; (3) lack of business entrepreneurship.

The following examples show that the enrichment approach is the only practical method of destroying these cancers of black poverty:

(1) Shopping centers, supermarkets, and discount stores have by-passed the ghetto for safer markets downtown or in suburban areas. The Negro does not use these outlets, either as a matter of choice, as in Harlem, or because of inadequate transportation, as in Watts. Plainly, it is necessary to find methods of establishing normal retail outlets *in* the ghetto. The integration choice would require an impractical program of bussing the Negro to Korvette's, Macy's, or the A&P in the suburbs.

(2) Reasonably priced credit must be made available to the Negro. The integration choice would force a Bedford-Stuyvesant resident to go to downtown Brooklyn or Manhattan and apply for a loan at, say, a branch of Bankers Trust Company. In time this must occur, but now a disadvantaged black is reluctant to go into any bank—even Harlem's Negro-controlled Freedom National Bank. The immediate objective, therefore, is ghetto credit enrichment, which would bring bank credit to the ghetto by installing newly chartered banks and new branches of downtown banks in the black core areas.

(3) The black economy lacks Negro entrepreneurs and capitalists. The resident of the ghetto almost never owns, as Richard Nixon stated during the election campaign of 1968, "a piece of the action." Our national policy should be to create Negro entrepreneurs as well as Negro executives. The economic-integration approach would set the Negro up in business on Main Street, but he would be certain to fail because current racial attitudes would ensure that a Negro entrepreneur operating in a white economy would find neither employees nor customers. The enrichment approach would establish him in business in the ghetto, where he would have employees and customers.

The enrichment theory would make sure that such needs as legal services, employment centers, family financial-counseling services, entertainment facilities, day care, and health centers remained in the ghetto when they are needed, and were not established outside.

The outstanding example of the economic "integration choice" is the present drive of American industry to provide hundreds of thousands of new jobs outside the ghetto for blacks who live inside the ghetto. Personnel officers frequently call these jobs "exits from poverty." Yet, considering the immobility of the hard-core unemployables, their anxieties about working in the normal economy, and the seemingly insuperable problem of moving eight million Negroes into suburban jobs, homes, and schools, job integration may not be the wisest choice. Certainly this is true if this route is pursued exclusively.

Polaroid Corporation, one of the more brilliantly successful and innovative companies of our time, has elected to pursue the choice of ghetto enrichment. At the AMA seminar in 1968, Arthur Barnes, a vice president of Polaroid, described a situation in Boston, typical of fifty major ghettos in the country, in which industry is located in suburban areas miles away from the inner city. He spoke of his company's dilemma and its preliminary solution:

We, like many others, have considered closing the Ten-Mile Gap by moving operations, now in suburban plants, into inner city plants. We have also considered establishing facilities for expansion in new locations in the inner city. Although both of these approaches are possibilities for us for the future, we at Polaroid have decided to start with a project that recognizes the probable continuance of the gap. We intend, therefore, to provide a bridge to cross the gap, a bridge to allow for inner city residents to reach the suburbs, and a bridge for us to reach the inner city. . . .

Offering opportunity and taking all of the appropriate permissive steps did not seem to really get at the problem for us. Therefore, we have now established a small manufacturing affiliate in the Roxbury area of Boston [the city's major ghetto] to make components for our film and camera assembly plants. This affiliate—Inner City, Inc. (I.C.I.)—has the responsibility to meet production schedules, to meet quality standards, to be in control of costs, to maintain proper facilities and to develop a work force to be proud of.

Parenthetically—although Polaroid Corporation will turn to I.C.I. to "pirate" its employees for jobs in Waltham or Norwood, we intend that it be possible for our "graduates" to go to other companies who can offer career jobs and the kind of continuing support needed to minimize the likelihood of stopping off at entry level jobs. . . .

This program recognizes, in an eminently practical way, that it is not feasible to attract, train, and hold the present hard-core unemployables if they must become commuters to the normal economy. The company has therefore chosen to build an economic bridge to the ghetto. It has established and committed capital to a plant in the ghetto where, in the most effective way, it will be possible to build Negro skills and economic power and even provide the option of changing jobs and competing with a former employer. These are the routes to the personal ownership of capital and power, in which lie seeds of ultimate ability to move with competence in an integrated economy.

An Experiment with
Income Certainty:
The Self-Executing Loan
Guarantee

I HAVE SUGGESTED earlier that wealth starts to grow in the normal economy when two vital conditions exist: (1) supply of front-end funds, risk capital, or margin money; (2) supply of debt financing or credit necessary to achieve leverage. The first condition, the creation of front-end money, occurs only when there are savings (funds exceeding normal living or staying-in-business expenses) which can be committed to a profit opportunity. In the normal economy, the simplest form of risk capital is margin money. This means funds used to purchase, say, convertible bonds carried at a bank on a margin loan. The second condition of leverage, the loan itself, occurs when income uncertainty required by the lender can be reduced to an insignificant risk. Stated more simply, the lender grants the privilege of leverage when he is relatively certain of being paid back. For example, in the normal economy credit funds for a borrowing collateralized by U.S. government bonds are virtually unlimited. A simple unsecured note of several hundred million dollars, signed by IBM, can be marketed at interest rates almost comparable to those ac-

142

corded the notes of the United States government. In both cases, the credit status of the borrower is such that income uncertainty is reduced practically to zero. The lender is assured of the regular payment of interest, and the eventual repayment of principal.

In the ghetto economy, risk capital is not generated internally because there is virtually no discretionary income. Risk capital does not move in from the normal economy because no profit opportunity, or even income certainty, exists. Also, in the slum economy, leverage is almost entirely missing, because there is virtually no person or indigenous business enterprise whose patterns of income are sufficiently reliable to assure repayment of a promissory note. The institutional lender, or banker, says, "I have trust funds to lend or invest. Show me how you can reduce my income uncertainty to zero and I will furnish you with unlimited leverage and take delight in watching you grow rich."

It is possible to develop a set of incentives which is effective in moving front-end money or risk capital into the ghetto. Risk capital is readily attracted by new profit opportunities which income tax incentives provide. This is demonstrated by the success of Puerto Rico's Operation Bootstrap, which brought vast new industry to an island ghetto through the promise of long-term income tax moratorium. But these incentives can operate on risk capital only when basic (almost risk-free) credit is available to pay the major cost of a new plant or other entrepreneurial effort. No system of incentives, however generous or comprehensive, is capable, in itself, of assuring the second condition of credit leverage when income certainty is missing.

Indeed, no tax incentive can make soft loans bankable. If a bank or insurance company commits an 80 per cent mortgage loan on a new shopping center in a hardened slum area, the institution's income-certainty requirement is obviously missing. The deal "begs" for a guaranteed lease from Safeway or some other nationally recognized supermarket chain whose promise to repay is almost without risk. Without the lease guarantee, the proposed supermarket loan remains soft. Since the loan will not pass the bank or insurance examiner, it will undoubtedly not be made in the first place.

143

If the interest rate established on a loan for a proposed new ghetto business is, say, 7.5 per cent and if a 3 per cent income tax credit is given the lender for each year the loan is outstanding, the over-all loan yield is in effect equal to 6¾ per cent after normal 50 per cent taxes. Depending on conditions, this may or may not be a sufficient after-tax yield to compensate a knowledgeable lender for the extraordinary risk in the loan. In all events, the loan is not bankable. Even if the income tax credit were 20 per cent, bank and insurance examiners would not pass the loan. These institutions may lend policy-holders' reserves and depositors' money only under conditions when income uncertainty, or risk of non-repayment, is relatively low (1 per cent or so). Regardless of how great the tax incentive, a loan to start up a new business in the ghetto is 100 per cent at risk from the day it is made.

In the past, this problem of making "soft" loans bankable or acceptable in an insurance-company portfolio (reducing income uncertainty virtually to zero) has been approached in a tentative way through the device of Federal Housing Administration insurance on residential mortgages and Small Business Administration guarantees of loans to ghetto businesses. But the inevitable encrustations of red tape and delays which have developed in FHA and SBA loan-approval procedures have augmented the ghetto credit risk-aversion of the banker on Main Street. To the lender, onerous procedures attendant on FHA and SBA applications have diminished the value of the subsidy or incentive of the federal repayment guarantee. Lenders and developers (the men who supply the equity and the leverage) have shunned transactions with these agencies. Also, institutions such as FHA and SBA, under Congressional prodding and scrutiny, have developed very rigid and conservative loan-guarantee policies. As a result, FHA-insured residential loans in slum areas have been insignificant, and SBA loans for new commercial projects in ghettos are running at the snail's pace of fifteen million dollars a year.

The answer does not lie in more federal-agency loan-guarantee programs. New federal institutions and agencies will take years to establish and will inevitably be subject to all the same delays, red tape, and vast bureaucratic expenses that have infected similar federal loan-guarantee programs in the past.

The solution, I suggest, lies in developing a system of self-executing loan-repayment guarantees. New legislation would provide that certain types of bank loans for predetermined enriching projects in designated ghetto poverty areas would carry (without prior application to any government agency) the automatic repayment guarantee of SBA and FHA up to 90 per cent or the full face amount of the loan. Under these conditions, the SBA-guaranteed loan to the ghetto businessman, which, typically, is needed to pay off the loan shark, could be committed on Thursday and disbursed on Friday, which is "loan-shark payday." The FHA loan could be committed in weeks instead of as much as a year. The function of FHA and SBA would be limited, at most, to post-audit loan review, which would assure that the loan complied with the law that commits an agency of the federal government to the repayment of the credit.

A program for a "federal blank check" or open-ended guarantee must obviously be approached with caution and experimentation. Unless the program is initially established as a demonstration or pilot effort, resistance in Congress will be formidable. I therefore suggest that a preliminary test program[1] be applied in the limited areas in which the most abject poverty occurs: one or more of America's Indian reservations. In this manner, the costs can be identified and limited and the results can be measured. If the program is feasible, it can be extended to other poverty areas.

I propose that, for a period of one year, loans to establish a new business, plant, or commercial facility in or adjacent to an

---

[1] This type of experiment has a precedent. Tests on the effect of the application of incentives or disincentives to the problem of poverty are currently being made. Under a grant of one million dollars a year from the Office of Economic Opportunity, the University of Wisconsin has selected, as a sample, one thousand poor families in several New Jersey cities. Most of these families are headed by an adult who does not earn enough to support his dependents at more than poverty standard. For the next three years, these families will receive a variety of income supplements. The precise amount will depend on work effort, family size, and the particular negative income tax plan the family is assigned in the experiment. The family's reactions will be watched closely by surveyors keeping records on changes in work effort, morale, spending (including food and drink), job mobility, and social attitudes.

Indian reservation should automatically carry a full repayment guarantee of interest and principal by the United States government, under the following conditions and safeguards:

(1) The loan must be made by a bank, insurance company, or other institutional lender regulated or supervised by state or federal law;

(2) If the loan is long-term (more than a year), it should carry an interest rate not to exceed that which is approved by Congress from time to time for FHA loans;[2]

(3) If the loan is short-term, the rate should not exceed 0.5 per cent of that paid on comparable U.S. government notes;[3]

(4) The loan guarantee would not be effective until the regularly established auditors of the lending institution and an independent licensed certified public accountant acting for the project sponsors had certified to the lender that the owners or sponsors of the new facility or plant had invested and paid for no less than 10 per cent of the proposed cost of the facility exclusive of working capital, inventory, pre-opening, training, advertising, and other start-up expenses.

In the absence of proof of fraud or collusion with the lending institution the auditors' certificates would be final and conclusive evidence of the validity of the federal government guarantee of repayment of the loan.

This program, which allows private industry to commit automatically the credit of the federal government to programs for rebuilding the ghetto, may seem drastic. Indeed it is. But administrators of FHA and SBA, with budgets of hundreds of million dollars a year, have not succeeded in protecting the nation against waste of federal funds. Nor have they succeeded in building any important ownership of residential or business equities in the ghetto. A combination of bank and insurance-company auditors (safeguarded by CPA's of project sponsors) are capable of doing

---

[2] Current FHA interest rates, increased in January 1969, provide an adequate incentive. The complaint of lenders is that administrative delays and red tape add extra lending costs—disincentives which reduce the value of the established interest rate.

[3] The extra one-half point is necessary to divert some money from competing federal government credit instruments, which are also free of the risk of nonrepayment.

146

a more effective and efficient job of policing costs and maintaining honesty. Under a program for self-executing government guarantees, the administrative costs saved by eliminating duplicating loan approvals would more than compensate for any extra losses on ill-conceived loans.

Banks and insurance companies, operating under goals defined by legislation set up by Congress, are capable of getting on with the job of building credit in the ghetto. But past experience assures us that, in the delicate process of building leverage, the weighty hand of government approvals must be excluded from reviewing, approving, or second-guessing credit decisions which already have been made by experienced and regulated credit institutions.

The Use and Misuse of
Ghetto Tax Credits

IT IS OFTEN DIFFICULT to keep an open mind on the vexing subject of tax incentives. The whole question of whether taxpayers should be given direct abatements in their taxes for doing certain things the government wants them to do has become charged with controversy. Often issues have been clouded by bitter disputes over oil-depletion allowances and accelerated-depreciation deductions. The usual attack on tax-incentive credits takes the form of accusations of "backdoor spending" and "privileges for special interests." These terms do not assist an analysis of this difficult subject. Seemingly, Treasury officials who, in past years, have rejected all tax-incentive proposals with the cry of "another loophole" would rather preserve the symmetry of the Internal Revenue Code—and their prerogatives to disburse public funds—than do some hard thinking about whether a carefully shaped tax credit might be the most compelling and effective way of achieving a vital national goal. The fact is that there are good tax-incentive credits and there are bad ones. The object of an oil-depletion credit is bad; the object of a ghetto-development tax credit is good. Some tax credits are broad and wasteful; others are carefully honed and effective. Therefore,

148

proposals for ghetto tax credits should not be dismissed out of hand. Practically no one will challenge the *purpose* of the slum-area tax credit. Criticism should be limited to the mechanism of the incentive. The object is to write and shape the credit so that it avoids the most serious objections of other tax incentives. The incentive must operate directly, effectively, and with minimum waste to accomplish a designated goal.

The techniques of federal compensating incentives or guarantees have been used for many years to implement various areas of our national economic policy. For example, after World War II, to increase foreign exports, the nation created the Export-Import Bank, which guarantees American exporters against loss on credit risks for sales abroad. To encourage permanent capital investments, we tax long-term capital gains at half the normal rate. To encourage charitable contributions, these grants are deductible from taxable income. To stimulate oil and gas exploration and real estate construction, we maintain the controversial depletion and accelerated-depreciation tax allowances. With the aim of stimulating investments in underdeveloped foreign countries, the federal AID program guarantees the domestic investor against foreign expropriation of investments, and restrictions on repatriating profits earned abroad.

The techniques of (1) guarantees against risk of financial or investment loss and (2) incentives or subsidies have been applied only in a peripheral way to the problems of the poor in America.

Under Lyndon Johnson's so-called "One-Stop Service for Businessmen," the government provided a haphazard collection of fringe incentives to private enterprise, all relatively inexpensive and none requiring Congressional approval or appropriations. Under the "One-Stop Service," the Federal Urban Mass Transit program was directed to provide transportation for workers to ghetto plants. The Department of Health, Education, and Welfare provided health service for ghetto employees. The Procurement Division of the Defense Department was directed to find items which could be produced in the ghetto and to grant special bidding benefits to plants near ghetto areas. To aid ghetto contractors, the federal government offered, occasionally, to pay

149

the cost of bonding slum-area employees. The Small Business Administration offered matching grants for funds raised by local non-profit business-development corporations and a limited program of equal-opportunity loan guarantees of private credits extended to ghetto businessmen. Probably the most important federal anti-poverty subsidy has been Department of Labor payments to employers who hire and train hard-core unemployables.

One of the most creative programs of OEO involved experimenting with variable profit incentives for companies contracting to operate federal Job Corps centers. Under this program, compensation to the private companies operating the training centers was directly related to their success in training and finding jobs for unemployables. An additional percentage fee, above the cost-plus-a-fixed-fee was established, based on the number of Negroes who were recruited, trained, and placed in jobs for at least six months. A sliding scale for measuring success was established. If 380 or more of the trainees held their jobs, the company was rewarded with a payment of 20 per cent above cost; if 360 found employment, the company received a bonus of 15 per cent of cost; and so forth. Obviously, this experimental plan was a sound and workable approach to the problems of providing business incentives to Negro training and hiring.

Employing the same technique, the OEO financed five thousand housing units in New York City; Cleveland; Durham, North Carolina; Washington, D.C.; Baltimore; St. Louis; Philadelphia; and Denver. This was achieved by providing two million dollars of "front-end money costs before mortgage" or seed capital (which FHA could not, by law, supply) for technical assistance in new housing projects.

In 1967, a pledge of more than three hundred of the nation's life-insurance companies to invest one billion dollars in new and rehabilitated slum housing was another attempt to encourage ghetto investments through the technique of the federal repayment guarantee. Without the catalyst of the FHA guarantee, the loans would not have been considered prudent commitments for life-insurance policy-holders' reserve funds.

Rent and interest subsidy programs for new housing, federal

Model City grants, and urban-renewal programs are further illustrations of publicly financed incentives to assure a business profit or minimum investment return on slum projects that, otherwise, would be economically unattractive and therefore would not occur.

Also, there are "disguised" federal incentive or guarantee programs that function in combating poverty, but whose anti-poverty impact is not so readily identified. For example, many new industrial plants, especially in the South, have been financed through the issuance of low-interest-cost tax-exempt bonds by the communities that benefit from the new plants. These plants reduce unemployment in southern rural areas, thus inhibiting Negro migration to the northern urban ghettos. Tax-exempt industrial bonds have financed new plants in the South for companies such as Armour, Allied Paper, and Olin Mathieson.

Even government techniques of periodically "heating up" the national economy, by reducing income taxes or increasing federal spending, act as a money incentive to business to hire people who might otherwise be unemployable. When the national economy is operating in high gear, workers are in short supply. Under these conditions, businessmen reach out for the unemployed, adopt more liberal personnel policies, and train the unskilled. But even though federal spending programs reduce unemployment and poverty, the impact of the spending does not focus on the hard-core unemployed, who are always the last to be rehired. Despite the level of federal spending and unemployment, the black unemployment rate continues to run twice as high as the white.

The foregoing shows the range of present and past incentive programs. The following analysis, essential to an evaluation of the program for categorical corrective incentives, suggests a set of principles which must be observed if incentives in the ghetto are to be workable, to be fair to all taxpayers, and to provide reasonable budgetary controls.

Ghetto Tax Credits Must Be Specific. Our current tax laws offer a 7 per cent investment credit as an incentive to industry to purchase or lease new machinery and equipment. This tax incentive is often justified as a necessary stimulant to national production and employment. Insofar as the incentive is directed at unemployment, it is too broad in its application. Under the Internal Revenue Code, so long as the equipment is new, the businessman is entitled to the tax deduction; it does not matter whether the new machinery will make jobs in a poverty area or in a labor-surplus area. The privilege I referred to earlier, which permits communities to issue tax-free bonds to finance new industrial plants, has the same defect. This tax exemption encourages plants to settle in the affluent northern suburban areas of high employment, just as it subsidizes new job facilities in rural or urban poverty areas. A prime objective, therefore, is to shape the incentive in such a way that its application is specific, or what I call *categorical*. The anti-poverty incentive must be geographically precise—that is to say, limited to specific poverty areas defined by the Department of Labor or Department of Commerce. The ghetto tax incentive must also be specific in its function and application within the poverty area.

For example, a ghetto tax credit which encourages start-up loans for new ghetto businesses, or which stimulates in the slum the formation of risk capital in the form of new savings accounts is more concentrated in its impact, and less wasteful than a broad national incentive directed at all new investments made in the ghetto economy. All tax incentives generate a certain amount of waste—usually in the form of loophole applications of the incentive to taxpayers and business activities which the incentive was not intended to benefit. The requirement that the incentive be categorical and specific reduces this waste.

Ghetto Tax Credits Must Be Applied Only to Centers of Profit. As a first step, Congress must identify those categories of taxpayers who are capable of committing either their skills or their capital to a national goal for enrichment of the ghetto. Having done so, Congress makes a covenant that if the taxpayer carries out these goals (under specific rules and safeguards determined by the Congress), the taxpayer receives a stipulated benefit in the form of the abatement of income taxes he would otherwise pay.

152

Clearly, if the taxpayer is operating at a loss, and has no immediate prospect of operating at a profit and therefore becoming obligated to pay taxes, the reward has no value. The incentive does not operate to achieve its goal.

It is remarkable how often this simple rule is overlooked. The Community Self-Determination Bill,[4] a proposal in Congress, having great promise, merit, and an excellent chance of enactment proposes an elaborate system of income tax incentives for newly established, federally chartered community-development corporations. These so-called CDC's are essentially conceived as ghetto-owned business conglomerates. They would acquire, create, and manage all businesses in their poverty areas. Each CDC would be owned by ghetto residents who would subscribe to one or more shares at five dollars a share. The CDC's would be entitled to income tax reductions determined according to an index of area unemployment and median income. The Community Self-Determination Bill deals importantly with the objective of "decolonializing" the economy of the ghetto—of establishing ghetto ownership and control of ghetto enterprises. Admittedly, federally chartered ghetto conglomerates should not pay taxes, but the incentive of tax reduction has no cutting edge because the ghetto conglomerate is likely to have nothing but "tax-loss carry-forwards" for a number of years after organization. To achieve a corrective impact, the tax incentive should be applied instead to taxpayers, either inside or outside the ghetto, who lend their organizational and managerial skills—and perhaps their money—to get the ghetto conglomerates established.

Later in this book I develop a specific program under which corrective incentives are applied to taxpayers in the outside economy in order to motivate them to build entrepreneurship and the ownership of capital within the slum. This principle of applying tax credits to healthy taxpayers means that if the objective is to move credit into the slum, the incentive is applied to the lender and not the ghetto borrower; if the object is to move risk capital into the ghetto the incentive is applied to the supplier of the risk capital, not to the ghetto conglomerate that needs it; if the objec-

4 Senate Bill 3876.

tive is to persuade the ghetto economy to save money and develop its own risk capital, the incentive should be applied to the interracial savings institution in the ghetto and not to the saver; if the objective is to encourage the outside economy to purchase materials or use services originating in the ghetto, the incentive should be applied to the profitable firm in the outside economy which you wish to persuade to "buy black." Applying the incentive to the wealth-maker in the outside economy may be bad politics; it may even encounter opposition within the ghetto. Yet, if the technique of the incentive is to be used, it is good economics.

Avoid Incentives for Fixed-Asset Investments in the Ghetto. Tax credits which encourage new plant construction and investments in machinery by allowing accelerated-depreciation deduction (a tax credit which permits a taxpayer to write off in the early years of ownership of a building or a machine twice the normal depreciation allowance) contain a number of serious defects. First, these tax credits are not specific, since the taxpayer gets the same depreciation-tax write-off for a new casino in Las Vegas that he would get for a supermarket in Harlem or for a new assembly plant in Watts. Second, the incentive applies to a fixed capital asset—land, buildings, and equipment. Fixed assets can be easily mortgaged. This means that a taxpayer who "craves" tax shelter can often borrow on the asset up to 80 per cent or 90 per cent of its value and repay the loan over a long period of time. Through the leverage achieved by long-term borrowing, the high-tax-bracket taxpayer may *multiply the value of the tax credit four or five times.* This results in an extra and unintended loss of federal revenue. In addition, fixed assets are uniquely subject to favorable capital-gains taxes which further increase the owner's tax shelter, to the detriment of other taxpayers. A tax system is unfair if it requires other taxpayers to pay extra taxes to compensate for a businessman in a high tax bracket who is enjoying an unduly large tax shelter.

In most cases, the categorical corrective incentives avoid applying the incentive to fixed assets invested in the ghetto. Instead, the incentives are applied, wherever possible, to other economic

154

measures of new production or commerce in the slum. This requirement is illustrated by the tax credits proposed for (a) business loans extended in the ghetto, (b) new ghetto savings accounts, (c) income derived by a national company from a ghetto business franchise, and (d) corporate purchases made from a ghetto subcontractor.

In my judgment, avoiding slum-area tax credits on fixed assets, or on other "hard" investments in the ghetto, reduces the risk of simply "gilding the ghetto" with new and unproductive plants. The incentive is more wisely applied to the items in a profit-and-loss statement that show the plant is viable and productive. A tax credit for ghetto-origin sales or ghetto-origin purchases has the advantage of *not yielding its tax-reduction reward to the sponsor until the production in the ghetto begins to flow*. A tax credit for new real estate constructed in the ghetto often gives you just that —bricks and mortar. The new construction is likely to be a monument to ill-conceived tax credits, rather than a new home for black capitalism and careers.

The Benefits of Ghetto Tax Credits Should Be Limited to Tax Brackets of 50 Per Cent or Less. Tax-incentive programs in the past have produced unintended windfalls as well as loss of revenue, as a result of our system of graduated income taxes. Individual taxpayers in high tax brackets have actually gone into the market and bought accelerated-depreciation tax deductions from other taxpayers whose income was already adequately sheltered by depletion or depreciation deductions. The primary objective of ghetto tax credits is to involve the industrial corporations, banks, and insurance companies in programs for enriching the ghetto economy. All of these institutions are taxed at a basic rate of 50 per cent or less. I suggest, therefore, that any program for ghetto tax credits be limited in principle to corporate taxpayers. Individuals and partnerships would be permitted to use the credit only in proportion to the taxpayer's income being taxed at less than 50 per cent. The ghetto economy needs the investment programs and entrepreneurial skills which the corporations can offer. The slum has much less need for the funds of the higher-bracket individual taxpayers, whose contribution to the ghetto economy is slight, and whose motive is a hunger for income tax shelter in the form of a slum investment.

In the next part of this book I turn to the specifics of the program for categorical corrective incentives. These incentives are categorical in that, as already indicated, they are specific. I also view them as categorical in the sense that they are compelling and necessary. These incentives are a natural development of our earlier economic overview of the ghetto economy. The plan looks behind the visible symptoms of ghetto business poverty—the decayed real estate, the sluggishness of commerce in the slum, the apathy of its residents. At the same time, it rejects a number of ghetto incentives that have been suggested in the past. I have done this because, in my judgment, those proposals have failed to meet the necessary guidelines I have suggested for an effective, fair, and workable incentive program. Congress has been beseiged with dozens of tax-incentive proposals for low-income housing, plants, and other real estate projects in the ghetto. Yet the absence of modern plants is only a symptom of a greater sickness in the slum economy. The incentive must go much deeper than the condition of ghetto real estate; it must attack the roots of entrepreneurial failure of the ghetto—the original vices which prevent the growth of plants and business enterprises, and which forbid, to almost everyone in the slum, the ownership of productive capital.

PART SIX

Twelve Magnets of Profit: A Program for Categorical Corrective Incentives

---

Injections of Leverage

Reducing the Risk on "Soft" Commercial Loans

"Adam Smith," the sage of Wall Street, tells us how to recognize a money crisis: First mortages are either unavailable or command interest rates of 12 per cent, offerings of real estate move like molasses, business values crumble, risk capital evaporates, and finally grass grows in the streets. If these conditions described the national economy during the crisis of 1933, they describe as well conditions in the credit economy of Watts and Bedford-Stuyvesant in the late 1960's. The fundamental malignancy in Negro business has been its chronic failure to attract, hold, and use institutional credit. This has occurred because the risks of non-repayment of slum-area business loans and the extra cost of servicing and collateralizing (and frequently salvaging) them are so massive that the banker faces the same dilemma as the businessman who would embark on programs for hiring or manufacturing in the ghetto. The ghetto economy has amassed such a pernicious array of risks, punishing any effort to introduce credit, that no interest rate is high enough to permit the banker to lend on a basis which is fair both to the ghetto borrower and to

159

the owners of the bank. No liberalization of the banking laws to permit high-risk slum-area business loans can, in itself, alter this dilemma.[1]

A few innovative banks, such as the First Pennsylvania Banking and Trust Company in Philadelphia, have made important and creative efforts to move commercial business credit into the ghetto. But since Negroes rarely come into the branches of the First Pennsylvania Bank, the bank has found that the most effective method of implementing its Negro business-lending program is to work through a loan-clearing house which is located in the ghetto. In Philadelphia, this clearing house consists of a non-profit association organized by a group of Negro businessmen who actively recruit potential businessmen who need credit. The local group examines these loans from the standpoint of feasibility and either recommends them to the bank or rejects them. The primary function of the bank is to supply credit, acting on the recommendation of people on the scene who understand the ghetto's special credit needs and risks.

This is a most effective program for forcing commercial credit into the ghetto. The program takes maximum advantage of the bank's economic power and, at the same time, negates the great disability which all banks share—an inherent reluctance of the loan officer to make a potentially soft loan. The bank assumes the

---

[1] However, expanding the powers of banks to make commitments in the ghetto provides the necessary legal environment in which ghetto credit incentives can operate.

In October, 1968, the author testified before the Senate Financial Institutions Subcommittee on proposals to amend federal banking laws in order to channel more bank credit into the black economy. At that time I recommended to the Committee: (1) expanding the investment powers of national banks to permit them to form credit-development subsidiaries to make high-risk commitments in poverty areas; (2) empowering national banks to directly acquire and develop real estate in designated poverty areas; (3) removing the limitations on maturities and repayment terms of slum-area mortgages held by national banks; (4) permission for a national bank to invest up to 2 per cent of its capital in shares of so-called interracial banks; (5) increasing Federal Deposit Insurance coverage of deposits in slum-area banks, and expansion of coverage to include debentures and capital debentures issued by these institutions; (6) modification of laws in certain states which forbid the operation of branch banks; (7) removal of Small Business Administration regulations which limit loans for start-up financing for small groceries, beauty parlors, and carry-out food shops in disadvantaged areas, and for financing change of ownership of a ghetto business.

credit risk, supplies the funds, and benefits in terms of greater city-wide business with the Negro community. But, unfortunately, one bank cannot reverse the direction of a massive ghetto economy that banished all commercial credit many decades ago.

Negro businessmen need bank credit for all the usual purposes —business start-up expenses, equipment purchases, and seasonal inventory requirements. Often, too, the Negro business needs credit for a special purpose which no downtown banker has ever heard of.

Bankers in the main economy favor so-called special-purpose loans—loans for new plant construction, acquisition of machinery, or expansion of markets. These are the loans that enrich and build the national economy and are therefore frequently exempted from voluntary credit restraints. However, loans to refund or pay off another loan do not create a net addition to the economy, and are looked on with less banking favor when credit is tight. In the ghetto economy, there is a special and legitimate need for refunding loans, since slum businesses are often started up with short-term and high-cost credit. In the ghetto business firm, the interest rate, as we have seen, may be 10 per cent a week rather than 10 per cent a year. Therefore, refunding or "clean-up" loans are especially enriching to the slum economy. The credits should not be viewed with the same skepticism that they receive in banks downtown.[2]

The importance of the refunding loan to the ghetto economy

[2] At an American Management Association Seminar in June, 1968, Thomas F. Murray, Vice President, Mortgages, of The Equitable Life Assurance Society, of the United States, described the most valuable type of "refunding loans" which the Equitable is making on ghetto real estate: "We soon found that the most expeditious way to get going was to invest in mortgages on one to four family residences. These mortgages usually permitted the owner or purchaser to obtain terms which were more favorable than were heretofore available, and often provided financing where none was obtainable before. We found, in many cases, that our mortgage refinanced a first and second, and possibly even a third mortgage whose combined monthly payments were practically impossible to meet for this Negro family that was seeking to establish itself as an owner in a community often characterized by absentee landlords. Very often our funds permitted the owner to rehabilitate his home, or he could use the decrease in monthly payments to modernize or improve his dwelling. We are delighted, accordingly, that our program has helped foster and support resident ownership in ghetto areas—nearly 85 per cent of our funds have gone into this phase of our ghetto lending program."

161

was illustrated a few years ago when most of the drugstores in Harlem were close to bankruptcy. A large proportion of drugs purchased in the ghettos of Harlem and the South Bronx are paid for under New York City's Medicaid or welfare program. At the time, the city was several months behind in its paperwork and disbursement, so the druggists were stuck with stale customer accounts four or five months old. They carried these accounts receivable by borrowing at exorbitant rates from local hip-pocket lenders. Through the brilliant work of McKinsey & Company, Arthur Andersen & Co., and James Talcott, Inc., a refunding-loan program was arranged, under which the loan sharks were paid off and reasonably priced commercial finance credit was substituted. This incident illustrates that often Negro business-men need commercial credit, not simply to start a new business, but to save a perfectly sound existing business which is being strangled by a special and unusual credit need.

Another special credit need of the black economy is for loans to finance the transfer ghetto business from white to black control. This type of loan also does not add to the "net worth" of the black slum economy. However, it satisfies a vital and urgent desire of the black man to control the marketplace and commerce where he lives. This type of bank credit is a necessary part of the black community's objective of working toward "decolonializing" the ownership of real estate and businesses in the slums. This program runs contrary to past—and, in my view, mistaken—policies of the federal Small Business Administration, whose rulings actually discouraged ghetto business loans to either repay pressing creditors or to buy an existing business in the ghetto. Bankers who normally discourage loans for the purchase of a business, or refunding credits, should take a more constructive view of these loans when they are sought by a black borrower.

Who are the potential lenders in a position to supply commercial business credit in the slum economy? Which institutions, for sound business reasons, do not lend in ghetto areas? The fourteen thousand commercial banks are the backbone of America's lending system. But since they operate under stiff regulatory restraints, they make direct business loans only to established businesses having "bankable" credit. Long-term mortgage loans come mainly from the savings banks and life-insurance companies, who, also, are highly regulated and restricted as to permissible loan risks. Personal-loan companies have found it difficult to lend in slum areas, in which legal limits on interest rates do not cover the unusual risks and expenses in making and servicing these loans. In some cases, these loan companies have shown remarkable mastery of the skills of making high-risk loans, but more often the economic anarchy of the ghetto credit economy has bested them.

Commercial finance companies are a most important group of business lenders. Respected institutions, particularly in New York City and Chicago, specialize in high-risk non-bankable business loans. These lenders measure business credit risk in terms of interest rates of 10 per cent and higher. They are considered expert in evaluating the ability of marginal or undercapitalized business to repay a loan. "Nimble" high-risk secondary lenders have played a vital role in the growth of small and untested businesses. Unlike the bank loan officer, who may be tied to more conservative lending practices, the secondary lender or finance-company officer often possesses great competence in appraising the promise of a business which will be operating in a cultural and economic environment completely foreign to his own experience. He often has special experience in loan "work-outs"—salvaging a loan and a business that is in trouble—a common problem with slum-area business credits.

In recent years, many banks have developed new expertise with the high-risk or "controlled-risk" loans. Banks such as First National City Bank in New York City and the First National Bank of Boston have moved into areas of risk financing which formerly belong to the secondary lenders and commercial finance companies. Special departments in these banks have developed great agility in taking unusual banking risks with appropriate compensation in the form of higher interest rates and valuable training privileges for junior credit officers. These banks are ideally qualified to establish additional programs of commercial lending to businesses in the disadvantaged areas of their cities.

163

I suggest that an automatic compensating credit incentive, pre-determined yet unregulated, is necessary to move vital business credit into the black markets. No incentive can give the ghetto lender the high degree of income certainty that his directors and his examiners normally expect of prime commercial borrowers. The incentive cannot insure the lender against riot, fire, or a business failure resulting in non-repayment of the loan. However, a credit incentive is capable of overcoming much of the ghetto risk-aversion. This incentive, operating together with the program I suggested earlier for self-executive federal repayment guarantees of ghetto loans, eliminates all of the legitimate arguments against lending in the slum economy.

I suggest that any federal or state regulated lender, such as a bank, insurance company, or loan company, should be entitled to a special annual addition to its allowable bad-debt reserve (over and above normal bad-debt reserve allowances) of 6 per cent of the average balance during the year of loans made to businesses and service establishments doing business in poverty areas designated by the Secretary of Commerce. This credit incentive would allow the corporate lender, who is normally in a 50 per cent income tax bracket, an additional 3 per cent after tax yield on commercial business loans made in ghetto areas.

This tax credit would be allowed even if the loan was secured by a mortgage, which would be the case for plants and supermarkets located in the ghetto. The bad-debt tax reserve credit would also be allowed any lender who successfully processed an application for a business-loan guarantee with the Small Business Administration. Such perseverance should be rewarded with both the incentive and the repayment guarantee of SBA. However, tax credit would not be available for residential non-business loans.

This program contemplates an "enforced" federally subsidized export of private business credit to the ghetto. In time, the "free market" interest rates of the ghetto credit merchants, who presently lend to ghetto shopkeepers at rates ranging from 50 to 250 per cent annually, would be replaced by those "near to prime" rates of 7 to 10 per cent that white businessmen pay downtown.

Hopefully, the country would finally achieve a reciprocating flow of credit from all parts of our cities so that the distinctions be tween the ghetto credit market and the mainstream loan markets would become blurred.

New Liquidity for Ghetto-Origin Installment Paper

During the bleakest period of the Great Depression, Walter Bimson, one of the nation's most creative bankers, sent a message to his staff at Phoenix's Valley National Bank:

> Make loans! That is the way to recovery, and I want this period of automatic loan refusal to end and end now. Make loans! The biggest service we can perform today is to put money into people's hands. Especially, let us go into mass-production on small loans. Plain people at this very moment need to borrow for all kinds of useful buying purposes. So great is their need for credit that some of them are paying heavy interest to loan sharks, and this is the bank's fault. This bank's credit capacity isn't what it will be, but we have some capacity, and I want it used. Use it to get buying under way, to get building under way, to get business and farm production under way.

The relevance of this plea to building installment loan credit in the ghetto economy is clear. But how do we get normal retail credit moving in the slum? In an area in which income certainty does not exist, collateral is weak, and few people can sign a bankable unsecured note for five hundred dollars, how do we rout the loan sharks and legally marginal lenders who destroy the possibility of building a reasonable system of installment credit?

Since the turn of the century, social workers have urged eliminating profit on consumer credit in the ghetto. They convinced the legislatures that criminal sanctions against usurious loans were the only method of rooting out the merchant credit gouger and loan shark. The nation's experience with legal prohibition of

165

liquor should convince us that criminal penalties for violation of credit laws are almost always futile and naive. These laws put loan sharks in jail, but do not remove the ghetto's need for credit, or add to the meager supply of loanable money. Enforced legal ceilings on interest rates do not reduce the buyer's determination for goods; he merely turns to those who exact an even higher price for credit. Recent laws which restrict the negotiability and liquidity of installment paper taken in unconscionable install-ment purchase transactions have the same effect of excluding normal credit in the slums. Institutions which lend at low rates, and which are unable to distinguish an unconscionable or frau-dulent sale of merchandise which is sold on credit shun the pur-chase of all installment paper originating in the ghetto. The loan shark accepts the paper and exacts his "toll."

Plainly, the objective is not to destroy the vestiges of low-cost bank credit that remain in the ghetto, but rather to build into the slum normal patterns of retail credit. A sound approach to this problem is to create new incentives or profit opportunities for lenders which will result in the export of low-cost credit from the normal economy into the ghetto. This can be achieved by com-pensating regulated commercial banks and finance companies for the extra credit risk they take in purchasing (discounting) in-stallment loans which originate in poverty areas. If the legitimate lender's compensating incentive is sufficient, ghetto installment loans will become attractive to lenders, or at least competitive with the safe loans available elsewhere.

I suggest that an institution which purchases an installment loan contract originating in an eligible poverty area should be entitled to an additional income tax deduction (over and above its normal bad-debt reserve deduction) on an annual basis equal to 6 per cent of the face amount of the purchased loan. This pro-gram would return to the lender a 3 per cent additional after-tax yield on installment loans originating in ghetto areas. The auditor of the lending institution would be required to certify that to his best knowledge:

(a) the loan was made directly to a resident of an eligible

poverty area and was secured by a first lien on new or used appliances, automobiles, or other hard goods; or

(b) the loan was purchased from an automobile or hard-goods dealer in an eligible poverty area and was so certified by the dealer.

The tax deduction would be claimed by the lending institution holding the paper at the end of his tax year. Since the special tax benefit would be negotiable and "ride along" as an endorsement on the installment paper, the tax credit would give extra value and buoyancy to retail commercial paper in downtown credit markets.

A criticism of this form of incentive is that the gouging appliance dealer in a ghetto area not only is perfectly free to overcharge the customer, but also is privileged to "lay off" the loan on a downtown bank anxiously bidding for the commercial paper because it carries the tax incentive. I suggest, however, that as a ghetto credit market develops and a supply of bank installment credit becomes available, the new credit will drive out the credit merchant, who will gradually lose his monopoly over ghetto loans. Since the credit gouger is a financial intermediary whose cost of capital is high, it will become impossible for him to compete at free-market bank rates. If it becomes feasible for downtown banks to lend in ghetto markets at, or near, downtown interest rates, new bank branches will open in the ghetto and existing branches will become aggressive lenders.

Stimulating Deposits in Slum-Area Banks

The specific credit incentives I have just proposed are designed to enforce exports of outside banking credit to the ghetto market. Obviously, these incentives do not work toward immediately creating new banking offices or deposits within the slum economy. Rather, they permit the credit-starved slums to tap the world's largest reservoir of private capital: the three hundred billion dollars of deposits held in fourteen thousand commercial banks in America.

Yet, we have also seen that white-controlled banks are not always the most effective vehicle to grapple with the problems of developing business loans in the slums. The ghetto's hostility to downtown banks, its opposition to the export of credit, the often excessive "ghetto credit risk-aversion" of the Main Street banker, and his inability or unwillingness to enforce collection of a loan from a ghetto borrower place limitations on our program for moving credit into the ghetto from the "outside" economy.

The internal banks of the ghetto, the so-called interracial or black-controlled institutions, have no such problems. The black banks recognize higher ghetto credit risks; they charge a higher interest rate on loans than prevails in the downtown economy without running afoul of charges of discrimination; they press regularly for collection of their loans. Moreover, the ghetto bank has greater skills, agility, and understanding in dealing with the special business and credit problems of the slum economy.

Although for blacks the ghetto banks have lending advantages over white-controlled banks, their power to change the credit economy of the slum is insignificant. To strengthen the lending capabilities of the slum-area banks, I propose an annual income tax credit for any corporation or person, including a correspondent bank, which maintains a deposit in any bank whose principal office is located in an eligible poverty area.[3]

[3] Ghetto branches of metropolitan banks are excluded because their principal offices are not in an eligible poverty area. Deposits in ghetto branches of the large metropolitan banks do not stick in the ghetto; they are more likely to flow back downtown seeking safer credit risks in the normal economy.

Under certain circumstances it might be desirable to expand the benefits of the tax credit to deposits made in *non*-ghetto banks where the deposit is earmarked for an unusually enriching program. An example would be bank deposits made under an innovative deposit program sponsored by the Bicentennial Improvement Corporation in St. Louis. This group arranges for undercapitalized blacks to obtain home ownership under conventional non-FHA mortgages. The Improvement Corporation sponsors individual and corporate deposits with ghetto mortgage lenders. The deposit is pledged as additional security for mortgage.

Of course the incentive would apply to any banks which might be established in the impoverished Indian reservations in the South or Southwest, or in any of the great rural poverty areas of Appalachia and northern California.

The income tax credit would operate as follows.

(a) *For demand deposits* (non-interest-bearing[4]). An annual tax credit to the depositor equal to 2 per cent of the average daily balance maintained, as certified in writing at the end of the depositor's tax year by the cashier of the ghetto bank.

(b) *For time deposits.* An annual income tax credit to the depositing individual, corporation, or correspondent bank equal to 25 per cent of the established interest rate on the time deposit. The tax credit would be limited to time deposits maintained for one year or more. The time deposit is more enriching to the ghetto economy than is the demand deposit, since it more closely approximates permanent capital. The relative permanence of this type of deposit gives the ghetto bank greater flexibility in making community loans.

(c) *Negotiable certificates of deposit or investments in ghetto bank debentures.* Holders of these instruments would be entitled to a year-end tax credit equal to 25 per cent of the established interest rate on the certificate of deposit or debenture.

Since many corporate treasurers would not feel comfortable with large deposit balances in the undercapitalized ghetto banks even if aided by the deposit incentive program, I suggest that the present Federal Deposit Insurance coverage limit of $15,000 be increased to $50,000 for demand deposits and time deposits maintained in banks doing business solely in the poverty areas.

The scope of Federal Deposit Insurance coverage could be expanded to include debentures issued by ghetto-area banks. The "capital debenture" route is becoming an increasingly more attractive method of raising bank capital. Allowing ghetto-bank debenture issues to carry, within limits, a Federal Deposit Insurance Corporation guarantee should be a most effective method of coaxing new funds into slum-area banks. The limited debenture guarantee would also reduce the cost of capital and give these banks the edge they need for lending in the profitless slum economy.

[4] By almost universal law in the United States, banks may not pay interest on demand deposits (usually checking accounts).

The program of tax incentives for deposits in ghetto banks, combined with increased Federal Deposit Insurance coverage, should persuade large metropolitan banks to establish healthy correspondent relations with ghetto banks. These correspondent bank balances deposits would place new funds in the hands of ghetto bankers who have a special expertise in handling the high-risk ghetto loan. A bank such as the First National in Boston cannot put out installment loan money in the Roxbury ghetto at, say, a 1 per cent premium over what it charges downtown. How ever, First National is in a position to maintain a one-million-dollar balance with the interracial Unity National Bank in Roxbury; Unity Bank, in turn, could then be in a position to spread this money around the Roxbury ghetto in installment loans at a one-percentage-point interest premium over the downtown rate.

The program for strengthening ghetto banks should also lure demand and time deposits from the treasurers of the great national corporations. Portfolio managers of life-insurance companies and other institutions[5] will improve their investment performance by acquiring low-risk tax-sheltered debentures issued by ghetto banks. Because of the new tax incentives available to depositors and investors, it is likely that credit markets will establish a beneficially low interest rate on debentures or certificates of deposit payable by ghetto banks.

[5] One of the most aggressive depositors in ghetto banks is the tax-exempt New York Synod of the Presbyterian Church. Without the impetus of tax incentives, the Church deposited $15,000 in Harlem's Freedom National in 1968, and spread $250,000 around in various slum-area banks and savings institutions.

Also in 1968, the Executive Council of the Episcopal Church deposited $675,000 in 45 ghetto banks. The Council's only requirement is that the deposits be federally insured and that the institution be locally owned and managed for the benefit of those who live in the community.

At last count, General Motors held cash and marketable securities of $2.3 billion. No published figures reveal how much of this resides in ghetto banks (probably more than the combined capital and surplus of any one of them), yet the ghetto banks hardly cause a ripple in our banking system.

Ghetto Development Bank: Public and Private

Our program has focused first on incentive credits for the direct development of commercial and business loans—a necessary element in building working patterns of black business and commerce. The next aspect of the credit program, the tax-incentive endorsement which rides on the back of ghetto-origin installment paper, is geared to encourage consumer credit in ghetto markets. It would reduce interest charges and ease repayment terms on the purchase of automobiles, appliances, and other hard goods. The next credit incentive is aimed at encouraging deposits in the interracial banks. This feature is designed to develop new and independent sources of credit within the slum, and at the same time to harness the special lending advantages of black banks.

The first three incentive programs should quickly aid and directly initiate our strategy of normalizing credit in the ghetto. However, there are vast urban core areas in America, housing hundreds of thousands of black people, where not one functioning commercial bank is evident. The ghetto is totally underbanked. Credit failure is so massive that an entirely new ghetto banking system is required.

Two basic approaches to this problem are available. One strategy calls for a completely new system of federal-, state-, or community-sponsored development banks. The other suggests an extension and expansion of the existing commercial banking system, with concurrent adoption of adequate lending incentives for the ghetto area.

Influenced by the success of the World Bank abroad, there is bipartisan support in Congress for creating a new bank, or a system of banks, to lend in the ghetto. A leading advocate of this approach is Senator Javits of New York. In October, 1967, the Senator introduced a comprehensive program for setting up a Domestic Development Bank and a separate Economic Opportunity Corporation to provide technical assistance to black businesses, and to develop ghetto entrepreneurship.

171

Under the Senator's plan, the Domestic Development Bank would be established, by an act of Congress, as a profit-making corporation for financing business and commercial projects (plants, equipment, and working capital) in or near poverty areas where capital is not available on reasonable terms. Loans would be made to companies of all sizes for job-producing enterprises. For smaller businesses, the Domestic Development Bank would be authorized to guarantee loans made by local banks.

A more recent proposal suggests a new national system of community-development banks, patterned after the National Land Bank Associations set up to provide farm credit during the depression years. These banks would be established as part of the Community Self-Determination Bill,[6] introduced in the Senate in July 1968. The bill contemplates setting up a series of Community Development Corporations owned by the residents of poverty neighborhoods. The CDC's would be essentially ghetto business conglomerates, with broad powers to control the economic development of their neighborhood. They would own the local community-development banks. These banks would be funded by capital contributed by the parent CDC, and by the sale of income bonds backed by a Federal Reserve escrow fund. A National Community Development Bank would also be established to assist the CDC program.

Proposals for a new federal development bank and, as an alternative, for a new system of community-controlled development banks, repeat some errors of anti-poverty programs of the past. It seems likely that a new federal development bank, independent of Congress and the Executive Branch, would yet develop many of the disincentives such as delays, red tape, and rigidity that have infected ambitious ghetto programs entrusted, in the past, directly to the Small Business Administration and the Federal Housing Administration. Greater disadvantages, in my view, are the delays inherent in recruiting and staffing, financing and launching a completely new nationwide system of banks. The community-development banks are not likely to attract the more

6 Senate Bill 3876.

172

effective wealth-builders to their loan staffs. Most important, the system of CDC banks does not take any advantage whatsoever of the lending skills of a hundred thousand or more trained American banking executives.

Supported by at least twenty senators, liberal as well as conservative, this program for establishing a new system of community-development banks stands an excellent chance of enactment during the 91st Congress, as part of the Community Self-Determination Bill. The thrust of the new banking legislation—a massive injection into the ghetto community itself—is sound. Despite its disadvantages, the program deserves total support from American business and banking.

The alternative, developing a system of private development banks that would undertake high-risk loans and investments in the ghettos, is philosophically opposed to legislation calling for a new system of federal or community-sponsored banks. Private development banks would be set up as subsidiaries of existing banks, or as joint ventures undertaken by a consortium of banks and insurance companies, all of which would have a common interest in the regeneration of a particular city or area. The private development bank could be established as a business corporation for profit, or as a non-profit community corporation. It would be largely funded from local banks, insurance companies, and other business corporations. The private development bank would commit for a broad range of equity loans, second mortgages, and front-end capital investments in the ghetto, which are presently illegal investments for life-insurance companies and banks.

The prototype of a bank-originated private development bank is the Citizens and Southern Community Development Corporation, formed by Georgia's one-billion-dollar Citizens and Southern National Bank. Capitalized in May, 1968, by its parent bank at one million dollars, the new unit makes second-mortgage loans and provides equity capital for new small businesses in the slums of Savannah. It will also lend second-mortgage and equity money to enable slum dwellers to buy their own homes. The bank antici-

173

pates that, on most home loans, first- and second-mortgage payments will be no higher than the rents now being paid. This program is a brilliant innovation, uniquely calculated to build
ownership and equities in the ghetto.[7]

A different approach has been taken by the non-profit Interracial Council for Business Opportunity in New York City. An
ICBO Fund had been organized which plans to raise about
$300,000 in capital funds. Unlike the Citizens and Southern Na-
tional Bank plan, the ICBO Fund does not lend directly to black
businesses. The Fund guarantees repayment of ghetto business
loans made by private commercial banks that have agreed to participate in the program.[8] Through the use of the guarantee technique, it is obvious that greater lending leverage is obtained. The
Fund estimates that $300,000 in capital will support one million
dollars in loan guarantees to Negroes. The ICBO Loan Guarantee Fund hopes to commit ghetto guarantees with a minimum of
red tape—possibly even by telephone request. The program puts
private banks and businesses directly in the role of recruiting and
funding loans to promising black businessmen. Since the guarantee makes the loan bankable, the credit can be committed at the
lower rates prevailing outside the ghetto. The ICBO program removes two fundamental weaknesses of the direct loan functions
and loan-guarantee program of federal agencies: (1) administrative delays in approving loan applications; and (2) the inability

[7] The program was approved by the Comptroller of the Currency in April,
1968. The plan is therefore legal for any national bank. It is doubtful if any
state regulatory authority would fault a parallel project undertaken by a state
bank provided the financial commitment was reasonable in relationship to the
sponsoring bank's capital funds. Under the Citizens and Southern plan, the
capital at risk is less than .01 per cent of the total assets of the bank.

[8] The original participating banks in the ICBO program were all in New
York City: Bankers Trust Company, The Chase Manhattan Bank, Chemical
Bank New York Trust Company, and Harlem's Freedom National Bank. A
similar guarantee fund, Puerto Rican Forum, Inc., has been established in New
York City to help finance small businesses operated by minority-group mem-
bers. The fund is sponsored by Manufacturers Hanover Trust Company and
San Juan's Banco Popular de Puerto Rico under a Ford Foundation grant. In
July, 1968, the first loan of $6,000 at 7.5 per cent simple interest was made by
Manufacturers Hanover to Tony Bonilla of 69 Irving Place, New York City,
for refinancing existing obligations of his printing shop. The Fund guarantees
half the loan on a pro-rated basis. The bank thus accepts one-half of the risk.

of government agencies to recruit and recognize promising Negro borrowers.

The concept of a nationwide system of private ghetto development lending institutions with broad powers to make "free-wheeling" risk loans and equity commitments carries extraordinary potential. New sponsorship of these projects should be encouraged through a specially tailored and controlled system of incentives.

I suggest that sponsors of private ghetto development banks be permitted to deduct from taxable income, spread ratably (amortized) over a three-year period the amount of any investment in the capital stock of any corporation chartered to take equity positions; make business, mortgage, or personal loans; or acquire real estate in the designated poverty areas. For maximum efficiency, I would suggest that the incentive apply only when 40 per cent or more of the capital stock, or debenture capital, of a new development bank is held by insurance companies, commercial and savings banks, and other institutional lenders regulated by law.

The subsidiary private banking development corporation would also be entitled to the benefits of the categorical credit incentives I suggested earlier to encourage ghetto installment credit, commercial and business loans, and deposits in slum-area banks.

Under present income tax laws, the type of private ghetto lending subsidiary formed in Georgia by Citizens and Southern National Bank is not encouraged. The initial commitment of funds is a non-deductible business investment, not a deductible charitable contribution. The parent bank obtains no tax deduction except as ghetto loans are written off as worthless, or unless the whole ghetto development subsidiary fails and is written off as worthless stock in the parent bank's income tax return. The tax premium therefore attaches to failure. There is no reward for initiating a successful slum business loan, except satisfaction from full repayment of the loan with interest (taxable at the usual 50 per cent rate). The plan I suggest of granting an income tax benefit to banks that organize ghetto development banks applies the tax incentive to a very early and difficult stage of the process we wish to encourage—actually forming and putting hard money into a ghetto development organization.

Unlike proposals for chartering a new federal or a community-sponsored system of ghetto development banks, the plan for private development banks makes immediate and effective use of the lending skills of both the white-controlled and the black banks. Staffing is not a problem, and the program can go into effect immediately. This program creates an immediate need on the part of the nation's banks and insurance companies to fund new high-risk subsidiaries uniquely qualified to build credit enrichment into the ghetto.

Front-End Incentives

Coaxing Savings in the Ghetto

THE BANKER'S ETHIC to the contrary, few people in the normal economy grow rich or even affluent through the simple process of faithfully and periodically depositing money in a savings account. Personal affluence is more likely to come from converting a stake of money or savings into a business or investment opportunity. A sum of savings enters the process of building wealth only when, by a bold act of the owner, the thrift fund is changed into risk capital or front-end money. The companion wealth-producing factor of leverage—typically a line of credit from a bank—operates only in conjunction with this risk capital. It is rarely possible to start up a new business on borrowed money unless someone supplies some element of margin money, equity, or front-end money. A tradition-bound economy, such as we find in the American ghetto, cannot grow and innovate without developing these discretionary risk funds.

If the formation of risk capital has been such a vital part of the process of growing affluent in the normal economy, then it is necessary to work on the available pockets of potential savings in the ghetto, so that they may find their way into a thrift institution or mutual-fund shares. Emerging opportunities for blacks in commerce and business tend to remove the argument, popular in the ghetto, that there is "no use in savings." But these entrepreneurial and investment opportunities must be reinforced so that the motivation for the savings will be for "investment" as well as for "security." The black man's need to have money in the bank for a rainy day is no greater than his need to have it so that he can seize an entrepreneurial opportunity. I develop later a specific set of incentives which are designed to make certain adjustments in ghetto economics so as to encourage Negro entrepreneurship. These incentives should boost motivation to save money in order to enter commerce; yet the importance of the very process of savings in reversing the direction of a declining or undeveloped economy commands a specific savings incentive program.[9]

It would appear that an inducement could be given directly to the ghetto resident and businessman to encourage him to save. The normal approach might be a federally subsidized bonus to the ghetto saver in the form of an increment of 1 per cent or more to the normal 5.5 per cent interest paid by the savings institution. But there are serious obstacles in administering a savings incentive which is applied directly to the depositor. Savings from the outside economy will too readily find means of acquiring the benefits of the savings credit by channeling funds through a ghetto resident or businessman. Moreover, I suggest that if the ghetto purchaser or businessman is willing to disregard the interest charge on his installment purchases from the ghetto credit merchant (which frequently varies from 20 per cent to 100 per cent per annum), no reasonable additional credit to the interest column in a savings passbook is likely to produce savings in the

---

[9] A program encouraging the development of savings in the ghetto will be more effective if it is combined with the more urgent program of bringing ghetto incomes above the poverty level and reducing immigration to the slums. The ghettos of America are unable to control either births or immigration, which now aggregate about half a million people a year. The program for generating savings in the ghetto must recognize that significant gains will not occur until the slum has first provided for minimum consumption needs. A federal program which encourages new plants (and jobs) in the South obviously tends to break the economic grip of the ghetto in the North.

ghetto in preference to spending discretionary funds.

For this reason, and for reasons of more efficient administration, the incentive is more effectively applied to the ghetto savings institution than to the saver.

To persuade the resident of the ghetto to open and maintain a conventional savings account requires some marketing skill and maybe a little sorcery. During the years after the 1933 Bank Holiday, when nobody trusted a savings bank, American banks showed great resourcefulness in coaxing savings from a poor economy. Banks advertised for savings; they merchandised savings by offering casseroles, clocks, and sets of dishes. The potential for building personal capital in an underdeveloped economy has been demonstrated in the Soviet Union, where one of world's largest pools of personal savings has been created in 70,000 government-owned savings banks. The Soviet banks aggressively advertise and merchandise savings—virtually the only exception to the communist prohibition against advertising. In the United Kingdom, banks traditionally have merchandised savings by giving the depositor the option of applying one-half of his interest dividend to the purchase of national lottery tickets. Banks cannot sell lottery tickets in the United States, but they do have access to trading stamps, television advertising, and a host of merchandising techniques which have never been used to encourage personal savings in ghetto areas.

At the present time, ghetto banking economics are so distorted that the ghetto institutions actually discourage savings accounts. Black banks have low profit margins because they are plagued with high bookkeeping and administrative costs incurred in servicing a large number of tiny, active savings accounts. Unlike other banks, those in the ghetto are not favored with a high percentage of the more profitable demand deposits or checking accounts, or with substantial and rewarding time deposits.

Therefore, I suggest that an incentive should be applied which compensates the ghetto savings institution for (1) the extra administrative costs of maintaining savings accounts in slum areas and (2) the extra marketing and promotional costs that are necessary to lure the money of ghetto savers away from the numbers operator and into a passbook account where, ultimately, it may be converted into risk capital or even into the purchase of mutual-fund shares.

The incentive to ghetto-area savings institutions would operate in the following way:

Every ghetto bank (savings bank, savings-and-loan association, or commercial bank with its main office and branch offices located exclusively in the designated poverty areas) would be entitled to a year-end payment from the federal government.[10] The federal credit would be 1.5 per cent of the savings accounts held by individuals who, at the time the account was opened, were residents of a designated poverty area. The credit would be smaller, 0.5 per cent, for year-end savings balances which admittedly originate from non-poverty-area depositors or from sources which the ghetto bank is unable to identify.

This incentive gives the ghetto institution a fund for promoting ghetto savings. It also compensates the bank so that it will no longer tend to discourage the small, active savings accounts which are so costly for the banks to maintain. The incentive will encourage the formation of new branch banks in the ghetto areas. It will also have the effect of causing the slum-area banks to persuade a few middle-class or affluent residents of the ghetto to transfer their savings accounts from downtown banking offices to slum-area or independent interracial banks. Giving the ghetto bank a bonus for funds deposited from *outside* the ghetto does not build thrift *within* the ghetto, yet it strengthens the capital structure of the interracial ghetto banks. The effect is a desirable infusion of capital into the slum banking community, where it will be available for commercial and mortgage loans.

The direct federal subsidy to ghetto banks for time deposits is in addition to the tax credit proposed earlier, which is applied directly to any person maintaining balances in ghetto institutions.

[10] The federal payment or subsidy to the ghetto bank would be made *outside* the federal income tax system because most ghetto banks show an operating loss. Therefore an income tax credit holds no advantages.

Ghetto-Origin Stock Placements

During such time as the ghetto economy remains poor and has very limited capability of generating savings and risk capital internally, the need to attract risk funds from outside the ghetto is urgent. Just as uncertain patterns of ghetto income and risks to invested capital block bank and other credit from moving into the slum from downtown institutions, so the nation's underwriting industry does not bring to the market new stock issues for financing new ghetto plants or real estate improvements. Until 1969, when a Wall Street brokerage house underwrote shares for a stock offering of Parks Sausages, Inc., a new "hot issue" in the shares of a Negro firm was unknown on Wall Street—or, for that matter, on 125th Street in Harlem.

The occasional public issue, or private placement of shares, in an untested Negro enterprise is not bought with any real expectation of profit. The underwriting is more often an act of philanthropy. A stock issue in Harlem's Freedom National Bank was marketed with difficulty in 1964, although Jackie Robinson, of Brooklyn Dodgers fame, was Chairman of the Board.[11] Mutual Real Estate Investment Trust (M-REIT), a publicly owned real estate trust formed to purchase white apartment buildings and open them up to all races, took two years to market its first share offering of four million dollars. In his efforts to prove that integrated housing can be profitable, the sponsor, Morris Milgram, offered a second stock issue of ten million dollars in 1968. *Business Week* reported that only one-tenth of the issue had been sold one month after the offering date, but that the assassination of Martin Luther King created new interest in this offering.[12]

These laborious efforts to market securities for enriching the

[11] The stock prospectus was hardly designed to excite stock traders downtown. It explained that Freedom National had been "planned as a community enterprise that will in every way belong to the people it is to serve. . . . Moreover, it is intended that these people shall be represented in the formation and administration of the policies of this bank to assure its role in helping to eradicate those financing practices that restrict the economic growth of the community and erode the money power of its members."

[12] *Business Week,* April 13, 1968, p. 118.

ghetto stand in sharp contrast to the current frenzy of new issues in the main economy. Hardly a week goes by that Wall Street markets do not make millionaires of men who have new ideas for a restaurant franchise or for an electronic product. Since new security issues are such an important catalyst of wealth in the normal economy, I suggest that incentives should be developed to start building normal patterns of new security issues for projects in the Negro market.

Our income tax laws now permit any investor in a qualified small business corporation to deduct in full against income any loss on the sale of stock in the corporation. This provision allows full tax benefits from the loss, even if the securities are sold "long-term." This incentive was enacted in 1958 in line with Congressional policy to encourage risk-capital investment in small business ventures.

I suggest that these special income tax privileges for small business corporations should be expanded for stock or debenture investment in all corporations formed to develop new plants, office buildings, apartment houses, retail outlets, or other new facilities in the certified poverty areas. Losses in these security investments should be allowed in full against the investor's ordinary income, plus an extra deduction against ordinary income of 10 per cent of the loss. Profits on resale of ghetto-origin stock investments should be taxed in the usual way but reduced by a special poverty-area tax credit of 7.5 per cent of the capital gain.

As a further inducement encouraging ghetto ownership of business and real estate equities, I propose that the poverty-area tax-loss deduction or credit on taxable profits be increased by 30 per cent in cases in which, after the financing is completed, 50 per cent or more of the equity securities of the issuing corporation are owned by ghetto residents or firms.

These specific incentives for new security issues should lure risk capital out of the normal economy and force it into the subsidiary ghetto economy. Investors in the normal economy will be encouraged to seek out creative new ways of combining their risk capital with SBA- and FHA-guaranteed credits to build examples of entrepreneurship in the urban slums.

182

The Core-Area Service Cluster

Leverage, or the compounding of value, develops most efficiently in concentrated form. Real estate men and city planners know that a concentrated five-million-dollar real estate investment in a blighted area will produce greater aggregate value or wealth than the equivalent money dispersed over the entire area. A massive concentration of investment in a ghetto neighborhood can basically reverse the direction of a decaying slum. Significant investments focused on a limited area produce new values in surrounding real estate. This added value of leverage is lost when programs for economic enrichment of the ghetto are dispersed in various pockets which gradually become overwhelmed by the decaying character of surrounding neighborhoods.

Several decades ago, Metropolitan Life Insurance Company's massive investment in New York's Stuyvesant Town added hundreds of millions of dollars in tax assessments, and transformed much of this Lower East Side ghetto of New York City. Value was added to properties many miles away from the actual point of investment. In 1959, the $175 million Lincoln Center project, built on Manhattan's decaying West Side, set off a rejuvenation of the area from 42nd Street to 79th Street. Billions of dollars of value was added to dilapidated real estate in an area shunned by institutional lenders. The proposed New York State government office building to be located at 125th Street has stimulated speculative interest in Harlem real estate, dampened only slightly by the riots following the assassination of Martin Luther King in the spring of 1968. The most significant rehabilitation of a ghetto area has been undertaken by the Bedford-Stuyvesant Restoration Corporation. This project, originally sponsored by Robert Kennedy, involves restoration of 640 square blocks of the nation's most depressed poverty area. The project ambitiously contemplates renovation of most of the area's deteriorated three- and four-story row housing. Planned are two "superblocks" linked to central green belts, two rehabilitation centers for skill training, a $4 million athletic and cultural center, and a huge office-and-

183

shopping center with perhaps a branch store of Macy's. The plan contemplates some twenty-five new businesses and plants, a network of health centers, a local TV station, and a four-year work-study college. The Bedford-Stuyvesant Restoration project was introduced in the fall of 1960. Progress has been slow. Aside from the support of foundation and government grants, the ultimate success of the project depends on the continuing drive of the businessmen and bankers who have been associated with it. But the future of a project of such magnitude should not rest only on the goodwill and voluntary desires of the businessmen who are "pledging" their time. Large core-area projects offer such potential of leverage for the complete and efficient transformation of a ghetto economy that special assistance and direct inducements should be applied.

I suggest a specific incentive program for new investments in contiguous facilities in an eligible ghetto area of $100 million or more in a city with a population of five million or more (the amount of required investment to be scaled down for smaller cities).

The incentive would apply to an investment in a cluster of facilities which includes three or more of the following:

(a) a department store, shopping center, or cooperative market;

(b) a plant, or business service facility, such as an automobile diagnostic service center;

(c) entertainment facilities (theaters,[13] bowling alleys, roller- and ice-skating rinks);

(d) medical centers, hospitals, and extended-care facilities;

(e) day-care facilities for children;

(f) low-income housing;

(g) new ghetto-resident-controlled banks and other regulated credit institutions.

This tax incentive should be directed to the supplier of the risk capital, as well as the participating lending institutions:

[13] The new New York City zoning code already encourages construction of legitimate theaters in new office buildings by granting the builder more liberal legitimate office-space allowances in new buildings which also contain a legitimate theater.

184

(1) The sponsor and owner (or consortium of owners) should be entitled to normal accelerated-depreciation deductions and new facilities tax credits, plus an automatic annual incremental tax credit of 5 per cent of equity investment cost without "strings," restrictions, or regulatory approvals. The effect of this incentive is to add a 5 per cent tax-free investment return on equity.

(2) Participating construction lenders and holders of long-term mortgages should be entitled to a tax exemption of 2 per cent of interest income received or accrued. The exemption on interest received would apply, whether or not the construction or long-term loan was insured under any existing federal or state programs for the guarantee of loans.

Corporations such as Alcoa, Gulf Oil, and ITT have expressed interest in building entire new towns and cities in America. The federal government must use its taxing powers to direct these efforts into the ghetto and poverty areas, where the greatest leverage for slum rehabilitation can be achieved.

The program I suggest for core-area clusters is an exception to the principle I suggested in Part Five, which excludes investments in leveraged real estate from the benefits of ghetto tax credits. The exception is made because the program for new ghetto service clusters offers such great opportunities for reversing decay in our cities.

Imparting the Skills of
the Entrepreneur

Aid for the Poverty-Area
Business Franchise Holder

YOUNG NEGRO EXECUTIVES are moving rapidly into the executive ranks of the large national corporations. This process of bringing the Negro into enriching positions in the downtown economy is proceeding without assistance from government subsidies or incentives. But, clearly, the other half of the over-all goal is putting the Negro in a business of his own. Lacking sufficient compensating incentives, the business and banking community has not moved to recruit and establish independent entrepreneurs in the slum areas, except on a token basis.

Since massive tariffs and extra risks facing a new ghetto business are formidable, early business failure becomes almost certain. Unless the new ghetto businessman is temporarily sheltered by outside management expertise or by some other economic umbrella which assures a market for his product, he has little chance of success. The risks facing new Negro businesses give assurance that the cause of black entrepreneurship will not be advanced by providing incentives for any and all new business start-ups in the ghetto. In most cases, nothing is accomplished by

186

simply giving money to a Negro who is untrained in techniques of production and marketing and expecting him to sell successfully in the poor markets of the ghetto or in the affluent markets of the normal economy, which are still unreceptive to black production and services. An impractical incentive program for building Negro entrepreneurship would only produce further recriminations. Loans and capital, pumped into the slums, would only run off back downtown as an aftermath of defaults and foreclosures.

A feasible program for putting the Negro in business must therefore:

(1) contain a built-in assurance that the new business will have not only adequate start-up financing, but continuing lines of credit;

(2) encourage new businesses which do not require large amounts of initial capital (ghetto entrepreneurs have already shown some success in businesses of this type);

(3) give the new ghetto entrepreneur a reasonably assured market for his product, intensive business training and guidance, and, if possible, the advantage of a well-known brand name.

This third element is essential if a man is to have a reasonable chance to build ownership of business capital and affluence in an economy which regularly and perniciously destroys the formation of wealth. He must have a "head start"—some extra compensating advantage.

These objectives will be best accomplished by creating and applying an incentive to the well-known system of business franchising. Under the typical business franchise, a national company, such as Dunkin' Donuts, Chicken Delight, Midas Muffler, or Carvel ice-cream stores, licenses its nationally advertised brand name to an individual who wishes to operate a small business. The recognized franchise name assures the operator of a reasonable level of patronage from customers who recognize the quality of the product, the service, and other positive factors associated with the brand name. The national franchisor also supplies the franchisee with vital management, financial, and accounting assistance, thus reducing the risk of business failure. The franchisor benefits by charging initial start-up fees, regular fees based on sales income of the franchisee, and often by selling products to the franchisee.

The American business-franchise system is already organized and staffed to recruit and train potential ghetto entrepreneurs. Of the thousand or more national franchise companies which license trade names and marketing techniques to small business operators, each of the two largest national companies has more field personnel training local or potential franchise operators than the entire field staff of the Small Business Administration.[14] To achieve maximum effect, an income tax incentive should be applied to the two established entrepreneurial and financial profit centers that are capable of packaging the new ghetto franchised business:

(1) The federal government should provide a tax credit for franchise income derived by the franchisor from the poverty-area franchised business. This compensates the national franchisor for the extra risk involved in entrusting the good will of his brand name to the inexperienced ghetto entrepreneur. It also compensates the national franchisor for the need to provide extra supervision, training, and financial guidance which normally persuades him to forgo the "soft" ghetto franchise in favor of the "hard" or profitable franchise always available in the normal economy.

(2) A second tax credit should be granted to the lender who provides the basic capital or start-up cost of the new franchised business. In the past, as we have seen, Small Business Administration equal-opportunity business-loan programs have not been sufficient to move this type of risk money into ghetto entrepreneurship.

The incentives would take the following specific forms:

(a) Any corporation regularly engaged in the business of licensing the use of its name, trademark, business, working techniques, and products would be entitled to an annual federal in-

[14] Remarks of Robert Rosenberg, President, Dunkin' Donuts of America, at American Management Conference held in New York City, June 3–5, 1968. Robert C. Moot, then Administrator of the Small Business Administration, stated at the same conference that the SBA had 150 field employees engaged in entrepreneurial training activities.

188

come tax credit equal to 5 per cent of the fees from franchise-fee income derived from a new franchise operation established in an eligible poverty area. The tax credit would be good for five years from the initial opening of the new ghetto franchise.

(b) Any bank (supervised by federal or state law) or licensed finance company would be entitled to a consecutive five-year federal income tax credit equal to 3 per cent of the year-end balance of loans made to establish or carry a new ghetto franchised business. The income tax credit thus amounts to an extra annual tax-free interest yield on ghetto business loans of 3 per cent. This loan must be made to a new business in a designated poverty area, franchised by an established franchisor with ten or more franchises operating elsewhere. To command the income tax credit, the loan may not carry an interest rate exceeding the prime rate established by banks from time to time. The purpose of the loan must be to assist the franchised business either to: (1) enter a new business under its franchise, or (2) purchase an existing business which is to receive a new franchise.

The income tax incentive to the lending institution would apply whether or not repayment of the loan was insured or guaranteed by any federal or private institution. This feature is necessary because the loan repayment guarantee—never an adequate incentive in itself—is nevertheless a valuable foundation on which the tax incentive can build. Moreover, the tax-incentive credit would not affect the lending institution's privilege of in cluding the loan in its normal bad-debt reserve allowance.[15]

Erecting the incentive program on an already established national franchise system with operative skills in building small-business entrepreneurship is a practical and effective method to encourage and establish business opportunities in the ghetto.

[15] Aside from normal burdens and delays in processing an SBA or FHA loan-guarantee application, a lending institution's incentive to make these loans has been curtailed in the past by Treasury efforts to disallow these loans as part of the lender's tax base for usual annual bad-debt deductions.

Encouraging the New Ghetto Business with a Protected Product Market

I have just explained the vast potential of the business franchise system for providing an inexperienced black with a branded trademark, accounting personnel, marketing advice, and other business skills which give sufficient assurance of success to justify applying the specific corrective tax incentive. Even lacking a franchise, the new ghetto entrepreneur has a "leg up"—a reasonable assurance of success—where he is guaranteed a market for his product. Patterns of white-buying discrimination, combined with Negro inexperience in product marketing, largely kill the chances of success of the unfranchised new business which has no guaranteed market for its production.

A limited, specific, and constructive tax incentive should be applied to companies in the normal economy to encourage the formation of new ghetto subcontracting facilities that have an assured long-term market for their production.

As in encouraging franchised ghetto businesses, this incentive to subcontract in the ghetto cannot be applied directly to the new ghetto facility owner, since reduction of income taxes is rarely a motivating consideration for an undercapitalized man who is venturing into a new business. Instead, the incentive should be applied to *ghetto-destination* payments made by the product-purchasing corporation in the normal economy to induce it to develop wealth-building subcontracting arrangements with firms in the ghetto.

The typical umbrella subcontracting incentive would function as follows. Assume that Sears Roebuck purchases a million tents a year for sale to its retail customers. The company needs an additional supplier and is willing either to consider setting up a tent factory in a Chicago ghetto, or to contract for purchases from a ghetto tent factory set up by someone else. The incentive is applied to persuade Sears to make the "ghetto option"—a selection in favor of a facility which will enrich the Chicago slum. The incentive must be bold enough to overcome usual ghetto disincentives—higher costs of recruiting, training, absenteeism, theft, and production failures—which always plague a new ghetto business facility. The guaranteed requirements purchase contract of, say, five thousand tents a month has a twofold advantage. It assures the marketing success of the ghetto project and also gives the ghetto facility the element of income certainty, which is the key to financing the cost of plant construction. The basic construction and long-term mortgage money necessary to build and equip the plant is available either through a direct Small Business Administration loan or an SBA-guaranteed bank loan. The loan application papers will move more rapidly through SBA approval procedures because of the strong sponsorship for the project. For the same reasons the equity and front-end money for plant start-up expense, initial training costs, inventory and working capital should now be available through a loan from a Chicago bank. Since Sears has committed to a specific program for purchase of its tent requirements, the borrower's income uncertainty is greatly reduced; the loan is no longer "soft." Although the loan does not carry a direct repayment guarantee by Sears, it is now bankable and should pass muster with bank examiners.

At the beginning of this Part, I suggested a specific *credit* incentive to encourage loans for building and carrying new ghetto facilities. Even when the new subcontracting incentive is operating to reduce the manufacturer's aversion to purchasing in the ghetto, the earlier poverty-area loan incentive is still required since the loan carries abnormal risks. The over-all ghetto franchise program I suggest harnesses two specific compensating incentives and applies them to the two key profit-making and tax-paying institutions—the manufacturer outside the ghetto and the Chicago bank. The incentives give the extra economic advantage necessary to justify a commitment of stockholder capital to an onerous program for building new businesses into the Chicago ghetto.

The specific program would operate as follows: A federal income tax credit would be assured to any manufacturer, wholesaler, or retailer, equal to 5 per cent of its annual gross purchases from a new plant facility located in a federally designated poverty

191

area. The tax incentive would be available only for purchases under contracts calling for an over-all purchase commitment equal to 80 per cent of the projected manufacturing capacity of the new ghetto plant or business. To assist in financing the new facility and to give the plant an assured purchase market for a reasonable period, the purchase contract should have a fixed term of not less than five years.[16]

The incentive should be available to a tent-manufacturing subsidiary wholly owned by Sears, provided the plant is located in an eligible poverty area. This kind of facility would provide Negroes with jobs, even though it does not carry the additional advantage of Negro ownership. However, I would suggest that if the tent-manufacturing subsidiary sells 10 per cent or more of its capital stock to ghetto residents or its employees (through payroll withholding or otherwise), Sears's income tax credit should be increased on a prorated basis. This is in line with the objective of building new black ownership of ghetto businesses and real estate.

The incentive for purchases from new ghetto business with a protected product market is designed to correct a specific and vital weakness in the ghetto economy—its inability to manufacture either for its own use or for export to the regular economy. The incentive also reduces the ghetto's inability to generate its own job-producing facilities. Under the specific incentive program, the risk of wasting federal funds on abortive new businesses in ghetto areas is minimized because of the obligatory feature of a long-term purchase-requirements contract. This umbrella feature effectively eliminates the lack of a product market, inadequate marketing skills, or white purchasing discrimination as causes of ghetto business failure. Finally, the augmented income tax incentive for minority interests in ghetto plants or businesses provides a start toward Negro ownership of capital.

---

[16] The contract should be terminable only by mutual consent or for unreasonable or repeated production failures, with disputes to be arbitrated by the American Arbitration Society.

New Equities in Ghetto Ownership

I have explained how beachheads of Negro entrepreneurship can be developed in the ghetto economy by the application of incentives to the industrialist in the normal "outside" economy. New business start-ups in the slums are achieved by applying a tax credit (a) to the income derived by a national franchisor from slum-area business franchises, and (b) to the gross volume of production purchases made by any company from a ghetto subcontractor.

However, many business activities do not lend themselves to the franchise or subcontracting opportunity. A number of corporations do not franchise or subcontract as a matter of corporate policy, especially businesses which wish to maintain tight central controls over production and marketing activities. These corporations may yet be willing to "risk a new ghetto plant" and share ownership, although not ultimate control, with ghetto residents and employees. Other companies may be willing to transfer majority, or even complete control, to the ghetto.

Partial or complete transfer of ownership of slum-area facilities to local residents and employees holds out great economic benefits. A new Montgomery Ward outlet in Hough enriches this community because it provides high-quality low-cost merchandise to an area which is currently victimized by gouging credit merchants. But the same new retail project is doubly beneficial if shares in the Montgomery Ward subsidiary can be marketed to Hough residents and employees of the store.

There have been only very limited examples of industry efforts to arrange stock-purchase plans for employees of new ghetto businesses. We have seen how Aerojet General's employee stock-purchase plan at its Watts manufacturing unit encountered major difficulties and was temporarily abandoned. In a joint venture with the federal government, the District of Columbia's Model Inner City Community Organization and Fairchild Hiller Corporation established an assembly operation for wiring harnesses and circuit boards in a converted warehouse in Washington's Shaw ghetto. The Fairchild subsidiary, with almost entirely black management, plans to sell stock in the ghetto and become a community-owned organization. Fairchild Hiller would ultimately retain only 10 per cent ownership.

Boston's nuclear-testing firm of Edgerton, Germeshausen and Grier has formed a new manufacturing unit in the South Boston black community. This plant will be the nucleus of a project for training Roxbury workers in metal-working, drafting, and welding. Twenty-five per cent of the stock of the subsidiary will be earmarked for employees. Here, too, the goal is to sell the plant to the resident workers. If EG&G is able to accomplish even part of this plan, the company will have introduced new economic forces into the underdeveloped Boston ghetto—far more significant to Roxbury and to the nation than the equally expensive company programs in Boston to hand out jobs to Roxbury residents and bus them to a suburban plant.

Since minority interests owned by ghetto residents and employees build such valuable economic leverage and incentives in the slum, I suggest a specific incentive to help these programs. The object is to encourage supermarket chains, oil companies, theater chains, and hotel companies to establish new facilities in partnership, or for ultimate sale to, residents of the ghetto.

The incentive would allow corporations a five-year annual income tax credit equal to 10 per cent of the annual carrying charges (interest, rent, plant maintenance, insurance, and payroll) of a new ghetto business facility, pro-rated for the percentage which the equity stock ownership initially marketed to ghetto residents or employees bears to the total stock ownership. For example, if the annual carrying charges of the ghetto subsidiary are $500,000 per year, and 10 per cent of the stock is marketed in the ghetto, the parent company would be entitled to an annual tax credit on its income tax return of $50,000 for five consecutive years during which the plant is maintained. If 50 per cent of the stock were marketed in the ghetto, the annual tax credit would increase to $250,000. Beyond that point no further tax credit would be given. However, I would suggest an additional benefit to the sponsoring parent corporation if, at any time, it sold the entire facility, or its remaining equity, to ghetto residents. The sale price would not exceed the amortized book cost of the facility. It would be paid over a period of not more than ten years with interest not to exceed the prime rate on corporate loans. Sale of the ghetto facility by a sponsoring corporation to members of the community on these terms would entitle the purchase-money note to carry an automatic repayment guarantee of the Small Business Administration. This would be achieved without any prior regulatory approvals. The agency's guarantee on the note should make it readily saleable by the parent sponsoring corporation in the normal markets for notes guaranteed by a government agency.

Developing Black Entrepreneurs

Negro magazine publisher John Johnson once tried to buy a funeral parlor from a white man who refused to show the property to a Negro. Johnson hired a white attorney, who was able to buy the building for $52,000. Before the deal closed, Johnson, who had never been inside the building, had his lawyer request that a maintenance man be allowed to look over the heating system. The owner agreed, and Johnson inspected his future home dressed in overalls. Johnson said, "I learned that there was no use just getting mad at somebody like that. You had to outthink him." This is the story of a black man who had learned to innovate and outwit—the essential act of an entrepreneur.

The remarkable success story of John Johnson obscures the catastrophic failure of Negro citizens to develop entrepreneurial skills and power.

New approaches to this problem have been only tentative. I have already reviewed the programs of the federal Small Business Administration to recruit, train, and finance potential black entrepreneurs. These efforts failed for lack of adequate financial support in Congress and, more importantly, because responsibility for developing black entrepreneurship was incorrectly assigned to a sector in our society which lacked understanding and competence in the processes whereby men in this country marshal capital, production, and marketing to achieve affluence.

Recognizing that a federal agency was not the most effective vehicle for building black entrepreneurs, the country is now looking elsewhere. One approach is creation of a network of federally assisted ghetto-controlled business conglomerates in poverty areas throughout the country. Community-development corporations would be an important feature of the proposed Community Self-Determination Bill.[17] I have mentioned earlier that the so-called CDC's would be legally and financially structured so that they would ultimately control all businesses in their areas. The Bill contemplates that existing ghetto businesses would receive federal financing on condition that they be sold to the local CDC as soon as the business had become viable. Tax advantages to ghetto businesses would be conditioned upon their operating under the aegis of a CDC. The entry of large outside companies into ghetto areas would be discouraged since income tax incentives would be conditioned on integrating ghetto branch business operations with the local CDC.

Entrepreneurship that now exists in the ghetto is essentially in the form of segregated businesses. There firms have survived because the blacks to whom they sold products or services could not buy these products or services in the white community. Now these ghetto businesses are weakening as white businesses begin to compete and seek out Negro patronage. The concept of a ghetto CDC with a legally protected and subsidized monopoly over ghetto business provides protection from this new competition. Also, the Community Self-Determination Bill wisely recognizes the forces of black economic power—the certainty that black men will not tolerate indefinitely a system where their entrepreneurial strength is derived from money and skills provided by a paternalistic white economy. In my judgment, the basic fault in the CDC proposal is its premise that creative entrepreneurship and black affluence can develop in a quasi-socialistic enclave where the production and marketing are community-controlled. The fact that ghetto residents will "own" the CDC's, subscribing

[17] Senate Bill 3876.

to shares at 5 dollars a share, does not alter this conclusion. The second weakness of the CDC program is its bias against the use of sponsorship, and management and technical assistance from outside the ghetto.

Another approach to the problem of developing black business skills is suggested by recent private programs. In New York City, Rockefeller and Ford foundation funds have organized the nation's most creative plan for building and training new Negro entrepreneurs—the Interracial Council for Business Opportunity. The ICBO has established business-development centers employing teams of business consultants, accountants, and lawyers in Bedford-Stuyvesant, Harlem, Hough, and Watts. ICBO consultants move into the ghetto and attack specific business problems. The Council's objective is not only to organize new minority businesses but also to strengthen existing businesses in major urban ghettos. The innovative thrust of the ICBO approach is illustrated by a Chicago newspaper report of a project of Benjamin Goldstein, who formerly headed a women's-wear specialty chain. Goldstein was called in as an ICBO consultant to a sportswear shop in Brooklyn owned by Floyd Ramsey and Jaime McDowell, two porters at New York's East Side Airline Terminal. Goldstein tells the story: "They were saying to me, 'Cure me,' and I was saying to them, 'Show me your wounds.' It took an hour before we were really able to talk to each other." Goldstein reported that the two proprietors ran an attractive operation. But one year, right after Christmas, they ran into trouble. Although the shop had enjoyed a good holiday season, nothing much had moved since; the two operators needed cash for a spring line. They were running a sale, marking down their prices by 5 and 10 per cent. Goldstein told them they would never move their goods unless they slashed prices by 50 per cent. "Frankly," Floyd Ramsey said later, "we wondered whether the man came to put us in business or out of business." The Chicago newspaper reports: "Today, the two men no longer wonder. Goldstein's advice started merchandise moving. Working together, the three men set up inventory controls and a sales reporting system to enable them to tell what sold well and what did not. Jay Schwamm, a financier and former chairman of American Trust Company, was brought in as a financial consultant and he guided the two embryo businessmen through the intricacies involved in securing a business loan. The store has flourished." [18]

Building on the prototype of the ICBO, I propose a specific incentive to induce the skilled, aggressive, and successful businessman to offer guidance to the Negro businessman in finance, production, marketing, accounting, and other business skills. The umbrella incentives for (a) nationally franchised ghetto businesses and (b) Negro subcontractors are valuable devices for protecting the future of the incipient ghetto business. But these incentives shelter the Negro businessman and, to some extent, preserve the benevolent monopoly—the economic dependency which he abhors. The broader goal is to attack and rehabilitate the basic business and commercial inadequacy of the minority entrepreneur. The incentive would give the ghetto resident direct access to vital business training from the business community—training now available only through the limited voluntary demonstration projects of ambitious, but less-experienced, non-profit organizations.

I suggest that an incentive be granted to any corporation which establishes an entrepreneurial development center in a designated poverty area. These centers (typically established in ghetto store-fronts) would evaluate business proposals, assist in preparing loan applications, help establish bookkeeping systems, and explore sources of financing for ghetto businesses. They would evaluate and make recommendations on locations and types of business needed in the community, and help develop and implement business programs which would improve economic conditions in the community by working with local groups, city, state, and federal agencies.

The incentives should take the following forms:

(1) An extra 25 per cent add-on income tax deduction for any business enterprise measured by the established salary[19] of any executive who gives consulting or business services through

[18] *Chicago Sunday Sun Times,* October, 1967.
[19] The net tax benefit of the incentive is actually 12.5 per cent of salary for a business in a normal 50 per cent tax bracket, since 100 per cent of the salary is deductible under present law.

an established store-front or permanent center in a designated poverty area. The incentive would also be available to self-employed professionals such as lawyers and CPA's. The deduction could be claimed by self-employed professionals, pro-rated for actual time spent in teaching or consultative work in the ghetto as certified in writing by any bona-fide association or tax-exempt organization with which the individual is affiliated. The certificate from the organization would be used in income tax return audits very much like the written statements given by recipients of charitable gifts.

(2) An extra annual income tax deduction equal to 25 per cent[20] of the carrying cost (interest, depreciation, rent, salary, insurance, real estate taxes) of any facility (business school or management of business counseling center) established and maintained in an eligible ghetto area by any individual, partnership, or corporate taxpayer.

This set of incentives minimizes reliance on the ambitious but often entrepreneurially ineffective personnel of charitable foundations. In moving toward the goal of black capitalism, the incentive draws directly on the management skills of American industry.

The credit incentives developed earlier are designed to move business credit from outside capital markets into the ghetto. But this commercial credit is meaningless unless it is made available to a Negro who has achieved an adequate level of business skills. The object of the incentives for black entrepreneurial training is to create the confidence necessary to assume risk—to incur business debt. In this way, a debt can be repaid and built on again. Only then will the minority businessman have achieved the secret of compounding wealth through leverage.

Store-Front Training Centers

A major symbol of ghetto poverty is the Negro dropout, seventeen to twenty-one years old, an age at which the rate of unem-

[20] Again, the net tax benefit is 12.5 per cent of annual expenditures for taxpayers in a 50 per cent income tax bracket.

ployment is twenty to thirty times as high as that of his white contemporaries in the normal economy. He probably reads at a fifth-grade level and has achieved second-grade arithmetic skills. He possesses no trade skills that have any commercial value.

The business sector has greater competence in on-the-job training of hard-core unemployables than any other public or private group. Today, industry is feeling the bite of the failure of urban schools to graduate a reasonable supply of trained labor. The largest corporations in the nation are filling this void by conducting basic classes in grammar-school subjects. Federal agencies are reluctant to yield training prerogatives to private industry, yet the Jobs Corps of the Office of Economic Opportunity was quick to recognize that the most effective program results would be achieved by delegating the job-training effort to private industry. The achievements of companies such as Federal Electric Corporation are extraordinary, not only in vocational training, but also in motivating young dropouts to perceive the connection between the subjects they are required to learn and their career expectations beyond the Job Corps.

It is also likely that the framers of the Economic Opportunity Act of 1964 foresaw that cost efficiencies would be achieved by allowing private industry to perform training functions that were closely related to business needs. For years, the great banks and utilities have had a long and successful record in vocational education, programmed instruction, and employee development. American industry is currently engaged in hundreds of programs for training unemployables. But in most cases these training programs are considered either as a form of "corporate community chest" or as a voluntary "self-inflicted tax" on the profits of the employer to achieve a public social goal. Neither these motives nor Department of Labor subsidies (and regulatory controls) provide industry with a sufficient continuing motivation necessary to sustain the massive rehabilitation, training, and retraining effort needed.

Moreover, the most effective manpower job-training programs are those that occur in the ghetto. Mobile and store-front training within the slum overcomes the Negro's anxiety of traveling to a white plant in the suburbs. Training in the ghetto also bridges the transportation barriers which provide an excuse for not taking advantage of a training opportunity. Store-front training centers in core areas carry signs, advertising to ghetto residents the concern and constructive action being taken by the business operating these centers.[21]

To make job training a prime and urgent responsibility of business, I suggest a training incentive limited solely to establishing store-front training centers in designated poverty areas. I would initially limit the program to store-fronts because of the special value to the Negro community in having large national corporations "hang out their shingle" in slum areas. Private-industry job-training centers in ghetto high schools, churches, and other corporate training activities outside the poverty area would not be eligible for the incentive because of inherent problems of administration.

Anyone who shows up for store-front training in the ghetto is probably worthy of the subsidy. Outside the ghetto, there is no way of computing or allocating the incentive—normal training expense versus expense of training unemployables—except by issuing "a green card" to the hard-core unemployable which entitles the employer to the tax benefit. The "green card" system was proposed by the Kerner Commission, but I don't think the country is ready for a system whereby its citizens carry a printed badge of poverty. The requirement of locating the store-front training center in an eligible poverty area gives reasonable assurance that federal tax funds will be devoted to the most fundamental training needs of the slum community.

I propose an annual income tax credit equal to 2 per cent of the annual costs—rent, real estate taxes, trainee's wages, depreciation (straight line), interest, allocated executive expense—in-

[21] Large metropolitan banks have been particularly effective in store-front education and training centers. New York City's Bankers Trust Company, Chase Manhattan Bank, and First National City Bank have demonstration training and education projects in Harlem. One of the most creative of the nation's privately financed ghetto skill centers belongs to the Security First National Bank of Los Angeles. At a location adjacent to a branch in the Watts South Central area of Los Angeles, the bank hires, recruits through local community-action groups, and trains girls for jobs as computer clerks and teller trainees.

curred by the taxpayer in maintaining new facilities in an eligible poverty area, used exclusively for vocational and job training. Under present law, all training expenses are deductible from taxable income. Thus, an automatic 2 per cent tax credit incentive to businesses which engage in training unemployed is roughly equivalent to the federal government hiring and paying a tax-free fee of 2 per cent of cost for doing the job. The automatic training incentive gives industry broad scope for experimenting in demonstration and innovative training and motivational programs without direction from welfare or community-action groups or administrative agencies. A federal job-corps system, operated by private enterprise on a fee basis, does not provide sufficient business incentives for the massive rehabilitation and training necessary to reduce the number of Negro unemployables. The training costs of a federal program are excessive because the compensation of the industry operator is based on a cost-plus-fee basis. Moreover, the major uncertainty experienced by most businesses, of whether the Department of Labor will allow reimbursement for various aspects of training costs, is avoided. The problems of red tape, forms and follow-up—of "prying the reimbursement out of the federal agency"—no longer act as disincentives to training efforts of the business community.

Conclusion

IN RECENT YEARS I have sat through dozens of business symposiums on the role of business in the ghetto. On this subject I have read endless articles and books. Of one thing I am sure: constructive ideas will emerge only if we can put aside all the semantics of business and ghetto poverty. The tiresome company jargon about "crash programs," "task forces," "target areas," and "business involvement" does not advance or validate anyone's program for enriching the economies of Black Bottom or the Central Ward. Results will come only if we dig a little, and expose the basic wealth-forbidding defects of American slums. Unless we try this, the corrective programs that develop will be no more rewarding than the daily routine of the untrained black who sweeps air in the suburban plant to which he is bussed from the ghetto every morning.

The businessman who views the ghetto economy as simply a pale reflection of the same economic forces that operate in the main economy could not be more wrong. One thing we know for certain is that poverty, especially ghetto poverty, changes all of the rules of classic economics. If the businessman thinks of ghetto poverty simply in terms of almost universal unemployment, he is considering a condition of slum poverty. Unless he also understands how the slum maintains, or increases, its rate of unemployment—at a time when the outside economy hungers for labor—the corrective action he takes will most likely be limited to more "community chest" programs of collecting and creating jobs for the unemployed. If the businessman thinks of ghetto economics only in terms of the decayed and putrid condition of its real estate, his solutions become as easy as they are wrong— weekend ghetto clean-up programs and the simple export (through tax incentives or otherwise) of more bricks and mortar to the slum. Indeed, if we are to avoid the exclusive strategy of more Christmas turkeys and charity for the black poor, the businessman must not think of ghetto economics only in terms of low incomes. He must not overlook the reverse face of poverty which states that almost no one in the ghetto is rich or affluent.

There exist in America today fifteen or more million people living in 163 isolated slums. Each of these black ghettos is structured to prevent the accumulation of wealth in that it is:

(1) Resolutely hardened in its determination to crush profit and incentive, and to oppose investment or technical assistance from the normal economy;

(2) Totally destitute of business patterns of "income certainty" which preclude the attraction of credit and risk capital;

(3) Almost wholly lacking in the ability or motive to save money, or convert even available thrift funds into venture capital;

(4) Completely deprived of any entrepreneurial skill—the essential ability to harness techniques of marketing and production for the formation of wealth;

(5) Wholly isolated from the main economy by a system of tariffs on retail sales, rents, consumer and business credit, and on employment—yet totally dependent on the main economy, from which it imports everything, and to which (in the case of the most deprived ghettos) it exports nothing.

These are the forces which I have often referred to in this book as the "disincentives"—the wealth-forbidding conditions that are present to a degree in any economy. However, in the economy of the slum they are dominant and persistent.

The forces of disincentive have preserved ghetto poverty for many years. Yet, a review of the history of legislation designed to change things in the slums shows that few programs have curbed ghetto poverty. In fact, the public effort has reinforced or sheltered the anarchical processes of the ghetto economy. In pursuit of minority entrepreneurship, government programs have introduced a new array of disincentives, or wealth-forbidding forces, into a market whose patterns of profitlessness, anarchy, and commercial conservatism had already snuffed out the spark of wealth.

Following the 1965 riots in Watts, the American business community, the so-called private sector, for the first time became an additional force on the scene of ghetto economics. The initial reaction of business was a predictable withdrawal of credit and commerce from the slums. Fire-insurance companies red-lined large areas of the ghetto, often making it impossible for ghetto entrepreneurs to finance the start-up or continuation of a business. Burned-out or looted branches of clothing stores and supermarkets withdrew from Watts, and never returned. Municipal bonds of American cities showing a strong black-nationalist profile dropped sharply in market value, reflecting a withdrawal of institutional capital—an overreaction of the investment officer to the credit risks in our cities.

The burning and looting of Detroit and Newark in the summer of 1967 focused the attention of businessmen of America, for the first time, on the basic economic causes of ghetto riots. The result was hundreds of new business-sponsored programs for ghetto unemployables. Of all the reasons that motivate business programs for the slums, none is more forceful than the commerce-crushing threat of the riot and the curfew. Yet riots, as a means of communication from black to white, rarely evoke, or persuade the businessman to undertake, programs of the kind that blacks need. The riots not only produced a massive withdrawal of commerce and capital from the slums, but at the same time gave birth to business programs which were more concerned with keeping "our windows from being busted," keeping the kids off the streets, and getting the blacks into temporary employment, than with reshaping and rebuilding the ghettos so as to expand the ability of blacks to build their skills, train their hard-core unemployables, and place them in career jobs.

The ghetto does not need, to any great extent, the anti-poverty efforts which the businessman's ethic or conscience persuades him to pursue. The businessman's sense of wanting to make amends for having excluded the Negro from employment in the past has produced "resident" Negro assistant vice presidents, token loans to ghetto entrepreneurs, more ghetto summer programs, and "cokes for the kids." The ethic of the old-timers in business—still a powerful force in corporate boardrooms—that associates poverty and unemployment with personal fault and lack of moral fiber called on him to invest in the blind or handicapped poor, the infant poor, or the old poor, but not in the entire economy of poverty. The needs of the entire slum economy for credit and infusions of capital often required the banker to invest against his ethic, and sometimes even against his prejudices.

The other forces which motivate businessmen—their sense of social responsibility, the need to build a strong corporate image, the desire of the organization man to "play it safe" with low-risk programs in the inner city—produced a vast network of business symposiums and conferences on urban poverty and a massive froth of publicity giving birth to ghetto-enrichment action of minor proportions. Even the great innovative corporations that have moved plants and commercial outlets directly into the slum community have a greater institutional need to "hang out their shingle in the ghetto" than to decolonialize the inner city by imparting their wealth-making skills and purchasing power to the advantage of a ghetto entrepreneur. Finally, the businessman's deep conviction that corporate programs in the ghetto interfere with management's prerogatives to hire labor and capital as economically as possible discourage constructive business programs for employment and investment in the black slums.

Clearly, the time has come to develop a new mechanism. Having identified the precise conditions in the slum which prevent its economy from operating in a normal manner, we must move to

206

dismantle the structure of the ghetto economy. The new mechanism must utilize the power and skills of American business. This is inevitable, since the business community is the seat of all wealth-making power in the nation. The great talent of the government to achieve political and social change—and, indeed, its vast economic power as the largest bank in the world—must not be confused with its meager ability for the job of building production and marketing skills—and blending these skills with credit and risk capital for the creation of wealth. The businessman wealth-makers are capable of achieving these objectives in the slums. But progress will not happen until the specific objectives and deficiencies are identified, and specific mandates are devised to use the initiative and skills of the business community to remove the functions that keep the ghetto poor.

If the Negro businessman fails because the outside community of abundance does not export capital, credit, and entrepreneurial training to the core areas, the new mechanism must include an enforced change in economics of the slum which will evoke a new need on the part of the businessman and the banker in the main economy to supply capital, credit, and business training. If the black businessman fails as a producer because he can't market in white communities, we must frame compelling attractions which create a need on the part of the manufacturer in the main economy to "buy black" from ghetto subcontractors and entrepreneurs. If the newly financed ghetto businessman is inevitably headed toward early business failure for lack of business skills, we must build a new and urgent need on the part of national corporations to provide the temporary umbrella of a ghetto business franchise. If the ghetto economy, following the pattern of other traditional and underdeveloped economies, fails to innovate for lack of savings and risk capital, it is necessary to seize those banking institutions in the main economy which are so successful in coaxing people to save, and persuade them to apply their skills to attractive programs of capital and savings development in the slums.

If the ghetto credit marketplace fails to function because it is isolated from the main economy, we must remove the ghetto credit-aversion of the downtown banker by adding an extra few "points" to his yield on slum-origin commercial paper. At the same time, acknowledging the unique capability of the undercapitalized ghetto bank to make enriching loans in the slums, we must strengthen the ability of these banks to lend in the ghetto by creating a new need on the part of large banks and corporations in the normal economy to entrust their money in high-risk time and demand deposits of ghetto banks. The tariff walls which permit a higher price for merchandise north of Ninety-sixth Street in Manhattan must give way by granting an extra increment of value to the income derived by a national supermarket chain from a branch or franchised market in East Harlem.

Since it is so clear that the economic anarchy and profitlessness of the ghetto economy banish the possibility of creating wealth and ownership of productive capital, we must develop new mechanisms to enforce stable patterns of income and expenses in the black communities. This must include a new system of "self-executing" loan guarantees which eliminates all of the disincentives built into the present loan-guarantee programs of the Small Business Administration and the Federal Housing Administration. So long as the black community is openly hostile to white sponsorship of new ghetto banks, brokerage firms, and shopping centers, the corrective program must take this opposition into account by abandoning programs which simply reinforce the condition of the ghetto as a dependent subsidiary of the main economy. The black militants' argument of white man's colonialism must be defeated by offering greater rewards to the outside economy when it shares its entrepreneurial secrets with the untrained black and builds businesses in the slums in partnership with, or for ultimate ownership by, residents of the ghetto. If white attitudes of guilt, "tokenism," or even a need to make reparations produce programs that withdraw promising black executives from the slum into non-career jobs on Main Street, the corrective system must include greater advantages and incentives to the businessman who finances and develops true career opportunities in the ghetto.

We must recognize at the same time that if we set up the Negro for an early business failure in a new bank, brokerage firm, or manufacturing establishment without benefit of a protective franchise, a long-term purchasing agreement, and an assured market for capital and credit, it is we who will have to foreclose and pick up the pieces. And in the end we simply will have reconfirmed the black theory that we intended to take over in the first place.

The system of categorical corrective incentives offers great promise of directing the businessman's efforts away from his own needs and focusing his skills and capital on the needs of the slum economy. It does so in a direct, efficient, and compelling manner. The system cuts directly at the wealth-forbidding processes of the ghetto economy, by-passing the laborious process of creating an expensive new network of federal banks and community-development corporations which must inevitably develop the same conservatism and poverty-preserving delays and disincentives which have infected less ambitious programs in the past. Above all, intelligent planning is capable of shaping the incentives so that they exclude those who hunger only for ghetto tax credits, and at the same time rewarding only those in the white economy who successfully engage in the agonizingly difficult puzzle of creating earned income paid to or from black entrepreneurs who are engaged in a viable and continuing commercial enterprise.

The system of categorical incentives focuses directly on the profitlessness of the slum economy. It totally rejects the preposterous and fatuous dream that the enormous profit potential of a federally sponsored Comsat-type corporation can be matched by selling shares to American investors in a corporation chartered to develop the economies of 163 undeveloped and impoverished black slums.

These categorical incentives will work only if they provide a compelling need on the part of American business to ruthlessly dismantle, brick by brick, the entire tariff structure of the slum economy. The mechanism must also remove the new breed of disincentives in the ghetto which a concerned but misdirected effort—both public and private—has imposed in only recent years. The success of the new effort will depend more on its magnitude than its magnanimity. It will surely fail if its foundation continues to rest only on a sense of generosity, on charity, or on the repayment of a debt for exclusions or injustices of the past.

A Selected Lexicon of
Business and Poverty

The reader is cautioned that seemingly innocent and straightforward definitions often reflect the bias of the author for the correct *strategy for building black enterprise.*

BAD-DEBT LOSS. A lender's annual ratio of uncollectable loans to total outstanding loans. In black-controlled banks, according to the Federal Reserve System, on average, 10 per cent of outstanding loans are overdue.

BASKET CLAUSE. A legal provision in the insurance investment laws of most states which permits an insurance company to invest a designated portion of its assets (often 1 per cent) in high-risk loan or equity commitments. With minor exceptions, American banking laws prohibit 14,000 commercial banks (with aggregate assets of $300 billion) from investing any portion of their assets in equities, second mortgages, or "non-bankable credits" in the ghetto.

BLACK CAPITALISM. The strategy which urges creation of new jobs and profit centers inside ghetto areas. The program also seeks to transfer the ownership of ghetto business from white to black control, at the same time building in the ghetto new banks, insurance companies, production, and service facilities. Today, black capitalism is an insignificant economic force in America.

BLACK LIFE-INSURANCE INDUSTRY. This is the only significant element of black capitalism in America today. The black insurance industry showed dramatic growth before 1950 when the low life expectancy of Negroes insulated the black life-insurance companies from white competition. Since 1963, black life-insurance companies' assets have grown at an average annual rate of 3 per cent, compared to 9.5 per cent for the industry as a whole. Although this industry is

211

the only form of black enterprise (other than ghetto banks) to employ substantial elements of capital in commerce, these companies have assets of only 0.2 per cent of the industry total. The largest Negro-controlled life company, North Carolina Mutual Life, of Durham, North Carolina, has assets of $90 million—about $\frac{1}{300}$th of the size of Prudential Life in Newark.

BLANKET GUARANTEE. The short-form loan-guarantee procedure developed by the Small Business Administration in 1968 to expedite approval of SBA guarantees of minority business-loan applications.

BLOCKED-OPPORTUNITY THEORY. The view that riots are a consequence of the prolonged exclusion of Negroes from the social and economic benefits enjoyed by the main economy.

BMIR (Below Market Interest Rate). A Federal Housing Administration rent-supplement program under which FHA pays subsidies to cooperatives, limited dividend corporations, and non-profit groups sponsoring housing projects (for the displaced, handicapped, aged, and tenement dwellers). The subsidy is the difference between a full market rental and 25 per cent of the tenant's income before taxes.

BRIMMER, ANDREW F. Black economist and governor of the Federal Reserve System, he first demonstrated to American business the ironic and destructive effect on black entrepreneurship of desegregation and white attitudes of equality.

BROWNSVILLE. The notorious ghetto area of Brooklyn, New York, singled out by sociologists as the fastest-decaying slum in America. Brownsville ranks at or near the top in juvenile delinquency, welfare cases, narcotics addiction, venereal diseases, and infant mortality.

BUSINESS AS USUAL. The quality of amnesia in the American business community which permits interest in urban programs to flag after one summer of relative tranquility in the ghetto.

BUSINESS SURVIVAL. The view that it is impossible to maintain a healthy growing total business economy in a nation so long as large numbers of people in the society are poor. Its proposal that business solutions to the urban crises are a necessary condition of business survival is the foundation for current ghetto programs of the National Alliance of Businessmen. The theory of "essential business survival" seriously retards federal incentive programs to build business and

212

commerce in the ghetto, since the strategy incorrectly assumes that the inherent threat of the urban crisis contains within itself an adequate motivating force to persuade businessmen to move forward with ghetto-enrichment programs.

BUY BLACK.   An ancient slogan urging Negroes to utilize their economic consumer power by purchasing only through black-owned shops, black entrepreneurs, and black producers. Currently, the movement is receiving significant support from the National Urban League and the Honeywell Corporation in Minneapolis.

CATEGORICAL CORRECTIVE INCENTIVES.   A proposed system of ghetto tax credits whose objective is a systematic isolation, identification, and dismantling of specific qualities which prevent slum economies from developing the ownership of capital. Unlike conventional ghetto-tax-credit proposals which concentrate on the creation of black jobs outside the ghetto and on white-controlled employment within the ghetto, this system expands the capability of the slum economy to use labor and create work. This system emphasizes, too, the need of the slum economy to expand its capability of using commercial credit, to develop its power to generate savings and risk capital, to enlarge its capability to produce for and market in the entire economy, and, most important, to break the grip of the traditional forces of economic conservatism which prevent the slum economy from beginning to innovate.

CENTRAL WARD.   This vast ghetto area of Newark, New Jersey, houses 400,000 blacks. Unemployment is officially set at 12 per cent, unofficially as high as 20 per cent. Seventeen thousand households live on incomes of less than $3,000 a year. The Central Ward and Brownsville, in Brooklyn, lead all ghettos of the nation in crime rate, venereal disease, and maternal mortality.

CHANCE TO FAIL.   This view insists that the Negro will never "make it" in business unless he is given an opportunity to compete on equal terms with the white entrepreneur. It ignores the unassailable facts that desegregation and the resulting new white competition for black patronage have (1) caused the total number of black businesses to shrink by 20 per cent between 1950 and 1960, (2) severely reduced the growth rate of Negro insurance companies, and (3) caused wholesale failures, during the past decade, of black service establishments such as funeral and nursing homes, dry cleaners, grocery stores, and hotels.

CHARITY IN THE GHETTO. The businessman's need to "do his part" and simply share his wealth with the ghetto poor, rather than share his knowledge of how to grow rich. The strategy of charity as a solution to the problems of the poor (currently reflected in the slogan of the Urban Coalition, "Give Money, Give Jobs, Give a Damn") dates to the earliest periods of Christian civilization. The first significant business departure from this policy of grants in the ghetto occurred in October, 1968, when the Ford Foundation announced a permanent program of *investing* in ghetto businesses and enterprises.

CLEAN-UP LOAN. A refunding loan. One of the most urgent credit needs of the slum economy. The normal economy borrows "long." The ghetto borrows "short," often pyramiding short-maturity loans collateralized by multiple liens on real estate or on a chattel. The ghetto borrower therefore has a frequent and urgent need to "stretch out" or consolidate existing loans.

CODE ENFORCEMENT. The theory that enforcement of building codes will force an abandonment of tenements by absentee slumlords and work a transfer of ownership to slum residents.

COLONIAL CONSPIRACY. The belief of black militants that white society deliberately preserves poverty in the ghetto, and retains absentee control and ownership of slum property and business, to assure the white economy of a continuing supply of black people to fill menial and domestic jobs. The theory views business job-programs for blacks as an effort to divert potential black activists. The banker's offer of capital and loans is further regarded as a bribe to the "Uncle Toms" to help the whites perfect their ownership and control of the ghetto economy.

CONTROLLED-RISK LOANS. An abnormally high-risk commercial bank loan extended to a borrower of untested credit, or to one who operates in an economic environment in which the risks of default are higher than normal. The unique capability of controlled-risk lenders is an ability to take quick and constructive measures to salvage the business and credit of a commercial borrower who threatens a default. The emerging talent of banks to deal with high-risk credits is a cogent argument for developing a system of private ghetto-development banks in preference to a national ghetto-development bank, in which the practice of taking unusual credit risks must inevitably become subordinate to the economic conservatism of a banking bureaucracy.

214

CORE-AREA SERVICE CLUSTER. The theory that greater leverage for ghetto enrichment is achieved by concentrating investment capital in a limited slum area. The premise of the core-area service cluster is that dispersed investments in the ghetto ultimately "return to the jungle," taking on the decaying character of surrounding real estate; whereas, through the force of leverage, a concentrated investment of the *same* funds adds new wealth to surrounding real estate. The most significant example in America of a concentrated core-area service cluster is the massive Bedford-Stuyvesant Restoration Corporation project in the black slum of Brooklyn.

COST PREROGATIVES. The essential and well-guarded privilege of American businessmen to maximize profits by purchasing labor, operating plants, and investing capital as efficiently as possible. The prerogative is a serious obstacle to (1) programs for training and hiring slum unemployables, (2) bank commitments to soft ghetto loans and mortgages, (3) locating production and service facilities in ghetto areas of high capital risk and low labor efficiency.

CREDIT-DISCRIMINATION DILEMMA. The essential reluctance of the white bankers to either (1) incur the community wrath (black and white) by charging the ghetto borrower with the high free-market interest rate which income uncertainties of the slum economy require, or (2) make a soft ghetto loan at low downtown rates which bank examiners, loan committees, and the public will criticize if the credit turns out to be uncollectable. The ghetto black-controlled bank is not burdened by the credit-discrimination dilemma because it recognizes the credit tariffs of the ghetto and therefore charges a higher-interest loan rate on commercial and personal loans than do white-controlled banks.

DECOLONIALIZATION. The process of transferring control and ownership of ghetto real estate and business from whites to blacks. The most significant example of ghetto decolonialization occurred in late 1968 when F. W. Woolworth completed a two-million-dollar sale and leaseback of its Harlem store to a black syndicate, Harlem Freedom Associates.

DEMONSTRATION PROJECT. An innovative business experiment for building new kinds of enriching facilities in a ghetto, or (invidiously) a commercial showcase which merely "dresses" or "gilds" the ghetto, advancing only the public image of the sponsoring corporation for "doing its part."

215

DESERVING POOR. The traditional beneficiary of corporate charity and federal aid. The ethic of the businessman and the bureaucrat that plain poverty is a sin, yet poverty of the handicapped is worthy, is a major barrier to constructive programs to rebuild the whole economy of ghetto poverty.

ECONOMIC CONSERVATISM. The essential debilitating quality of the black economy. The failure to innovate commercially occurs at all levels of ghetto commerce.

ECONOMIC-INTEGRATION CHOICE (also GHETTO-DISPERSAL CHOICE). This theory holds that the greatest economic good for blacks would be achieved by writing off the ghetto as an archaic and obsolete economy, and working toward programs that would absorb Negro entrepreneurs and workers into the entire economy.

ENTREPRENEURIAL SEGREGATION. The protective commercial monopoly formerly enjoyed by the ghetto service business. See *Ghetto Business Monopoly*.

FEDERAL DEPOSIT INSURANCE. The precedent for the proposal of self-executing federal loan guarantees. Under a federal law dating back to the Great Depression, a depositor may, by the simple act of depositing money in a bank, acquire a promise by an agency of the federal government that his deposit will be repaid.

FEDERAL HOUSING ADMINISTRATION. An agency of the federal government with broad powers and capabilities of generating ownership of highly leveraged home equities. FHA has mostly rejected equities in the cities, favoring short-term leases for the urban poor.

FIVE-PERCENTER. In the loan shark's lexicon, someone who lends money at an interest rate of 5 per cent a week (260 per cent a year).

FLIPPING (or SWITCHING). The small-loan companies' practice of persuading the inexperienced borrower to convert an installment sales contract to a more profitable small loan. The technique of flipping decreases monthly payments, but enlarges the over-all debt.

FREEDMEN'S BANKS. A system of black-owned-and-controlled banks established after the Civil War. Most of the Freedmen's Bank units failed in the panics and the depressions of the past seventy-five years.

216

FREEDOM NATIONAL BANK. The largest Negro-controlled bank in America, with its principal office in West Harlem and one branch in the Bedford-Stuyvesant ghetto of Brooklyn. Freedom National has assets of $27 million, and, in size, ranks 1,733 among banks in the United States. Although a magnificent monument to black capitalism, its capability of bringing commercial credit into New York's ghetto areas is almost insignificant.

GARNISHMENT. The legal process whereby a creditor may compel an employer to pay wages owed to an employee directly to the creditor to whom the employee is indebted. In the ghetto economy, according to the Federal Trade Commission, the process of garnishment is used at the rate of one garnishment suit for every $2,600 in consumer sales. The garnishment rate is one suit for every $232,000 in the economy as a whole. In recent years, many states have properly restricted the creditor's remedy of garnishment. The effect has been to restrict further the availability of normal credit in the ghetto.

GHETTO BUSINESS MONOPOLY. The immunity enjoyed by ghetto businesses from white competition. Since 1950, attitudes favoring social integration and new laws banning discrimination against blacks have opened up the entire economy to black patronage. The monopoly which was formerly assured to ghetto hotels, banks, life-insurance companies, and restaurants has all but disappeared.

GHETTO CREDIT ABDICATION. The ultimate decision of an institutional lender to withdraw all credit from the ghetto economy rather than face the social opprobrium of establishing, or enforcing, a compensating interest cost which society would consider usurious.

GHETTO CREDIT CARD. A plan advocated by the Washington, D.C., branch of the National Urban League proposing the organization of a federally subsidized bank or foundation to issue consumer-purchase credit cards to ghetto residents. The plan would substitute a monthly credit charge of one per cent or more as a substitute for the present ghetto consumer credit system which, through the system of "add-on" interest charges, levies an effective interest cost of up to three to four times the rate prevailing in the normal credit economy.

GHETTO CREDIT GAP. The failure of credit to move from the normal economy into the black slum. A condition that is due more to

217

higher lending costs and lower loan-repayment capabilities in the black economy than to credit discrimination on the part of the downtown banker.

GHETTO DEALERSHIPS. The automobile or appliance dealer, the essential example of small-business entrepreneurship in the normal economy, is missing in the black economy. Of the 17,500 authorized automobile dealers in the country, seven are black (seven times as many as there were in 1966).

GHETTO-DEVELOPMENT BANK (Private). A privately owned financial institution (usually formed and controlled by one or more banks) with broad chartered powers for making high-risk ghetto loans and equity investments which are outside the regulatory control of bank and insurance-company examiners. The prototype private ghetto-development bank was formed in May, 1968, and capitalized at one million dollars by the Citizens and Southern National Bank of Georgia.

GHETTO-DEVELOPMENT BANK (Public). A proposal advocated by Senators Jacob Javits and Charles Percy for the Congressional chartering of a federal bank, similar to the highly successful World Bank, with broad powers and capability of lending and investing in the underdeveloped slum economies. The proposal is premised on the belief that the nation's private banks (with or without the benefit of subsidies and ghetto loan-repayment guarantees) can never overcome their deep-seated ghetto investment risk-aversion.

GHETTO-ENRICHMENT CHOICE. This strategy gives priority to programs for building in the ghetto normal patterns of commercial credit, Negro ownership of capital, and new economic facilities to make it possible for blacks to develop so that they will be able to produce and market in the entire economy. The theory rejects the strategy of immediately integrating blacks into the main economy, particularly in the form of "bussing" them to suburban jobs.

GHETTO INVESTMENT RISK-AVERSION. The undeniably logical and correct view of the institutional lending officer that an unsubsidized, or non-guaranteed, commitment of private credit or capital to a ghetto enterprise is an imprudent investment of stockholder capital. The institutional investor's ghetto risk-aversion is often reflected in an overreaction to the inherent risks of income uncertainty and rioting in the slum economies.

218

GHETTO LOAN-PRODUCTION OFFICES. Branch banking offices (of questionable legality in many states) which solicit and originate consumer and commercial loans in slum areas.

GHETTO-ORIGIN COMMERCIAL PAPER. Time loans and promissory notes executed by a ghetto borrower as consideration for the purchase of high-priced items in the slum economy. Because bankers are reluctant "to pull the string" on a Negro borrower, they increasingly refuse to discount or purchase slum-origin commercial paper. As a result, ghetto credit merchants and factors take the paper at exorbitant interest rates and pass these charges on to the ghetto consumer.

GHETTO PAYMENTS DEFICIT. The adverse flow of money and capital from the ghetto economy into the normal economy. The ghetto's unfavorable balance-of-payments gap is reflected in these ways: (1) Negro-owned life-insurance companies invest ghetto premium revenues in government bonds and corporate obligations rather than in core-area mortgages; (2) white-controlled banks with branches in slum areas reinvest ghetto savings outside the ghetto; (3) absentee owners of ghetto businesses and real estate deposit profits in banks downtown rather than in interracial banks doing business in the ghetto.

GHETTO PROFIT OVERKILL. The technique whereby the ghetto economy—speaking through its power to riot; its inability to marshal risk capital, credit, or marketing and production skills; its excessive costs of capital; its unreliable labor; its anarchical consumer markets; and its opposition to economic support from the white economy—excludes the development in the black slum of normal patterns of commerce, personal affluence, and the ownership of capital.

GHETTO TAX CREDITS. Proposals for the amendment of federal tax laws (either in the form of extra depreciation allowances or direct credits on taxes otherwise payable) which grant tax abatements to corporations and individuals who pursue certain anti-poverty (or ghetto-enrichment) programs. This system grants a direct self-executing subsidy to the project sponsor. The theory of ghetto tax credits is opposed, in principle, to the extension of the present system of federal aids which makes a subsidy benefit available only through an intermediate federal agency (typically the Small Business Administration and the Federal Housing Administration) which must give prior approval to the ghetto expenditure or investment.

219

GHETTO UNDERBANKING. The almost total absence of deposit-oriented institutions in the black slum areas. In New York City as a whole the ratio of commercial banks is one for every *five thousand* residents. In Harlem, the financial center of the black economy, the ratio is one commercial bank for every *thirty thousand* residents. The Brooklyn Bedford-Stuyvesant ghetto of 400,000 inhabitants, the country's most pernicious slum (slightly smaller in population than the entire city of Cincinnati, and all black), has one commercial bank.

GUARANTEED GHETTO BANK DEBENTURES. A proposal which recognizes the ability of ghetto banks (not enjoyed by white banks) to make high-risk, high-interest-rate loans in the slum economy, without being accused of credit gouging—and therefore urges an automatic federal repayment guarantee of debentures issued by indigenous poverty-area banks. The purpose of the federal guarantee is to facilitate the ability of the weak and undercapitalized ghetto banks to compete nationwide for capital and deposits.

GUARANTEED INCOME MAINTENANCE. A national goal, now advocated by leading businessmen, which would put sufficient income directly into the hands of the poor so as to bring the annual income of all families of four up to the poverty threshold of approximately $3,300 a year. The cost of this program, which would replace the present national welfare system, has been calculated from $13 billion to $30 billion a year. Aside from cost, the serious problem in this strategy is how to prevent the beneficiary of guaranteed income maintenance from reducing his work effort to zero.

HARD-CORE AFFLUENCE. A condition of personal wealth, existing almost entirely in the normal white economy, under which the negative forces of extravagant personal spending and sometimes confiscatory income taxes fail to diminish the ability of the rich to grow richer. The system of corrective incentives has as a goal the production of elements of hard-core affluence in the ghetto, as well as the elimination of its hard-core poverty.

HIGH SOCIAL YIELD. A euphemistic expression that notes the collateral benefits to be derived from an economically unsound "soft" loan or business investment made in the slum economy. The premise of high social yield is not an adequate or a durable motivation for moving credit or investment capital into the ghetto economy. The expression obscures the urgent need for "hard" credit subsidies or incentives.

HIP-POCKET LENDER.   The loan shark, who presently dominates the ghetto credit economy. Hearings in 1967 before the Clark Senate Committee produced testimony that a large percentage of new business start-ups in the Puerto Rican and black economies of New York City are financed by sharks.

HOTEL THERESA.   A Harlem hotel, once the social center of New York's black community, but now in bankruptcy—a symbol of the damaging effect of social integration on black businesses and entrepreneurship.

INCOME CERTAINTY.   A borrower's pattern of stable business income which gives reasonable assurance to a loan officer that a credit will be repaid with interest. The income uncertainty of the ghetto entrepreneur is so great (or so widely unpredictable) that it is impossible to set credit terms that are at the same time fair to the ghetto borrower and to the stockholders of the ghetto lending institution.

INSTANT REHABILITATION.   An innovative tenement-rehabilitation technique whose feasibility was first demonstrated by United States Gypsum and the Carol W. Haussamen Foundation in New York City. The process permits removal of the core of a tenement building and the substitution of a prefabricated tier of kitchen-bathroom units —all in a period of 48 hours.

INTEREST SENSITIVITY.   A time-honored economic principle which states that a well-advertised increase of one-half a percentage point in interest rates (which competition fails to meet) will move millions of dollars of savings and capital across a continent. *Interest Sensitivity* operates to attract money only in a highly developed economy of sophisticated credit markets. The ghetto economy is almost totally interest insensitive. This is one of the most serious obstacles to framing workable incentives to encourage the formation of savings and credit in the ghetto.

INVESTMENT AND LOAN QUOTAS.   The view that banks, insurance companies, and other financial institutions "affected by the public interest" should be required by law, as a condition to enjoying a continued public franchise, to earmark a specific percentage of their assets to investments and loans in urban core areas.

INVESTMENT DIVERSION.   A form of charitable pledge of capital funds to the ghetto economy. The process under which a bank or

221

institutional investor shifts the normal flow of investment capital from "hard" and competitive loans or investments in the normal economy to "soft," non-competitive investments in the ghetto economy. The 1967 pledge by the nation's life-insurance companies of one billion dollars of mortgage funds to ghetto areas is an example of this process. Investment diversion runs counter to the theories of Self-Inflicted Taxation and the Ghetto Investment Risk-Aversion.

JOBS NOW.　A nationwide private business effort to put blacks in jobs. An important billion-dollar annual expenditure which nevertheless fails to give necessary emphasis to an expansion of the employment capabilities of the ghetto economy.

JOHNSON, JOHN H.　The pre-eminent American Negro entrepreneur. He heads a publishing empire (*Ebony, Jet,* and *Tan*) and is Board Chairman of the $34 million Supreme Life Insurance Company of Chicago.

LEVERAGE.　The use of borrowed money, in combination with risk capital, to magnify the value of an initial stake. The technique of leverage (in the sophisticated form of a high-risk commercial loan or unsophisticated form of a 90 per cent FHA home mortgage) is a common route to wealth or affluence in the normal economy. The ghetto economy almost never uses leverage to acquire (or magnify the value) of real estate or capital goods.

LO-BALLING.　A marketing device of the ghetto merchant gouger. The promise of a service—usually on an automobile—at an outrageously low price. The work is performed, but only as a ploy to gain possession of the automobile in order to charge the owner for additional, unneeded repairs.

MAXIMUM FEASIBLE PARTICIPATION BY THE POOR.　A fundamental concept of the *Economic Opportunity Act of 1964* which encourages ghetto residents to aid each other, thus drawing together and strengthening the slum.

MOBILE SAVINGS UNIT.　A mobile bank savings unit (illegal in many states) operating in the slum economy to encourage savings accounts in ghetto areas.

ONE-BANK HOLDING COMPANY.　A corporate device which permits a commercial bank to become a subsidiary of a parent holding company. By forming a "sister" subsidiary, the bank may engage indirectly in high-risk investment, lending, and other activities which the law would not permit it to perform directly.

PARKS, HENRY G. A black entrepreneur who first demonstrated that a black could produce and market in the white economy. From Baltimore Mr. Parks sells $7.5 million of sausages a year ("More Park Sausages, Ma") to blacks and whites. In early 1968, Mr. Parks's firm sold shares publicly through a leading New York underwriter.

PARKS, MRS. ROSA. On December 1, 1955, Mrs. Rosa Parks boarded a Cleveland Avenue bus in Montgomery, Alabama. The Negro revolt properly dates from this day when Mrs. Parks said "no" to the bus driver's demand that she get up and let a white man have her seat.

PASSBOOKS SAVINGS ACCOUNTS. The dominant form of bank account employed by most ghetto businesses and individuals. In the Brownsville section of Brooklyn, up to 98 per cent of bank accounts take the form of small, active, high-cost savings accounts. The ghetto bank's high ratio of active high-cost savings accounts to non-interest-bearing and low-cost checking accounts is one of the most destructive tariffs which the ghetto economy imposes on the operations of its financial institutions.

POST-AUDIT REVIEW. A proposed system of government audit and review, by which the function of federal agencies guaranteeing ghetto loans is limited to a compliance audit or review of a ghetto credit *after* the credit has been committed. This device gives assurance that the lending institution is acting under pre-established guidelines in accordance with declared ghetto-enrichment policies of the United States. The purpose of the post-audit review of ghetto loan commitments is to eliminate present Federal Housing Administration and Small Business Administration procedures which require time-consuming paperwork and delays in obtaining approvals of federally insured ghetto credits.

POVERTICIAN. In the lexicon of the ghetto, one who deals in, or profits from, the politics of poverty.

PRIVATE LOAN GUARANTOR. A private organization (usually a charitable institution) or syndicate of guarantors which acts as a guarantor of the repayment of a third-party business loan made in the ghetto economy. The function of the private loan guarantor is

223

to convert a "soft" ghetto loan into a bankable credit acceptable to bank loan officers and examiners. The prototype ghetto loan guarantor is the Interracial Council of Business Opportunity in New York City.

REVERSE FACE OF POVERTY. The view of ghetto poverty which notes the ability of the ghetto economy to bar hard-core affluence, as well as its power to guarantee that successive generations of its residents will live in hard-core poverty.

RIFFRAFF THEORY. The view that rioters are irresponsible deviants, unassimilated migrants, emotionally disturbed persons, or members of an underclass. This "theory" opposes the view that ghetto rioting is a result of blocked opportunities or economic exclusions.

RIOT. The single most *ineffective* method of communicating the real economic needs of the ghetto to the main economy. Forty or more American ghettos are still convalescing from the massive outflow of business and capital that resulted from summer rioting in 1966 and 1967.

RISK CAPITAL. The wealth-building process, almost totally lacking in the ghetto economy, of generating discretionary income and converting it into venture capital for commitment to a business opportunity.

SECOND-MORTGAGE DEPENDENCY. The essential reliance of the black slum economy on secondary liens as collateral security for home and business loans.

SELF-EXECUTING LOAN GUARANTEES. A device which would permit regulated credit institutions, particularly banks and insurance companies, to commit, by their own act, the credit of the government to certain investments which Congress designates as usually enriching to the ghetto economy. An essential feature of the proposed system of categorical corrective incentives.

SELF-INFLICTED TAX. The view that American business cannot and will not indefinitely pursue expensive programs of training and hiring the hard-core unemployed and continue to invest in inefficient core-area production facilities, since the expenditure is, in effect, a form of self-taxation—a voluntary and inefficient dedication of private capital for a public good.

224

SMALL BUSINESS ADMINISTRATION. An agency of the federal government established to finance and assist small businessmen in America. For many years, its loan programs have been plagued by red tape, onerous bureaucratic procedures, and inadequate funding from Congress.

SOCIAL ENGINEERING. Business anti-poverty programs regarded by most businessmen as a "soft science" having nothing to do with the conduct of his business.

SOFT LOANS. A retail or commercial credit extended in the ghetto economy to a black borrower whose credit profile is considered unbankable. The soft loan is, in reality, a charitable gift, except that it is not deductible for tax purposes until it fails—and is written off against the lender's bad-debt reserve. This is the essential irony of an income tax system which subsidizes charity for the poor (which has never worked) and leaves soft loans (which might work) solely to the conscience of the benefactor.

SUBMARGINAL LOAN. A soft loan or a high-risk loan. A credit that falls short of being "bankable" or "hard" because of weakness in the collateral that secures it, a poor credit rating of the borrower, or the fact that it originates in an undeveloped economy. The loan is submarginal when the cost of originating and servicing the loan, in combination with the lender's allocated cost of capital, overhead, and expected bad-debt loss, exceeds the achievable interest charge on the loan.

STORE-FRONT CREDIT ACADEMIES. A ghetto banking office, not legally qualifying as a branch bank, where banking executives instruct ghetto-area residents and businessmen in techniques of credit and family financial planning.

TRADITIONAL ECONOMY. An underdeveloped or economically conservative economy, typically a ghetto economy, which fails to innovate because it has too much to lose by risking savings on labor-saving machinery or in a new business opportunity.

TRANSPORTATIONISTS. Those who believe that the most important inroads toward normalizing the ghetto economy can be achieved by improving and increasing public transportation facilities between ghetto areas and the white economy.

225

VIGORISH. The installment of interest that a ghetto (or non-ghetto) borrower pays to his loan shark every Friday.

WOODLAWN. A Chicago black ghetto, until the 1940's a desirable residential extension of the University of Chicago community. Now the principal "port of entry" for blacks migrating to Chicago from the South.

An Overview of Black Entrepreneurship and Company Programs in the Ghetto

Following is a selected listing of examples of black capitalism in America today. I have also included programs for black entrepreneurship and capital ownership which have been developed by white-controlled companies and non-profit institutions. Government efforts have been listed where the program thrust was to put blacks into commerce or equities. Generally, projects which simply repeat the efforts of other firms have been omitted. Five thousand or more company programs for hiring hard-core jobless have been excluded except when they are unusually large, innovative, or include a collateral effort to develop black business. Modest efforts which move toward building equities, risk capital, and credit-leverage in the ghetto have been favored over more costly programs contemplating new white-controlled jobs and plants.

I make my apology now to the dozens of distinguished and creative efforts which have not come to my attention, and therefore have not been included.

ACCORD INC. This Detroit-based corporation has sold stock at $1 a share in its drive to raise $10 million for slum rehabilitation and development of black-owned businesses.

ACTION INDUSTRIES. Labeled a "ghetto conglomerate," this community-controlled corporation runs a wide variety of businesses in the depressed Venice section of Los Angeles. Public financing is to be provided by a $1 million sale of preferred and Class A stock—but control will rest with the Class B shares, all of which are restricted to a non-profit community organization, Project Action.

227

AETNA LIFE & CASUALTY COMPANY. This large Hartford insurance company has attacked the problem of the hard-core unemployed in a unique manner. Informed by the Connecticut state labor department that many jobs go begging because the unemployed lack driving licenses, Aetna set up a five-week driver-education course for Hartford high-school dropouts, with the candidates recruited by the Urban League.

AIM—JOBS. Leading manufacturers in Cleveland—General Motors, Ford, General Electric, TRW, and Republic Steel, among others— banded together after the Hough riots of 1966 to form Action in Manpower—JOBS, to find jobs for the unemployed. The companies have lent executives to AIM, continuing to pay their salaries. Backed by government manpower-training funds, AIM placed more than 1,400 persons in its first year of operation.

ALBINA ECONOMIC DEVELOPMENT DEMONSTRATION PROJECT. This OEO-funded project in Portland, Ore., is an effort to create new resident-owned businesses in a depressed inner-city area. Albina Corp. is engaged in wood- and metal-fabricating and has started production of fiberglass boats. An innovative feature is the Albina Investment Trust, set up as an employee deferred-compensation trust. Using OEO grant funds, the Trust will purchase the stock of Albina Corp. on behalf of the employees. The Trust will administer the stock and will eventually be able to use expected earnings for further economic development in the community. Employees will share in the Trust and will have the option of making additional contributions of savings to the Trust to build further equity.

AMERICAN AIRLINES, INC. AA became the first airline to hire a black pilot—in 1964. The company now has nine. The number of black stewardesses went from 25 in 1967 to 53 in 1968.

AMERICAN DREAM SOAP CO. A black-owned Cleveland soap company formed in December, 1968, by Cecil King, a 33-year-old former bank loan teller and real estate agent, and Dr. Ralph Gardner, ex-Sohio chemist. The first products are a soap for dishes (Dream Liquid), a laundry detergent (Jet Power), a facial soap (Dream), and a deodorant (Dreamex). Until American Dream gets its own plant, all products are being manufactured by Theobald Corp., Kearney, N.J., and Duveen Soap Corp., Brooklyn, N.Y.

228

AMERICAN INSTITUTE OF ARCHITECTS. The Institute has established community design centers throughout the country. Located in ghetto store-fronts or in AIA chapter offices, the centers provide design guidance to people too poor to pay for it. Projects range from housing rehabilitation to the planning of parks.

AMERICAN TELEPHONE & TELEGRAPH. As the largest employer in the nation, AT&T probably has trained more hard-core unemployed than the federally financed Job Corps program of the Office of Economic Opportunity. Between 1964 and 1967, the Bell System's black employment went from 29,000 to 51,000. AT&T units around the country and Bell subsidiary Western Electric have been active in a broad range of programs to fight poverty in urban areas. Much of this effort has been directed to education, with Bell companies working closely with public-school officials. AT&T's corporate policy-makers have featured Negroes in AT&T ads, published a monthly internal magazine, *The City,* and sponsored a highly acclaimed TV series on the urban crisis, replacing the long-standing Bell Telephone Hour.

ARMSTRONG CORK CO. One of the country's largest producers of building materials, Armstrong Cork is developing prefabricated products in an effort to drive down the cost of housing. The company has utilized these products in the conversion of a deteriorated Philadelphia building into apartment units and the rehabilitation of nine row-houses in its home city of Lancaster, Pa.

ASSOCIATION TO ASSIST NEGRO BUSINESSES. A New York City syndicate of 13 guarantors who arrange, service, and back loans to small business enterprises in New York City ghetto areas. Its stated object is to short-cut delays and red tape under Small Business Administration applications. The Association sells the loans to interracial Freedom National Bank in Harlem, enabling the bank to move commercial credit into ghettos without assuming the entire risk. Freedom National has indicated that once the loan is partially repaid and the borrower has shown substantial progress, the Association guarantors will be released from the guarantee and then will be in a position to back other loans.

AVCO CORPORATION. Avco's Economic Systems division put a one-million-dollar printing plant into Boston's Roxbury ghetto in early 1968. One year later the plant was operating with a staff of nearly 200 men and women recruited from the ranks of Roxbury's hard-core unemployed blacks. Avco reported it had applications from 1,300 others.

B. GREEN & COMPANY. This major Baltimore food wholesaler helped small Negro grocers take over ghetto supermarkets in the wake of the rioting which followed the assassination of Martin Luther King, Jr. A key aid was the supply of $30,000 of inventory credit.

BANK OF AMERICA. In July, 1968, the world's largest bank earmarked $100 million for residential mortgages in California's blighted ghettos. The bank set up a special cadre of more than 100 lending officers to implement the move on a statewide basis.

BANKERS TRUST COMPANY. This New York City bank is turning one of its ghetto branches (after normal banking hours) into a schoolhouse to train and develop black businessmen. The New York City Interracial Council for Business Opportunity will sponsor seminars at the bank branch at Madison Avenue and 116 Street in Harlem to teach Negro small businessmen the art of business organization, use of credit, methods of merchandizing, law, and accounting.

BCIC. The Bicentennial Civic Improvement Corporation was created in St. Louis by leading businesses to serve as a real estate developer and broker for the poor. BCIC buys rundown buildings for an average of $1,500 per dwelling unit, rehabilitates them for another $5,000, and then makes them available to tenants for about $70-a-month rent. Special financing arrangements make possible 100 per cent mortgages at 6 per cent over 15 years.

BEDFORD-STUYVESANT DEVELOPMENT & SERVICES CORPORATION. Devised by the late Senator Robert F. Kennedy, this is the nation's most successful and innovative program for black capitalism. A community-development corporation, with impressive support from business and banking leaders, it has resulted in the start of at least a dozen new enterprises in the Bedford-Stuyvesant slum of Brooklyn, N.Y. Projects include the establishment of manpower-training centers; the rehabilitation and renovation of rundown homes; the opening of a 300-man IBM plant; and the launching of "Inside Bedford-Stuyvesant," a community-produced television program that "tells it like it is."

BETTER HOMES FOR SPRINGFIELD, INC. Companies in Springfield, Mass., formed this corporation in 1966 to establish a revolving fund

230

for the improvement of housing for low-income families. Financial institutions, led by the Springfield Institution for Savings, have backed the group, providing not only the necessary credit but help in the development of black contractors to do the building.

BETTER ROCHESTER LIVING, INC. This program encourages the poor to become home owners and teaches them property maintenance and rehabilitation. BRL acquires, rehabilitates and sells one- and two-family homes for $10,000 to $11,000 each, under 6 per cent, 25-year FHA mortgages. Tenants with annual incomes of $4,000 to $6,000 rent the homes, with option to buy. Tenants renovate their property themselves when possible, financed and supervised by BRL. BRL also provides counseling on credit and home maintenance. More than 400 Rochester families have taken steps to improve their earning power and credit rating in hopes of qualifying under this low-cost housing program.

BLACK COALITION. An economic development program designed to secure jobs, houses, education, and health services for the disadvantaged in Philadelphia. The Black Coalition was launched with a pledge of $1 million from 60 Philadelphia banks and businesses, with the drive spearheaded by R. Stewart Rauch, Jr., president of the Philadelphia Savings Fund Society.

BLACK ECONOMIC UNION. A non-profit organization started by ex-football great Jim Brown, it has offices in six cities helping Negroes to start their own businesses.

BLACK PEOPLE'S UNITY MOVEMENT. This self-help organization was started in Camden, N.J., with the support of leading businesses in the area. One of its first moves was the opening of a black-owned African-style garment factory.

BLACK STAR COOPERATIVE. Money raised in Detroit's black community has helped this cooperative launch a supermarket, a gas station, and a clothing-manufacturing plant. The enterprise is headed by Rev. Albert Cleage, black militant leader and pastor of the Church of the Black Madonna.

BLACK SUPERMARKETS. Giving blacks a stake in food retailing is recognized as an important step in ghetto economic development. Supermarket chains have moved in this direction in a number of cities. Safeway has aided black grocers in San Francisco and Wash-

231

ington, D.C. Giant Foods also has a major program in Washington, D.C. Jewel Tea assisted black stores in Chicago. In Chicago, A&P stores in the black ghetto now stock the products of 17 black-owned companies, among them Joe Louis milk, Baldwin ice cream, Conway's pine oil and Golden Crown lemon juice. In New York, the Waldbaum grocery chain has concentrated on the development of black managerial personnel.

BOARD FOR FUNDAMENTAL EDUCATION. A non-profit organization based in Indianapolis, BFE specializes in on-the-job instruction in reading, writing, spelling, arithmetic, and basic grammar. It has trained more than 80,000 workers, as well as 4,000 teachers, in plants all over the country.

BOSTON BANKS URBAN RENEWAL GROUP. This group of 20 lending institutions was organized in Boston in 1962 to assist financing of homes for low-income families. A total of $20 million has been set aside for this program. One of the group's prime accomplishments has been to take on unqualified applicants (those with poor credit ratings) and reconstruct their financial picture so that they are eligible for credits. The banking group, operating out of a store-front office in Roxbury, grants a personal interview to every applicant. Example of activity: in December, 1966, 72 mortgages were assigned to member banks with a financing total of $1,127,350.

BOWERY SAVINGS BANK. Bowery is one of the more venturesome of New York City thrift institutions participating in a statewide savings-bank program to rehabilitate deteriorating properties in disadvantaged areas. Altogether, Bowery has completed ghetto-rehabilitation loans totaling more than $11.2 million. In an unusually dramatic demonstration project, Bowery made an $800,000 loan to rehabilitate two vacant, boarded-up tenements consisting of 42 dwelling units at 438–444 East 120th Street in East Harlem.

BRISTOL-MYERS COMPANY. The drug and cosmetic producer gave $100,000 to the New York Urban Coalition, which was used for an "Operation Better Block" program and "Operation Sports Rescue," a project which brought name athletes into the ghetto to talk to groups of youngsters. In Stamford, Conn., home of Bristol Myers' Clairol plant, the company gave $22,000 to a non-profit Negro corporation for acquisition of a 53,000-square-foot site where a 90-unit low-income cooperative will be built.

232

BROWN SHOE COMPANY. This major shoe producer, which moved out of St. Louis in 1956, returned in 1968, breaking ground for a new $1 million facility in the heart of the city's Yeatman slum. Some 200 ghetto residents are expected to be employed.

BURP. Boston Urban Rehabilitation Program, a 3,000-unit rehabilitation program in the Roxbury ghetto of Boston. The project, heavily endowed by Eastern Gas & Fuel's affiliate, Boston Gas Company, will use only gas for heating purposes. Eli Goldston, Eastern Gas president, adopted the now-famous slogan, "when you BURP, think GAS!"

BUSINESS & JOB DEVELOPMENT CORPORATION. This black-led organization is Pittsburgh's first major effort to promote black capitalism. Funded by both federal and private sources, BJD seeks to bring plants into the ghetto and to start more Negro-owned businesses. With close ties to Pittsburgh business leaders, BDC aims to serve as a bridge between the establishment and the black community.

BUSINESS DEVELOPMENT CORPORATION. This profit-making Philadelphia company is owned by 3,000 Negro stockholders who each put up $2 a share. It has arranged more than 140 loans for fledgling Negro businessmen, 100 of them through the First Pennsylvania Banking & Trust Company. Most credits have been made to small "Mom-and-Pop" enterprises, but one loan was made to a warehouser whose sales are now $1 million a year. Another credit helped Data Preparation Corporation, a key-punch business with present annual volume of $375,000.

CAPITAL FORMATION, INC. A foundation formed by Samuel S. Beard, formerly Staff Associate to Robert Kennedy, to strengthen black entrepreneurship in all areas of New York City. The foundation also has branches in Cincinnati and Hartford. Through a volunteer staff of 270 lawyers, brokers, and accountants, Capital Formation recruits black business borrowers and assists them in preparing applications for Small Business Administration loans. In some cases the foundation makes direct loans to ghetto businessmen—usually for the purpose of paying off personal creditors so that the borrower will be in a position to obtain SBA credit.

CENTRAL CITY FOODS. This black-owned supermarket in St. Louis has plans for 20 black-financed and black-operated supermarkets in the nation's 20 largest cities. Central City Foods is headed by James

E. Hurt, Jr., who is a member of the St. Louis Board of Education. A Central City market will be one of the main stores in a giant shopping center being developed by an all-Negro businessmen's group in the blighted Grandel Square area of St. Louis.

CHASE MANHATTAN BANK. Chase has put into operation a far-ranging urban program. It conducts the equivalent of a full-fledged school for high-school dropouts at its headquarters premises in Wall Street; it gives financial advice to black businessmen; its small-business arm has financed new black-owned enterprises in Harlem and Brooklyn; it sponsors bookmobiles for ghetto areas; it publishes the quarterly *Action Report* to prod other businesses; and it has brought community residents together in conferences exploring the effectiveness of direct political action.

CHRYSLER CORPORATION. To bring "money power" to the ghetto, Chrysler Corporation is depositing $100,000 each month in three black-owned banks—in Atlanta, Los Angeles, and Detroit. The money is earmarked for company excise-tax payments, but meanwhile the ghetto banks use it for short-term loans. Chrysler also has more black car dealers than any of the other auto makers. Chrysler holds the largest subsidy contract under the government-business drive to hire the hard-core unemployed: $5.8 million to train 3,000 men in six company plants and dealerships in 50 cities.

CIRCLE ASSOCIATES. A black investment company raising money from whites to buy up small businesses in Roxbury, Mass. Circle plans to transform itself into a mutual fund, with its shares to be held by the black community.

CITIZENS & SOUTHERN CAPITAL CORP. Launched by the $1.3 billion Citizens & Southern National Bank of Georgia, this subsidiary investment corporation provides high-risk loans and investment capital to minority-owned small business concerns. C&S Capital Corp. is the prototype bank-sponsored private community-development corporation.

COALITION VENTURE CORPORATION. Funded by the New York Urban Coalition, CVC makes soft loans to slum enterpreneurs on favorable terms. One of the first loans was $15,000 credit to a consortium of black contractors. The CVC's companion organization is Coalition Development Corporation, which provides technical and managerial advice to minority businessmen.

234

CONTINENTAL ILLINOIS NATIONAL BANK & TRUST COMPANY and FIRST NATIONAL BANK OF CHICAGO. Two of the largest banks in Chicago head a group of 15 Chicago-area banks which have committed $100 million in interim financing for low-income housing.

CONTROL DATA CORP. This computer-manufacturing and service concern has established major new facilities in the ghettos of Minneapolis and Washington, D.C. Both are staffed primarily by local residents, many of them previously unemployed.

CORE. The Congress of Racial Equality is one of the principal black groups moving aggressively to build black entrepreneurship. CORE was one of the architects of the Community Self-Determination Bill submitted to Congress in 1968 with the backing of 25 U.S. Senators. This bill would set up community-development corporations in poverty areas to acquire, create, and manage all businesses in their areas. Each CDC would be owned by neighborhood residents, who would buy stock at $5 a share.

CORN PRODUCTS CO. One of the world's largest food processors, this company has backed enterprises whose business is remedial education or manpower training. Corn Products developed MIND (Methods of Intellectual Development), a company which relies heavily on taped lessons to raise academic levels of workers. Corn Products also took a minority position in Woolman Systems, a specialized job-training and basic education organization. Corn Products owns 25 per cent of Information Science, a company which developed a computerized information system to match jobs with those who need jobs.

CORPORATION FOR URBAN DEVELOPMENT AND RESEARCH. This unique agency was created by law in New York State. It has extraordinary powers to override local zoning regulations to get housing units built for low- and middle-income families. The corporation utilizes a "turnkey" approach. It will contract with private developers who agree to limit their profits for construction of housing which the corporation will buy upon completion. The completed property would be leased back to the developers at regulated rentals or to a tenant-managed cooperative. In some cases the corporation will run the project itself.

COUNCIL FOR EQUAL BUSINESS OPPORTUNITY. A Ford Foundation project funded through the Potomac Institute, CEBO provides coun-

235

seling for minority businessmen in Baltimore. It has helped to start —or stay—in business 75 black contractors, a wood-pallet manufacturing company, a plastic-molder, a Negro auto dealer, and a chain of 10 black-owned supermarkets.

EBONY BUSINESSMEN'S LEAGUE. Negro businessmen in Hartford, Conn., formed this organization in 1968 to provide business management advice and develop new ghetto businesses. Ted Pryor, an executive at Aetna Life & Casualty Company, is board chairman of EBL, which set the following goals: $250,000 from the black business community for the city's first black professional building, $250,000 from the Chamber of Commerce to cover administrative costs for the first five years.

EG&G, INC. This Boston-based company opened a metal-fabrication plant in the Roxbury ghetto in 1968, pledging to reduce its holdings to 25 per cent in five years through various stock offerings to workers and community residents.

EL MERCADO DE LOS ANGELES. This marketplace in the Mexican-American section of east Los Angeles houses 40 small businesses under one roof. Opened in 1968, it is organized as a local development corporation under the Small Business Investment Act of 1958. Federal loans to El Mercado totaled $1 million, and $260,000 was raised in the community. The marketplace features Spanish architecture, strolling mariachi players, and a wide assortment of Mexican wares.

ENGLEWOOD COMMUNITY CORPORATION. Under the initiative of W. Norbert Engles, president of Chicago City Banking & Trust Company, merchants and property owners on Chicago's southwest side financed this neighborhood agency to the extent of $435,000, with the bank itself lending an additional $300,000. The corporation was then able to purchase an eyesore—a vacant lot at the corner of 63rd Street and Halsted—and begin renewing the area that was rapidly deteriorating into a slum.

EPISCOPAL CHURCH. Black banks need funds, and the Episcopal Church has helped by depositing $675,000 in 45 ghetto banks and savings-and-loan associations in 24 dioceses. The primary purpose of the program is to encourage local economic development.

236

EQUITABLE LIFE ASSURANCE SOCIETY. The country's third-largest insurer, Equitable has created a special fund to make grants to national and local urban coalitions and other urban action groups. Company chairman James F. Oates was credited by *Fortune* as the originator of the insurance industry's $1 billion slum investment program. Equitable's share under this program is $83 million. The company has taken great strides to integrate its work force, tripling the number of black employees since 1963.

F. B. MCKISSICK ENTERPRISES. Organized by the former national director of CORE, this profit-making company seeks to organize black-owned businesses on a national scale. One of its unique ventures contemplates the purchase of a tract of land in North Carolina for the development of a new town, thereby helping to reverse the massive rural-to-urban, south-to-north movement.

FAIRCHILD-HILLER CORPORATION. This company has opened a Washington, D.C., ghetto subsidiary, Fairmicco, to manufacture wood pallets and other products. Plans call for sale of the majority of the company's stock to area residents.

FIRST BANK SYSTEM, INC. This Minneapolis bank holding company received preliminary approval to establish a bank affiliate in a predominantly Negro area of Minneapolis. Before the new bank was established, the holding company's lead bank, First National Bank of Minnesota, opened an office in the area to provide credit counseling to residents. This facility had an advisory board representing minority groups. It is intended that white personnel will withdraw from the new office as Negro personnel are able to assume control.

FIRST HORIZON ASSOCIATES. Twelve Wall Street lawyers, bankers, and businessmen formed this New York partnership to invest $400,000 in the stock market, with profits realized to be reinvested in ghetto enterprises. The venture was stimulated by Capital Formation, Inc., the New York City non-profit organization which assists minority businessmen.

FIRST NATIONAL CITY BANK. This giant bank offers a broad range of programs designed to promote economic independence in the ghettos of New York. It backed a store-front academy in Harlem, and it sponsored JOIN (Job Orientation in Neighborhoods), where dropouts were put into special training programs and placed in bank positions with only their supervisors aware of their status. It has one of the most impressive hard-core training programs in American business, graduating 200 at a clip from a 26-week course conducted on the second and third floors of a former Chinese nightclub on the edge of New York's Chinatown.

FIRST NEW HAVEN NATIONAL BANK. This New Haven, Conn., bank headed up a group of five banks which made available a pool of $1 million for high-risk loans to commercial borrowers. Although the loans are guaranteed by the Small Business Administration, the banks are paying the administrative costs and have set a maximum interest rate of 8 per cent.

FIRST OPPORTUNITY INVESTMENT, INC. A small-business investment company formed in Washington, D.C., early in 1969 to specialize in the development of minority businesses. The company is a subsidiary of New York-based Educational Sciences Programs, Inc., a firm actively engaged in the "knowledge industry." Mark Battle, a Negro who formerly administered the Labor Department's Bureau of Work Training Programs, is president and chairman of First Opportunity Investments.

FLANNER HOUSE HOMES. An Indianapolis organization which first developed the technique of "sweat equity" to put blacks in home ownership. Begun in 1947, Flanner House Homes enables families with meager incomes ($3,500 to $4,200) to build and own their own homes. Indianapolis businessmen contributed a revolving fund of $200,000 to purchase materials, and the city's largest banks, including American Fletcher National Bank and Indiana National Bank, funded the mortgage loans.

FORD FOUNDATION. Long a prime source of funds for education, the Ford Foundation, under the leadership of McGeorge Bundy, is earmarking more of its resources for programs designed to help the poor, including Negro business development. Under a new policy emphasizing investments rather than grants, the Foundation has made a $1 million loan to the Congaree Iron & Steel Company of Congaree, S.C. (a firm that hires former convicts), and a $300,000 stock purchase in Progress Enterprises, Philadelphia. Ford also committed $300,000 to a consortium of black contractors in Oakland, Calif.

FORD MOTOR COMPANY. Among large corporations, Ford has the highest proportion of black employees—23 per cent. As chairman of

238

the National Alliance of Businessmen, Henry Ford II has led the American business community into creative new approaches to problems of minority-hiring. A Ford executive, Leo Beebe, was the working head of NAB during its first crucial year of recruiting businessmen to hire the hard-core unemployed.

FREEDOM INDUSTRIES, INC. Operators of a small electronic assembly shop, black-controlled Freedom Industries is negotiating to acquire two supermarkets with annual sales of $4.5 million in the Roxbury ghetto of Boston.

FREEDOM NATIONAL BANK. Largest of the nation's black-owned banks, with deposits of $28 million, Freedom is the prototype of the half-dozen core-area black banks formed in large cities in recent years. Under the leadership of well-known black banker William Hudgins, Freedom has been active in promoting economic development in Harlem, having made more SBA-guaranteed loans to ghetto businessmen than any other bank in the country—but its capital resources are not sufficient to make more than a dent in the economy of the largest ghetto on the east coast. Freedom National does not even rank as one of the 1,000 largest banks in the country.

GAP. Group for Advertising Progress was formed in New York City by black people working in the advertising business, to speed the employment of Negroes in that industry. Two big agencies, J. Walter Thompson Company and Doyle Dane Bernbach, have signed government contracts to train minority-group members for jobs on Madison Avenue.

GENERAL ELECTRIC CO. With plants located all over the country, GE has mounted an impressive urban-affairs program involving black economic development, hiring and training of the hard-core unemployed, support to education, and improvement of housing conditions. It was GE that made possible the launching of the first black-owned aerospace company, Progress Aerospace Enterprises, by awarding $2.5 million of sub-contracts. Other GE efforts have ranged from designing a business management system for the OEO's Head Start program in Bolivar County, Mississippi, to running what is virtually a high school in the facilities of GE's Hotpoint division facilities in Chicago. GE is co-owner, with Time Inc., of the General Learning Corp., an educational company which runs the Job Corps center at Clinton, Ia.

239

GENERAL MOTORS COMPANY. GM has been a leader in the hiring of the hard-core unemployed, putting 21,700 unemployables on the payroll in eight months ending November 30, 1968. GM elected not to accept government-offered training subsidies. "The responsibility for hiring and training personnel is ours alone—the cost as well," said GM. During 1968, GM also gave a boost to black economic development by placing an order for 247,000 glove-compartment boxes with the Watts Manufacturing Company of Los Angeles.

GPEDC. Greater Philadelphia Enterprises Development Corporation, a non-profit organization formed to expand black entrepreneurship. Funded by a variety of sources, local and federal, GPEDC has developed two inner-city shopping centers for black retailers, simultaneously selling shares at $1 apiece to neighborhood residents. GPEDC also provides management advice for black entrepreneurs.

GREATER HARTFORD HOUSING DEVELOPMENT FUND. GHHDF, launched in 1966 by Hartford business leaders, is now funded by commitments of $1.5 million from 26 businesses. The fund provides seed money to promote development of non-profit low-income housing projects.

GREEN POWER FOUNDATION. Founded by a charter group of 140 businessmen, mostly black, Green Power has established a baseball-bat factory in the Watts section of Los Angeles. It also runs a bus company and plans to start manufacturing plastic products and printed electronic circuits. Executive director is Norman Hodges, a Negro research engineer on leave from North American Rockwell.

H. G. PARKS, INC. One of the largest black-owned companies in America, H. G. Parks is a Baltimore maker of sausage and scrapple, with sales now in excess of $7 million a year. In early 1969 the company went "public" through an underwriting by Allen & Co., which sold 220,000 shares (or 37 per cent of the company) at $8. The stock bounded immediately from $10 to $12 on the over-the-counter market.

HARLEM COMMONWEALTH COUNCIL. A community-development corporation formed to provide economic self-help programs. Its aim: "To plug the leaks by giving black people control over capital instruments." HCC has devised plans for a chain of service stations, children's shoe stores, and an automobile diagnostic center. HCC acquired one of the biggest manufacturing units in Harlem, New

240

Acme Foundry, with loans from Morgan Guaranty, the Episcopal Diocese of New York, and the Urban Coalition.

HARLEM FREEDOM ASSOCIATES.   Pledged to the economic development of Harlem, this is a limited partnership bringing together leading black citizens and the Wall Street investment house of Carter, Berlind & Weill. A first move in its objective of "decolonializing" the ghetto was the $2 million purchase of the 125th Street store and property of F. W. Woolworth under mortgage financing provided largely by the Equitable Life Assurance Society. The store is being leased back to Woolworth, and the property has been turned over to the Canaan Baptist Church, with the income from the property to be used for the benefit of the entire Harlem community.

HARLEM RIVER CONSUMERS COOPERATIVE.   This giant cooperative supermarket, organized by Negro lawyer Cora Walker, opened in Harlem in 1968 with the backing of 3,800 resident shareholders. Litton Industries Credit Corp. assisted with an equipment loan of $160,000.

HARLEMDATA.   A ghetto loan factoring business formed by the Harlem Commonwealth Council, and McKinsey & Co., James Talcott, Inc., and Arthur Andersen & Co. to refinance Harlem pharmacists who were on the edge of bankruptcy as a result of carrying their Medicaid accounts receivable through ghetto loan sharks.

HAUSSAMEN FOUNDATION.   A fund established by Carol W. Haussamen, a leading New York City real estate developer and civic leader. Utilizing techniques of "instant rehabilitation," the Haussamen and Frederick Richmond Foundations initiated in 1965 a four-year rehabilitation project on 114th Street in West Harlem. The two funds renovated 37 rundown buildings housing 1,600 people on the entire block between Seventh and Eighth Avenues. Not one person was permanently displaced during the work.

HIGH-SCHOOL "ADOPTIONS."   A number of companies have offered their help to schools located in slum areas. In Detroit, both the Chrysler Corporation and Michigan Bell Telephone Company "adopted" high schools, working with education officials to prepare the students for jobs. In Cleveland, the General Electric Company donated a warehouse to the public-school system as a training facility. In Hartford, Aetna Life & Casualty "adopted" a high school.

241

HOTEL CORPORATION OF AMERICA. In 1968 this international hotel chain announced plans for a new $4,500,000 hotel in the heart of Harlem at 125th Street and Third Avenue.

HOUGH AREA DEVELOPMENT CORPORATION. A neighborhood-development corporation formed in the Hough ghetto of Cleveland in April, 1967, to promote economic development in the community. The corporation has plans for a combination shopping center and public housing project, and it has developed a contractor loan-guarantee program which will provide local building contractors with access to needed operating capital.

HOUSING NOW, INC. A non-profit corporation formed in 1967 by the Greater Hartford Council of Churches seeks to put tenant families with large families into a home-ownership position by means of grants which meet home down-payment requirements. Funded by a local foundation, Housing Now has help from many sources: The Hartford Society for Savings arranged for one of its officers to serve as treasurer; the Urban League provided an office; and the city of Hartford is paying the salary of an interviewer who screens applicants.

"INFILL HOUSING." This is a program in Boston to build low-income apartment houses on some 250 tax-foreclosed vacant city lots. A number of banks and savings-and-loan associations have backed the project, with the biggest commitment, $5 million, coming from the Worcester Federal Savings & Loan Association.

INNER CITY BUSINESS IMPROVEMENT FORUM. This non-profit development corporation was formed after the 1967 riots in Detroit with the objective of building $1 billion in black-owned business assets within 10 years. Projects in the blueprint stage are a super-market, shopping centers, a computerized bookkeeping service, and a local development company to be financed with matching funds from the Small Business Administration.

INSTITUTE FOR INTENSIVE ENTREPRENEURIAL TRAINING. This institute was organized by former New York City Finance Administrator Roy M. Goodman for developing Negro and Puerto Rican "Capitalists." The school will be privately financed by grants from foundations, corporations, and banks. Goodman says, "We aim to produce black capitalists and hopefully a few black millionaires."

242

INTERNATIONAL BUSINESS MACHINES CORPORATION. In recent years IBM has doubled the number of black people in its work force, bringing the ratio up to 4 per cent, which Thomas Watson states is "not good enough." IBM has set up a computer sub-assembly plant in Brooklyn's Bedford-Stuyvesant, creating ghetto jobs for 300, and it sponsored a store-front school in Harlem. In Los Angeles, IBM loaned more than $500,000 of equipment to help the Urban League open a computer job training center.

INTERRACIAL COUNCIL FOR BUSINESS OPPORTUNITY. Operating in New York, Newark, and other cities, ICBO is probably the largest and most active organization in the country dedicated to building black enterpreneurship. ICBO utilizes the talents of volunteer businessmen to help Negroes get—or stay—in business. In a novel approach, the New York ICBO set up a special fund which guaranteed to a group of banks that ICBO would absorb 50 per cent of any losses on loans made to black businessmen whose credit applications it approved.

JOB LOAN CORP. A private corporation formed by eight large Philadelphia commercial banks, which pledged to make $2 million available through the corporation for loans to minority entrepreneurs. In its first five months, Job Loan Corp. authorized 83 loans totaling $880,000.

JOHN HANCOCK MUTUAL LIFE INSURANCE COMPANY. Boston's John Hancock was a major participant in the billion-dollar 1967 commitment of the life-insurance industry for slum-area mortgages. Hancock was also a major subscriber to stock of Boston's new multiracial bank, Unity Bank. The firm has set up a skills bank where aspiring minority-group entrepreneurs can draw on the talents of lawyers, accountants, investment specialists, and other business experts.

JOHNSON PUBLISHING COMPANY. Base of one of the largest centers of Negro economic power in the United States, Johnson grosses more than $12 million a year in *Ebony, Jet,* and other magazines. The company, which is headquartered in Chicago, is owned and controlled by John H. Johnson, who also runs a successful black-oriented cosmetics company, Supreme Beauty Products, and an insurance company, Supreme Life Insurance.

243

JOINT SAVINGS BANK–SAVINGS AND LOAN COMMITTEE ON URBAN PROBLEMS. Following a 1968 White House meeting with President Johnson, the mutual savings banks of the country joined with savings-and-loan associations to set up this committee as a stimulus to their members to mount financing programs meeting the housing needs of lower-income groups. Thrift institutions across the country have responded to this challenge. The committee has collected many examples of creative lending programs in a booklet called *Urban Financing Guide*.

LEVI STRAUSS & CO. San Francisco jeans-maker stamps its purchase orders with a legend informing suppliers that Levi Strauss requires its suppliers to be equal-opportunity employers.

LIFE-INSURANCE INDUSTRY. In September, 1967, 163 American life-insurance companies pledged $1 billion for slum mortgages and rehabilitation. A year later, the companies had committed or disbursed $658 million for projects in 215 cities. These loans made possible 46,800 housing units and 16,060 new jobs.

LING-TEMCO-VOUGHT. LTV's Aerospace division not only recruits and trains unskilled workers, but also has imported them from 500 miles away for permanent jobs in its Dallas facilities. The company brought Mexican Americans and their families from the depressed Rio Grande region to Dallas, providing transportation and a living allowance until the first paycheck.

LOCKHEED AIRCRAFT CORPORATION. One of the leaders in the aerospace industry's drive to employ more blacks, Lockheed conducts special training programs for the hard-core unemployed at its Sunnyvale, Calif., plant and in Marietta, Ga., where it is the Southeast's leading employer. Lockheed was the first company to join Plans for Progress, the voluntary equal-employment arm of business. The aerospace giant has opened a subsidiary, the Ventura Manufacturing Co., at San Antonio, Tex., where 140 hard-core workers are employed.

MAINSTREAM, INC. This organization, located in Columbus, Ga., specializes in finding Negroes capable of running their own businesses. Mainstream advertises in Negro publications and refers promising candidates to banks, other financing sources, and franchising concerns.

MANHATTAN TRIBUNE. This weekly, calling itself "the nation's first black-white newspaper," began publication in 1968. Published by poverty expert William Haddad and Roy Innis of CORE, the paper covers the news of black Harlem and the Upper West Side of New York. It also plans to serve as a training laboratory for aspiring Negro reporters.

McKINSEY & COMPANY. One of the leading management consulting firms in America, McKinsey has made personnel available to various projects designed to promote black economic development. The firm was a prime mover in the formation of the Harlem Commonwealth Council.

MARTIN MARIETTA CORPORATION. This conglomerate has opened a woodworking factory, DICO, in the slum area of Washington, D.C., with the provision that, if profitable, the plant will be turned over to employees within three years.

MENSWEAR RETAILERS OF AMERICA. An extended credit pool of $20 million has been set up by this group under its Ownership Opportunities Program, designed to aid minority-owned retailers. More than 25 minority-controlled men's-wear stores across the country have been opened since the program went into operation in 1968.

MERCK & COMPANY. This New Jersey chemical and drug company gave $50,000 to the Interracial Council for Business Opportunity to guarantee bank loans to minority businessmen. The money should form the base for $200,000 in ghetto business credit leverage.

METRO-NORTH. A New York City rehabilitation program for the most depressed blocks of East Harlem—99th Street to 102nd Street from Third Avenue to the East River. The program includes vest-pocket public housing, mixed with both rental and cooperative middle-income housing and the use of schools, playgrounds, and parks on a soundly planned and integrated basis within the neighborhood.

METROPOLITAN LIFE INSURANCE COMPANY. The Met is a big contributor to the life-insurance industry's $1 billion commitment to core-area mortgages. Its share of this loan program is $160 million, the bulk of which has gone to financing homes and low-income apartment units. The company has followed through by appointing Negro mortgage loan correspondents in New York and Atlanta—the first insurance company to do so. On the employment front, Metropolitan Life has brought more than 3,000 minority-group members into its

New York home office, where it runs a wide variety of training and recreational programs.

MEYERHOFF, H. PETER. A Honeywell Inc. engineer, Meyerhoff personally launched a "buy black" campaign in Minneapolis, in 1968 as a reaction to the assassination of Dr. Martin Luther King, Jr. He compiled a directory of 200 black-owned businesses in the Minneapolis–St. Paul area and distributed 15,000 copies, urging whites to patronize black merchants. The National Urban League picked up the program for use in other areas, and Honeywell gave Meyerhoff a three-month leave, with pay, to develop the program further.

MOBIL OIL COMPANY. This giant petroleum company has stepped up its recruiting at Negro colleges, has opened up service-station dealership for blacks, and has been one of the principal supporters of the New York Urban Coalition. One of its top executives, Christian Herter, Jr., was loaned to the Coalition for six months.

MORGAN GUARANTY TRUST COMPANY. Traditionally a bank for corporations and millionaires, Morgan has made exceptions to its normal practices in order to stimulate Negro entrepreneurship. The bank solicits loans to Negro businessmen, it has made construction loans in New York slum areas, it gave a start-up grant to the Harlem Better Business Bureau, and it has offered to finance an important new cultural center in Harlem.

MREIT. Mutual Real Estate Investment Trust, was organized in New York in 1965 by Morris Milgram with the specific purpose of buying apartment houses and integrating them. Through direct sale of shares at $20 apiece to 7,700 shareholders, it raised $8.4 million, $1 million of which was subscribed by the Ford Foundation. In early 1969 it secured an underwriting through Edwards & Hanly, which offered the public 750,000 shares at $10 each. At the end of 1968, MREIT owned 13 properties in five states containing 1,600 apartments.

NARTRANS. A training, service, and support subsidiary, NARTRANS was established in 1968 in East Central Los Angeles by North American Rockwell Corporation. Capitalized at $750,000, NARTRANS provides jobs and training (including remedial education) to jobless blacks and Mexican Americans. The work—keypunching, plastic-bag fabricating, tool-grinding, carpentry—is secured from North American's aerospace plants in southern California.

246

NATIONAL ALLIANCE OF BUSINESSMEN.   President Lyndon B. Johnson mobilized this blue-chip panel of business executives to fight the
war against unemployment. Operating in the nation's 50 largest cities,
NAB reached some 12,000 companies in 1968 and got them to
provide more than 100,000 jobs for the hard-core unemployed. The
target is 500,000 jobs by 1971. Government funds underwrote much
of the training costs.

NATIONAL ASSOCIATION FOR THE ADVANCEMENT OF COLORED
PEOPLE.   The NAACP has helped to organize regional consortiums
of black-owned construction companies, with the idea of securing
contracts for major public projects which previously would have gone
to construction companies employing members of segregated unions.
Prototype for the idea is a consortium of 63 Negro-owned construction companies in the San Francisco–Oakland area.

NATIONAL BANK OF DETROIT.   The largest bank in Detroit plans to
finance reconstruction of an entire block burned out in Detroit's riot
area. The block, which once contained a branch of the bank, is
bounded by West Grand Boulevard, Grand River Avenue, Dexter
Avenue, and Lothrop Boulevard. Initially, most of the two-acre block
would be a parking lot, with a few stores and a new drive-in branch
of the National Bank of Detroit.

NATIONAL BUSINESS LEAGUE.   A private development association
for minority entrepreneurs, the National Business League provides
management and training advice, and through its newly instituted
Project Mainstream seeks the establishment of local development and
investment companies to aid minority businessmen. Berkeley G. Bur-
rell, a Washington dry-cleaner, is president of the NBL, which has
about 10,000 members in more than 50 chapter cities.

NATIONAL ECONOMIC GROWTH & RECONSTRUCTION ORGANIZATION
(NEGRO).   This is a New York-based holding company or ghetto
conglomerate which now encompasses 15 different operating units,
including an advertising agency, bus company, apparel-maker, and
paint company. The founder is Dr. Thomas W. Matthew, Negro
neurosurgeon.

NATIONAL HOUSING PARTNERSHIP.   A far-reaching scheme developed in 1968 by President Johnson to spur the construction of
housing for the poor. The plan brought together leaders in business,

247

banking, labor, and education in a government-sponsored corporation that hopes to finance the construction of 20,000 to 50,000 low-income housing units annually. Stockholders include such concerns as Kaiser Industries, Wells Fargo, Chase Manhattan Bank, Ling-Temco-Vought, Loeb Rhoades, and World Airways. The corporation plans to raise an initial capital of $200 million. It then plans borrowing of $4 billion with government loan guarantees.

NATIONAL URBAN LEAGUE. Under the banner of "New Thrust," the Urban League launched in 1968 new programs with greater emphasis on economic development of blacks. The Urban League training programs put 18,000 jobless to work during the 1964–68 period, and the League is now training 7,000 in 26 cities under the largest single disbursement ever given by the Department of Labor: $9.1 million.

NEIMAN–MARCUS INC. This prestigious Dallas store has informed its more than 2,000 suppliers that it "would rather do business with a company which is actively pursuing policy of equal opportunity than to continue to do business with one which is not." This policy of using corporate buying power to advance minority opportunities also has been adopted by two other big department stores. The Dayton Company of Minneapolis and F. & R. Lazarus of Cincinnati have informed their suppliers that equal-opportunity hiring practices would be considered when placing purchase orders.

NEW YORK INSTITUTE FOR CONSUMER EDUCATION. Funded initially by the Office of Economic Opportunity, this Harlem-based organization has spawned a cooperative association with great economic potential. The brainchild of Stephen Press, a community worker, the Institute set up the Cooperative Association of East Harlem with a loan of $35,000. The Association, which is selling shares to neighborhood residents at $5 a share, has opened a furniture store which is now grossing between $5,000 and $10,000 a week. The Association has also set up a meat and fish market. Soon to come is a credit union.

NEW YORK LIFE INSURANCE COMPANY. One of the "big five" of the life-insurance industry, New York Life is active in projects to advance black capitalism. The company made a $75,000 loan to former basketball star Willie Nauls to enable him to open a restaurant in Watts; it financed, to the extent of $3.5 million, the construction of a 12-story office building by a Negro-owned bank in Atlanta; it made numerous other mortgage loans across the country to finance low-income housing. At its home office, New York Life did the following during 1968: appointed its first three Negro officers, doubled the number of black agents to 200, and added four blacks to the personnel staff. Minority employment in the home-office white-collar staff has reached 18 per cent, triple what it was in 1963.

NORTH CAROLINA MUTUAL LIFE. This company, based in Durham, N.C., is the largest of the 50-odd black-owned insurance companies. With assets in excess of $90 million, North Carolina Mutual is one of two black-owned-and-controlled insurance companies—Supreme Life is the other—which operate nationally.

OPERATION BREADBASKET. An economic-development arm of the Southern Christian Leadership Conference, Rev. Jesse Jackson's Operation Breadbasket is based in Chicago and pressures stores and manufacturers to hire Negroes and to sell the products of black-owned companies.

OPPORTUNITIES INDUSTRIALIZATION CENTER. A Negro self-help organization founded in Philadelphia by Rev. Leon Sullivan, OIC trains and upgrades workers often in conjunction with businesses. It now has branches in 70 cities. Sullivan's OIC is generally conceded to be the most significant example of new black capitalism in America today.

P. BALLANTINE & SONS. This brewery, based in Newark, N.J., does more than half of its business in the black community. It has been awarded a $100,000 grant from the Office of Economic Opportunity to test-market a line of high-protein soft drinks aimed at under-nourished residents of deprived areas.

PACT, INC. Plan of Action for Challenging Times is a five-year-old black-organized non-profit organization that provides a wide range of counseling services in the San Francisco area. PACT has compiled a directory of black businesses, and advises companies on what they can do to promote economic development in ghetto communities.

PILLSBURY COMPANY. This Minneapolis flour-miller has announced a far-reaching "credo" pledging itself to actively recruit minority-group employees, seek out the so-called "unemployables," train them, locate plants where they will help the disadvantaged, develop new products that meet the needs of the disadvantaged, and support "public policies that we believe will quickly mobilize our society to

249

effectively achieve the American ideal for all citizens." Pillsbury had 286 minority-group employees in 1965; today, it has more than 400.

PLANS FOR PROGRESS. Operating under the aegis of the federal government, this is a voluntary equal-opportunity organization of business. The 441 companies which make up the membership employ 9.7 million persons—and more than 10 per cent of this labor force is now composed of blacks and other minorities. Since 1966, PFP members have increased their minority work forces by 35 per cent.

PROGRESS AEROSPACE ENTERPRISES. This is the first black-owned-and-operated plant for the manufacture of aerospace components. More than 600 Philadelphia Negroes invested in it under the leadership of their pastor, Rev. Leon Sullivan. PAE started up with $2.6 million worth of sub-contracts from General Electric. Another Sullivan-initiated company in Philadelphia is Progress Garment Manufacturing Company, a small clothing factory.

PROGRESS LABORATORIES. Black-owned, this pharmaceutical company was started in 1968 in Los Angeles. Marketing prescription and proprietary drugs, Progress Laboratories is headed by a former Calbiochem chemist, Clarence Lofton. Financing was provided by International Rectifier.

PROGRESS PLAZA. A North Philadelphia shopping center tenanted by black businesses and established corporations opened in 1968 as another facet of the self-help program launched by Rev. Leon Sullivan and his investing parishioners. Financing was provided by the First Pennsylvania Banking & Trust Company. The Ford Foundation helped by purchasing $300,000 of shares in Sullivan's community-owned and community-controlled profit-seeking corporation, Progress Enterprises.

PROJECT ABLE. Organized at the University of Massachusetts, ABLE (Accelerated Business Leadership Education) is a special training course in business management for non-white college graduates. Recruits will achieve a master's degree in 15 to 21 months. The university seeks to persuade companies to sponsor students for the course.

PROJECT OWN. Acronym for a new drive initiated in 1968 by Small Business Administrator Howard Samuels to create 10,000 black-owned businesses in a year. In Newark, the SBA guaranteed all loans which came out of a $1 million fund set up by three banks to help ghetto businessmen. In Louisville, an SBA loan of $390,000 breathed new life into Negro Products Company, a new black-owned pillow manufacturer. This is the kind of loan activity SBA previously eschewed.

PRUDENTIAL INSURANCE COMPANY.   Number one in the insurance industry, Prudential has also led the way in the industry's commitment of $1 billion in loan funds to fight urban blight. Prudential has been particularly aggressive in its home city, Newark, N.J. It has been a mainstay of the Greater Newark Urban Coalition, with a program to renovate some 10,000 housing units in Newark. It also finances Negro-owned businesses. Prudential has committed funds for "high-risk" projects which would not have been considered several years ago, such as a store-front rehabilitation center for narcotics addicts.

RBOC.   The Rochester Business Opportunities Corporation is a business and banking coalition organized in Rochester, N.Y., to help black-owned businesses get off the ground. More than 20 Negro businessmen have received aid. RBOC helped to establish FIGHTON, a new company geared to do $1 million a year in the production of electrical transformers and metal stampings.

R. J. REYNOLDS TOBACCO COMPANY.   Number one in the cigarette industry, R. J. Reynolds was shocked by black riots which swept its home city of Winston-Salem, N.C., in November, 1967. The result was a new commitment by the company to fight poverty in Winston-Salem. The Urban Coalition formed in Winston-Salem was funded by Reynolds at $1 million, the largest contribution of its kind in the country.

ROCHE LABORATORIES.   This Swiss-owned pharmaceutical maker runs an "Indigent Patient Program" under which physicians may order any Roche drug free of charge for patients who cannot afford to buy it. In a related program, Roche reimburses hospitals for 25 per cent of the cost of Roche drugs used by Medicare patients.

SANDERS ASSOCIATES.   This is a joint venture of four Negro investors in Boston, one being the Boston Celtic basketball star Tom Sanders. The group is engaged in rehabilitating homes in Roxbury under an FHA loan guarantee of $1 million, the largest loan commitment FHA ever made to a black venture. Supplying financial and

251

technical aid are four Boston banks and the utility Eastern Gas & Fuel Associates.

SAN FRANCISCO CONTAINER CORPORATION. This new company manufactures chipboard and cardboard cases in a San Francisco ghetto area. The company is owned by 25 Negro investors.

SHEARSON, HAMMILL & Co., INC. This Wall Street brokerage and underwriting house plans to open a branch in Harlem, with provisions to return a share of the office's profits to the community through a black-controlled foundation to guarantee loans to black businessmen. Under an agreement with Harlem CORE, the office will eventually be sold to blacks. At its non-ghetto offices, Shearson boasts a 13 per cent minority rate among its 857 workers and employs about one-fifth of the nation's Negro brokerage salesmen.

SMITH, KLINE & FRENCH LABORATORIES. This Philadelphia-based pharmaceutical producer has been working since 1966 to roll back the blight in the Spring Garden section where its headquarters are located. In addition to helping rehabilitate homes, SKF has given training and remedial education to many high-school dropouts, and it runs an information service for the community, which is predominantly Negro and Puerto Rican.

SPECIAL IMPACT. Under this program of the U.S. Department of Labor, the government subsidizes up to 15 per cent of a company's investment in a new ghetto-based plant, providing the company agrees to train a specified number of hard-core employed, pay higher than minimum wages, promote qualified workers to supervisory positions, and—in some cases—promise to offer profit-sharing or stock-option plans to employees. Under the initiative of Harold Levitt, senior partner of the Dempsey Tegeler investment house, five companies took advantage of this program to establish plants in the Watts ghetto of Los Angeles. The Bubble-Up soft-drink company put a $6.5 million plant into Watts; A&E Plastic Pak, producer of transparent meat trays, will employ more than 300 in its Watts subsidiary; the other companies were Udico Corp., Torite Enterprises, and Sahagen Industries.

THIOKOL CHEMICAL CORP. A chemical manufacturer for the aerospace industry, Thiokol has created a special division to oversee its operations in educating and training the disadvantaged. These activities include a Job Corps training center in Clearfield, Utah; a vocational and home-living skills training complex for American Indians at Roswell, N. Mex.; a wood and tile workers' training program at San Antonio, Tex.; and a Gulfport, Miss., pilot program to build maintenance and management skills among residents of a low-income housing project.

TRI-FAITH EMPLOYMENT PROJECT. This non-profit job-finding service of the Chicago Conference on Religion and Race grew from a local center in the basement of a church to a network of six fully staffed neighborhood offices. At its peak, the centers were making 1,500 full-time job placements a month, referring job-seekers to more than 5,000 firms.

UNITED AIR LINES. The largest carrier in the United States hired its first black pilot in 1965; it now has eight. United had 57 black stewardesses in 1967, 83 in 1968.

UNITED BLACK BUSINESSMEN'S ASSOCIATION. The UBBA has been formed in the Minneapolis–St. Paul area to promote Negro economic development. An outgrowth of the "Buy Black" campaign conducted there, it seeks job-training contracts and plans to build a shopping center.

UNITED METHODIST CHURCH. The church's Board of Missions has established a $100,000 fund with New York's Manufacturers Hanover Trust Co. to guarantee up to 10 per cent of the bank's SBA-guaranteed loans to minority entrepreneurs. An additional $400,000 has been set aside by the church for similar agreements with other banks.

UNITED STATES GYPSUM COMPANY. A building-materials supplier, U.S. Gypsum has been active in New York, Cleveland, and other cities in rehabilitating slum-located houses. The company put up $2 million for "instant rehabilitation" of six Harlem tenements. In Memphis, Gypsum and John Hancock each invested $1 million in a low-cost, computerized housing development.

UNITY BANK & TRUST COMPANY. This interracial bank opened in Boston's Roxbury ghetto in 1968. Its stockholders are 65 per cent black, 35 per cent white. This brought to 20 the number of black-owned banks in the nation, although in January, 1969, new ones were in the process of formation in eight other cities. In addition, there are 36 Negro savings-and-loan associations and 43 Negro mortgage banks.

253

URBAN COALITION. Born of the summer riots of 1967, the Urban Coalition brings together leaders from diverse and often unrelated endeavors to catalyze and coordinate action on urban problems. Besides the National Urban Coalition, headed by former HEW Secretary John W. Gardner, there are local coalitions in 39 cities and communities throughout the country.

WARNER & SWASEY COMPANY. This machine-tool manufacturer in Cleveland has invested $300,000 in the development of a subsidiary, Hough Manufacturing Company, a small machine shop, with the plant eventually to be turned over to employees.

WATTS MANUFACTURING COMPANY. A pioneering example of black capitalism created by Aerojet-General after the 1966 riots in the Watts ghetto of Los Angeles. This black-managed-and-staffed company has built up a now profitable business making tents and other products for the federal government. Aerojet-General plans to sell 51 per cent of the company's stock to employees.

WESTINGHOUSE ELECTRIC CORP. This major electronics producer has put special stress on programs that answer social needs. The company feels that eventually these can be profitable activities. Of the 616 contracts awarded to train Peace Corps volunteers, Westinghouse holds 10. It runs two Job Corps centers and helps to prepare VISTA volunteers. It has a subsidiary working on ghetto housing and urban-renewal problems. Westinghouse Learning Corp., which handles training services, has a volume of $16 million a year.

XEROX CORPORATION. This Rochester, N.Y., firm has one of the most progressive programs in industry on the social-action front. It has sought out Negro employees, developed special training materials, guaranteed $500,000 in purchases to a new black-owned manufacturing company, FIGHTON. The company also sponsored the seven-part CBS-TV series "Of Black America."

Further Reading and Sources

Background

THE WORKS of Louis O. Kelso and Patricia Hetter are an essential starting point for reading on black enterprise. These are *How to Turn Eighty Million Workers into Capitalists,* by Louis O. Kelso and Patricia Hetter (Random House, 1967), and a companion essay, "Equality of Economic Opportunity Through Capital Ownership" appearing in *Social Policies for America in the Seventies: Nine Divergent Views,* edited by Robert Theobold (Doubleday, 1968). The authors develop the wealth-making technique of credit leverage as one of the most efficient and direct methods of producing affluence in a poor society. The program is brilliantly creative and specific.

The writings of Georg Simmel, a German philosopher and sociologist who died in 1819, first exposed the failure of charity as an anti-poverty strategy. A translation of his very important essay entitled "The Poor" appears in *Poverty, Power and Politics,* by Chaim I. Waxman (Grosset & Dunlap, 1968).

One of the finest books published in recent years on the general subject of poverty is *Poverty U.S.A.,* by Thomas Gladwin (Little, Brown, 1967). The author develops the problem of the businessman's dilemma—the obstacle to conducting commerce in the slums on a basis that is fair to the businessman and to his customers in the ghetto. Another important current work on the subject of the role of private enterprise in manpower retraining and ghetto development is *White Power/Black Freedom: Planning the Future of Urban America,* by Arnold Schuchter (Beacon Press, 1968). This book also is an encyclopedia of anti-poverty strategies.

On the function of savings in developing poor economies, see a monograph by John Kenneth Galbraith, *The Underdeveloped Country* (CBS Publications, Toronto, 1967). On the same subject, see *Man's Struggle for Shelter in an Urbanizing World,* by Charles Abrams (MIT Press, 1964). In *The Rich Nations and the Poor Nations* (Norton, 1962), the British economist Barbara Ward explains the function of capital, credit, and savings to achieve an economic breakthrough in a traditional society.

The importance of reducing ghetto income uncertainty as an anti-poverty strategy is developed by Hyman P. Minsky in a monograph entitled *Poverty: The "Aggregate Demand" Solution and Other Non-Welfare Approaches,* published by the Institute of Government and Public Affairs, University of California, Los Angeles, April, 1965.

Black Entrepreneurship

Kenneth B. Clark's *Dark Ghetto: Dilemmas of Social Power* (Harper & Row, 1965) develops the protective economic monopoly provided by ghetto segregation. Background discussion of the reasons for black entrepreneurial failure is in *Black Bourgeoisie,* by E. Franklin Frazier (Macmillan, 1962 edition).

For the history of black entrepreneurship, there is *The Negro as a Capitalist,* by Abram L. Harris, published by the American Academy of Political and Social Science in Philadelphia. This book contains a complete history of Negro banking. Also, see *The Negro in American Business,* by Robert Kinzer and Edward Sagarin (Greenberg, 1950).

Two essays, "Desegregation and Negro Leadership," by Andrew F. Brimmer, and "Common Themes," by Eli Ginzberg, develop the destructive effect of desegregation on ghetto business enterprises and expound the importance of expanding the capacity of the ghetto community to use labor. These essays appear in *Business Leadership and the Negro Crisis* (McGraw-Hill, 1968). A book directed more toward the techniques of building black capitalism is *The Achieving Ghetto,* by Eugene P. Foley, published by The National Press, Inc., Washington, D.C. A practical soft-cover manual for the black businessman is entitled *How the Negro Can Start His Own Business,* by Thomas P. Jones, published by Pilot Industries, Inc., 347 Fifth Avenue, New York. This book highlights ghetto franchising operations.

Ghetto Economics

The most comprehensive presentation of ghetto economics in America is found in the early parts of the Kerner Commission Report published under the title *Report of the National Advisory Commission on Civil Disorders: U.S. Riot Commission Report* (hardcover, Dutton; paperback, Bantam Books; also U.S. Government Printing Office).

Illuminating testimony exposing the workings of the slum economy is found in the printed transcript of the Clark Senate Subcommittee on Employment Manpower Poverty of the Committee on Labor and Public Welfare of the United States Senate, July, 1967 (Government Printing Office). Of particular importance is the testimony beginning on page 1833 and on page 3027 relating to the Equal Opportunity Loan Program of the Small Business Administration.

A complete exposure of ghetto markets including the ghetto credit system is developed by David Caplovitz in *The Poor Pay More* (Macmillan, 1967). With particular reference as to why the ghetto economy does not function rationally, see *Tally's Corner,* by Elliot Liebow (Little, Brown, 1967).

Slum Credit Economics

Background materials of ghetto credit economics, including a number of suggested solutions to the problem of moving more credit and capital into the slum economy, is the U.S. Senate Committee Print, *Financial Institutes and the Urban Crisis: Hearings before the Subcommittee of Financial Institutions of the Committee on Banking and Currency,* United States Senate, 90th Congress, 2nd Session (Government Printing Office, 1968). These hearings were held September 30 through October 4, 1968.

During the hearings, Dr. Irwin Friend, Wharton School of Finance, University of Pennsylvania, and Stephen C. Miller, Executive Vice President, Comac Company of Birmingham, Michigan, articulated the problems of the bankers' ghetto-investment risk aversion and of duplicating approvals in Small Business Administration ghetto loan-guarantee programs. The statement of Sherman J. Maisel, Member, Board of Governors, Federal Reserve System, explains the ghetto lending gap—the reasons why the amount of private credit made available in the ghetto falls short of the amount of lending believed necessary on social grounds. Governor Maisel also develops the deterrent effect of the social opprobrium attached to possible usurious loans. In the same hearing, Donald J. Graham, Chairman of the Bankers Committee on Urban Affairs, American Bankers Association, and Chairman of the Board, Continental Illinois National Bank and Trust Company of Chicago, explains the credit deficiency environment in the ghetto— the relationship of urban decline to the flight of credit. He also develops the need to change the basic market characteristics of the ghetto in order to permit its residents to bid for capital and credit.

257

Ghetto Tax Credits

One of the most comprehensive contemporary expositions of the potential of tax credits to restructure poverty areas is a speech delivered by Robert F. Kennedy in the U.S. Senate, Wednesday, July 12, 1967, entitled "Industrial Investment in Urban Poverty Areas." The speech, which appears in the *Congressional Record,* July 12, 1967, was given in support of a proposed bill submitted by Senator Kennedy entitled The Urban Employment Opportunities Development Bill of 1967.

Periodicals

Those who wish to follow current examples of black capitalism and company anti-poverty efforts are referred to the bi-weekly report on business and social responsibility, *Business and Society,* 477 Madison Avenue, New York, N.Y. 10022, edited by Milton Moskowitz. There are other newsletters and periodicals touching on corporate programs dealing with urban programs. None has the stature of *Business and Society.*

258

Index

Accelerated depreciation, 148; defect as a tax incentive, 154; effect on high-bracket taxpayers, 155

Accord Inc., 227

Action Housing, Inc., 105–106

Action Industries, 227

A&E Plastic Pak Co., 252

Aerojet General Corporation, Watts project, 114, 132, 193, 254

Aetna Life & Casualty Co., 228, 236, 241

AIM-Jobs, 228

"Aladdin's Lamp Loans," 48

Albina Economic Development Demonstration Project, 228

Allen & Company, 240

Allied Paper Corporation, 151

Aluminum Corporation of America, 185

American Airlines, Inc., 228

American Dream Soap Co., 228

American Fletcher National Bank, 238

American Institute of Architects, 229

American Management Association, 7–8, 161, 173

American Motors Company, 113

American Psychiatric Association, 26–27, 80

American Telephone and Telegraph Corporation, 229; basic education programs in the ghetto, 121; programs for hard-core unemployables, 116; public relations and regulatory benefits in ghetto-hiring programs, 128

Anti-Poverty strategy, 92; burden of ultimate cost, 85; civic responsibility as a motivation, 129; effect of antitrust laws, 84–85; effect of a business oligopoly, 84–85; effect of charity, 3; enrich-

Anti-Poverty strategy (*continued*) ment choice, 137; government coercion of business, 91; integration choice, 137; liberalization of banking laws, 160; manufacturing corporations, 115; patriotism as a motivating force, 129; "playing it safe," 206; riots as, 113; statistics on government programs, 93–94; utilities, 115

A&P Food Stores, 42

Appalachia, 22

Armour Corporation, 151

Armstrong Cork Co., 229

Arthur Anderson & Co., 162, 241

Association to Assist Negro Business, 229

Atlanta Model Cities program, 96

Auditor of lending institution, 166–167

Automatic loan guarantee; *see* Self-executing loan guarantee

Automation: effect on ghetto employment, 76; effect on overall poverty problem, 89

Automobile dealerships, 61

"Back-door spending," 148

Bad-debt loss, at black banks, 211

Bad-debt reserve: addition to for ghetto loans, 164; effect of ghetto tax credit, 189

Ballantine, P. & Sons, 249

Banco de Ponce: ghetto interest rates, 55; operating handicaps, 52

Banco Popular de Puerto Rico: ghetto loan problems, 54; participation in loan-guarantee program, 174

Bank of America, 230

Bank debentures, 169

Bankers Fire Insurance Company, 62, 67

259

261

GAP (Group for Advertising Progress), 239
Garnishment, 217; percentage of suits in ghetto areas, 34
General Adjustment Bureau, 133
General Electric Company, 239, 241, 250; basic education programs in the ghetto, 121
General Foods Corporation, mobility in terms of ghetto risks, 117
General Learning Corporation, 239
General Motors Corporation, 240; "after-market" for products in ghettos, 42; AIM-Jobs project, 228; ghetto hiring program, 114; need for ghetto assembly plants, 10; rejection of Department of Labor training subsidy, 4, 125
Ghetto business conglomerates, 153, 172
Ghetto business franchise, as beneficiary of tax credits, 154–155
Ghetto business monopoly, 217
Ghetto credit abdication, 217
Ghetto credit card proposal, 217
Ghetto credit gap, definition, 217
Ghetto credit economy: export from white areas, 55; merger with main credit economy, 165
Ghetto credit-risk aversion, 44; the "prudent man" rule, 77
Ghetto dealerships, 218
Ghetto decolonialization, effect of Community Self-Determination Bill, 196
Ghetto-development bank, 171; private, 218; public, 218
Ghetto economy: absence of ghetto entrepreneurs, 60; absence of profits, 49; banking patterns, 45; characteristics of anarchy, 21; credit patterns, 45; effect of black nationalism, 65; effect of Negro immigration, 88–89; inhibitions against developments of risk capital, 56; isolation as a characteristic, 31; lack of economic power, 90; patterns of entrepreneurship, 60; patterns of savings, 56, 95; theories of the origin, 88

Ghetto-enrichment choice, as anti-poverty strategy, 218; *see* Enrichment choice
Ghetto entrepreneur; *see* Black entrepreneur
Ghetto franchise: "soft" franchise, 188; tax credits for, 186
Ghetto investment-risk aversion: definition, 191, 193, 218; department store chains, 86; expressed as "diversion," 86; reaction to riots, 205
Ghetto loan-production offices, 219
Ghetto loan-risk aversion, 49, 168; mortgage loan officer, 77–78; tendency to overcompensate, 87
Ghetto-origin installment paper, 207–208; proposed tax credit, 165
Ghetto-origin purchases, application of proposed tax credits, 155
Ghetto-origin sales, application of proposed tax credits, 155
Ghetto payments deficit, 219
Ghetto profit overkill, 219
Ghetto store-front training centers, 199
Ghetto subcontractor, as beneficiary of proposed ghetto tax credits, 154–155
Ghetto supermarkets: Harlem experience, 43; problems in operations, 42
Ghetto tax credits, 151–152, 154, 219; abuse of, 148; application to building loans in the ghetto, 154–155; application to business franchises, 154–155; application to corporate purchases from ghetto subcontractor, 154–155; application to ghetto savings accounts, 155; application to items of profit rather than fixed assets, 155; avoiding application in connection with capital gain opportunities, 154; avoiding application to taxpayers in brackets exceeding 50%, 154, 155; deposits in slum-area banks, 167; effect of Small Business Administration loan guarantee, 164; encourage

265

267

THEODORE L. CROSS

Born in Newton, Massachusetts, in 1924, Theodore L. Cross is a graduate of Deerfield Academy, Amherst College, and Harvard Law School, where he was an editor of the *Harvard Law Review,* 1948–50. After a period of private and corporate law practice in Boston and New York City, he became in 1960, at the age of thirty-six, Vice President, General Counsel, and member of the Finance Committee of the Board of Directors of Sheraton Corporation of America, which he now serves as Vice President Legal Affairs and Treasurer. In 1959 he founded the *Atomic Energy Law Journal,* and since 1963 he has been editor-in-chief and publisher of *The Bankers Magazine,* the nation's oldest journal of banking and finance. He founded and is currently chairman of the Banking Law Institute, which sponsors courses of continuing legal education for lawyers and bankers, and since 1964 he has been a director of the Bank Tax Institute. In October, 1968, Mr. Cross was among a group of American banking authorities who were called to testify before the U.S. Senate Banking and Currency Committee on means of channeling bank credit and institutional capital into ghetto areas. He lives in New York City with his wife and two daughters.